'This insightful book offers a critical multi-level account of the institutional complexity of ever-changing research funding conditions across Canada, Finland, Sweden and the UK. The work provides a fresh look at the gendered repercussions of external research funding imperatives and thus is a must-read for higher education policymakers, managers and researchers alike.'
– **Liudvika Leišytė**, *Professor of Higher Education, TU Dortmund University, Germany*

'Shines a powerful light on unexamined gender dynamics of who – and what – secures research funding and how this contours academic lives and careers. Essential reading for everyone invested in understanding inequalities in knowledge production and how such inequalities can be challenged.'
– **Maddie Breeze**, *Senior Lecturer in Public Sociology, Queen Margaret University, UK*

'In an era marked by a global competition based on publications and growing concerns for equity, diversity and inclusion, a nuanced and detailed exploration of the links between research funding and gender is more than necessary. Drawing on a diversity of qualitative approaches, these 23 respected scholars with varied expertise and experiences have produced an insightful comparative work structured around compelling themes such as stability and change, care and conflict, and funding and defunding. I strongly recommend *The Social Production of Research: Perspectives on Funding and Gender* to all current academics, future academics, and reflective practitioners, whether they work in granting agencies, government, higher education institutions or unions.'
– **Olivier Bégin-Caouette**, *Associate Professor, Université de Montréal, Canada*

'Acquiring competitive research funding is a must in today's hypercompetitive academia. *The Social Production of Research: Perspectives on Funding and Gender* explores the deeply gendered dynamics and experiences of that endeavour. This insightful book should be on the reading list of all higher education scholars and leaders.'
– **Terhi Nokkala**, *Senior Researcher, Finnish Institute for Educational Research, Finland*

'This book provides a broad and up-to-date account of gender and research funding by drawing attention to the gendered dimensions of the neoliberal research funding context. The use of qualitative methods makes it an important complement to existing bibliometric studies on the connection of gender and funding.'
– **Charlotte Silander**, *Associate Professor, Linnaeus University, Sweden*

The Society for Research into Higher Education (SRHE) is an independent and financially self-supporting international learned Society. It is concerned to advance understanding of higher education, especially through the insights, perspectives and knowledge offered by systematic research and scholarship.

The Society's primary role is to improve the quality of higher education through facilitating knowledge exchange, discourse and publication of research. SRHE members are worldwide and the Society is an NGO in operational relations with UNESCO.

The Society has a wide set of aims and objectives. Amongst its many activities the Society:

• is a specialist publisher of higher education research, journals and books, amongst them Studies in Higher Education, Higher Education Quarterly, Research into Higher Education Abstracts and a long running monograph book series.

The Society also publishes a number of in-house guides and produces a specialist series "Issues in Postgraduate Education".

• funds and supports a large number of special interest networks for researchers and practitioners working in higher education from every discipline. These networks are open to all and offer a range of topical seminars, workshops and other events throughout the year ensuring the Society is in touch with all current research knowledge.

• runs the largest annual UK-based higher education research conference and parallel conference for postgraduate and newer researchers. This is attended by researchers from over 35 countries and showcases current research across every aspect of higher education.

SRHE *Society for Research into Higher Education*
Advancing knowledge Informing policy Enhancing practice

73 Collier Street
London N1 9BE
United Kingdom

T +44 (0)20 7427 2350
F +44 (0)20 7278 1135
E srheoffice@srhe.ac.uk

www.srhe.ac.uk

Director: Helen Perkins
Registered Charity No. 313850
Company No. 00868820
Limited by Guarantee
Registered office as above

THE SOCIAL PRODUCTION OF RESEARCH

The Social Production of Research offers critical perspectives on the interrelations between research funding and gender, in a climate where universities expect accountability and publishing productivity to be maintained at peak levels.

Drawing upon a range of qualitative methods, contributors investigate experiences with research funding; the nature of institutional, funding body and country contexts; and the impact of social change and disruptions on research ecosystems and academic careers in Canada, Finland, Sweden and the UK. Nuanced accounts call attention to the social, emotional and political conditions within which research is produced, while identifying the ways academics enact, shape, negotiate and resist those conditions in their everyday practice.

Featuring thought-provoking and critical insights for an international readership, this volume is an essential resource for researchers, academics, administrators, managers, funders, politicians and others who are concerned about the future of research funding and the importance of gender equity.

Sandra Acker is Professor Emerita, University of Toronto, Canada.

Oili-Helena Ylijoki is Senior Research Fellow, Tampere University, Finland.

Michelle K. McGinn is Professor and Acting Vice-President, Research at Brock University, Canada.

SOCIETY FOR RESEARCH INTO HIGHER EDUCATION SERIES

Series Editors:
Rachel Brooks, University of Surrey, UK
Sarah O'Shea, Curtin University, Australia

This exciting new series aims to publish cutting-edge research and discourse that reflects the rapidly changing world of higher education, examined in a global context. Encompassing topics of wide international relevance, the series includes every aspect of the international higher education research agenda, from strategic policy formulation and impact to pragmatic advice on best practice in the field.

Titles in the series:

Exploring Diary Methods in Higher Education Research
Opportunities, Choices and Challenges
Edited by Xuemeng Cao and Emily F. Henderson

Marginalised Communities in Higher Education
Disadvantage, Mobility and Indigeneity
Edited by Neil Harrison and Graeme Atherton

Student Identity and Political Agency
Activism, Representation and Consumer Rights
Rille Raaper

The Social Production of Research
Perspectives on Funding and Gender
Edited by Sandra Acker, Oili-Helena Ylijoki and Michelle K. McGinn

For more information about this series, please visit: https://www.routledge.com/Research-into-Higher-Education/book-series/SRHE

THE SOCIAL PRODUCTION OF RESEARCH

Perspectives on Funding and Gender

Edited by Sandra Acker, Oili-Helena Ylijoki and Michelle K. McGinn

LONDON AND NEW YORK

First published 2024
by Routledge
4 Park Square, Milton Park, Abingdon, Oxon OX14 4RN

and by Routledge
605 Third Avenue, New York, NY 10158

Routledge is an imprint of the Taylor & Francis Group, an informa business

© 2024 selection and editorial matter, Sandra Acker, Oili-Helena Ylijoki and Michelle K. McGinn; individual chapters, the contributors

The right of Sandra Acker, Oili-Helena Ylijoki and Michelle K. McGinn to be identified as the authors of the editorial material, and of the authors for their individual chapters, has been asserted in accordance with sections 77 and 78 of the Copyright, Designs and Patents Act 1988.

All rights reserved. No part of this book may be reprinted or reproduced or utilised in any form or by any electronic, mechanical, or other means, now known or hereafter invented, including photocopying and recording, or in any information storage or retrieval system, without permission in writing from the publishers.

Trademark notice: Product or corporate names may be trademarks or registered trademarks, and are used only for identification and explanation without intent to infringe.

British Library Cataloguing-in-Publication Data
A catalogue record for this book is available from the British Library

ISBN: 978-1-032-31172-2 (hbk)
ISBN: 978-1-032-36143-7 (pbk)
ISBN: 978-1-003-33043-1 (ebk)

DOI: 10.4324/9781003330431

Typeset in Galliard
by Taylor & Francis Books

CONTENTS

List of contributors	*x*
Editors' acknowledgements	*xvi*
Series editors' introduction	*xvii*

PART 1
Introduction   **1**

1 Editors' introduction   3
Sandra Acker, Oili-Helena Ylijoki and Michelle K. McGinn

2 Research funding and gender: Insights from the literature   20
Sandra Acker

PART 2
Stability and change   **35**

3 Here today, gone tomorrow: The vicissitudes of funding in
gendered higher education contexts – a view from Sweden   37
Gabriele Griffin

4 Discourses of university research in precarious times: A
spatial/temporal analysis from the United Kingdom   51
Barbara Read and Carole Leathwood

viii Contents

5 Gender inequalities, research funding and organisational
   practices: Academic mothers in Finnish universities   66
   *Marja Vehviläinen, Hanna-Mari Ikonen and
   Päivi Korvajärvi*

6 Casting a long shadow: COVID-19 and female academics'
   research productivity in the United Kingdom   81
   Kate Carruthers Thomas

PART 3
Care and conflict   **97**

7 Funding journeys in health technology in Finland: The
   atypical stories of Sara and Heidi   99
   Oili-Helena Ylijoki

8 Caring about research: Gender, research funding and labour
   in the Canadian academy   113
   Marie A. Vander Kloet and Caitlin Campisi

9 The gendered affective economy of funding: Conflicting
   realities of university leaders and researchers in Finnish
   academia   127
   *Johanna Hokka, Elisa Kurtti, Pia Olsson and
   Tiina Suopajärvi*

10 Black women academics, research funding and institutional
   misogynoir in the United Kingdom   142
   Shirley Anne Tate

PART 4
Funding and defunding   **157**

11 Status hierarchies, gender bias and disrespect: Ethnographic
   observations of Swedish Research Council review panels   159
   Lambros Roumbanis

12 Tracing excellence and equity in research funding: Policy
   change in the Canada Research Chairs Program   173
   Merli Tamtik and Dawn Sutherland

13 Women academics under RAE and REF: The changing
   research funding policy landscape in the United Kingdom   189
   Lisa Lucas

14 Research funding organisations as change agents for gender
   equality: Policies, practices and paradoxes in Sweden   204
   Liisa Husu and Helen Peterson

Index   *221*

CONTRIBUTORS

Sandra Acker is Professor Emerita in the Department of Social Justice Education, Ontario Institute for Studies in Education, University of Toronto, Canada. She has worked in the United States and United Kingdom as well as Canada and has published widely on gender and education, teachers' work and higher education. Her current research interests encompass careers and change in academic work, the social production of research, women in academic leadership and journal editors' decision-making. Her most recent research project as principal investigator is Academic Researchers in Challenging Times, funded by the Social Sciences and Humanities Research Council of Canada.

Caitlin Campisi is Associate Academic Dean at the Cégep Heritage College in Gatineau, Canada. Prior to joining Cégep Heritage College, she was a PhD candidate in the Department of Social Justice Education at the University of Toronto and the Executive Director of the Association of Part-Time Undergraduate Students at the University of Toronto. Her focus in her professional and research work is to make post-secondary education more accessible and equitable.

Kate Carruthers Thomas is Senior Research Fellow in the College of Law, Social and Criminal Justice at Birmingham City University, UK. Her research focuses on gendered issues in contemporary higher education, and since 2020, on experiences and impacts of the COVID-19 pandemic on female academics. She is a Co-Convenor of the Higher Education and COVID-19 Pandemic (HEC19) research network for the Society for Research into Higher Education. She also specialises in creative research methodologies and research dissemination. She published the graphic novella *Five 'Survive' Lockdown* in 2021.

Gabriele Griffin is Professor of Gender Research at Uppsala University, Sweden, and Extraordinary Professor at the Centre for Gender and Africa Studies at the University of the Free State, South Africa. From 2017 to 2022, she was Coordinator of the NordForsk-funded Nordic Centre of Excellence Beyond the Gender Paradox. She is Coordinator of the Graduate School in Gender, Humanities and Digital Cultures (2023–2027), which is funded by the Swedish Research Council. She researches women's cultural production, feminist research methodologies, and artificial intelligence and cultural heritage.

Johanna Hokka is a postdoctoral researcher in the Faculty of Social Sciences at Tampere University in Finland. Her research interests cover urban studies and science studies. In her PhD thesis, she examined how good sociology is defined among the elite of sociology in Finland and in Sweden. Currently, she is working on a project funded by the European Research Council that studies conflicts and co-existence in diversified urban neighbourhoods in Finland, Sweden and France.

Liisa Husu is Senior Professor in Gender Studies at Örebro University, Sweden, and an affiliated researcher at the Hanken School of Economics, Finland. She has been engaged in gender issues in academia in research, policy and civil society since the early 1980s in Nordic countries, Europe and internationally. Her research and publications focus on gender dynamics, inequalities and sexism in academic organisations, careers, research funding and research policy. She has been advising ministries, national/international agencies, funding organisations and universities, and has contributed to European research development and actions on gender and science since the late 1990s, in European Commission expert groups, networks, numerous gender and science research projects and conferences. She is scientific adviser to the European Women Rectors' Association (EWORA) and the Gender Initiative for Excellence (GENIE) at Chalmers University of Technology, Sweden.

Hanna-Mari Ikonen is Associate Professor of Social Sciences of Sport, University of Jyväskylä, Finland. She has also been a researcher and Senior Lecturer in Gender Studies at Tampere University, including research through the NordForsk-funded Nordic Centre of Excellence Beyond the Gender Paradox. She has published on the working life and living out enterprise discourse among young adults, mother entrepreneurs, rural people and women academics. Her current research projects are concerned with the phenomenon of in-work poverty and precarity in a post-industrial welfare state, funded by the Finnish Cultural Foundation and the Finnish Ministry of Agriculture and Forestry.

Päivi Korvajärvi is Professor Emerita in Gender Studies, Unit of Social Research, Faculty of Social Sciences, Tampere University, Finland. She has published widely on changing gendering practices in work including a variety

xii List of contributors

of white-collar and clerical work, call-centre work, future expectations of young adults in work, and research and innovation work. Most recently she has participated in the NordForsk-funded Nordic Centre of Excellence Beyond the Gender Paradox (2017–2022), which investigated gender equality and women's career opportunities in research and innovation inside and outside academe.

Elisa Kurtti is an Information Specialist at the Open Science Center at the University of Jyväskylä, Finland, and a doctoral researcher in social psychology in the Faculty of Social Sciences at Tampere University, Finland. She has studied workplace team interaction, Zoom-mediated interaction, and affects related to universities' strategies in Finland. In her dissertation, she examines affects in relation to research funding and research collaboration in the context of Finland. Before her dissertation project, she was a research assistant in several other projects.

Carole Leathwood is Professor Emeritus in the School of Social Sciences and Professions at London Metropolitan University, UK. With a disciplinary background in sociology and women's studies, her research has focused primarily on inequalities in higher and post-compulsory education. Her publications have encompassed the experiences of minority ethnic staff in further education; issues of social class, access and participation in higher education; gender, emotion and academic subjectivity; and the impact of research policy on academic work. Her most recent research, in collaboration with Professor Barbara Read, has examined academic precarity and the equity implications of the casualisation of academic labour.

Lisa Lucas is Associate Professor in Higher Education and Co-Director of the Centre for Higher Education Transformations (CHET) at University of Bristol, UK. She is a sociologist of higher education and has done extensive research on higher education policy and evaluation and the impacts on academics and academic careers. Her research is also focused on social justice in higher education with recent projects, Access4All (exploring equity and access to higher education for students across Europe) and Southern African Rurality in Higher Education (SARiHE).

Michelle K. McGinn is Professor and Acting Vice-President, Research at Brock University, Canada. Her primary interests include research collaboration, researcher development, mentorship, scholarly writing and ethics in academic practice. She is a co-investigator on the nationally funded project Academic Researchers in Challenging Times exploring the careers, practices and identities of social science scholars and research administrators in Canada. Related prior projects include Life on the Academic Periphery: Multiple Stories of Identity, Participation, and Belonging; Becoming Social Science Researchers: Learning and Enacting New Practices and Identities; and Research Ethics on the Ground: Partnerships, Plans, and Practices in Global Population Health.

Pia Olsson is Professor of Ethnology in the Department of Cultures at the University of Helsinki, Finland. Her research interests cover varied themes dealing with experiences of everyday life, such as teenagers' experiences of their social life in comprehensive school and meanings given to the close environment by urbanites. Methodologically she has been involved in ethnographic processes and archived oral histories.

Helen Peterson is Professor of Sociology in the School of Humanities, Education and Social Sciences, Örebro University, Sweden. She has researched the Swedish higher education sector and the European science and innovation sector through a gendered lens for over ten years. Her focus has been on academic management and leadership, women's careers in male-dominated fields, gender mainstreaming and policy implementation. Drawing on multiple national and European research projects, her work has been published in national and international peer-reviewed journals. She has served as an expert on national and international boards and committees addressing gender equality in higher education.

Barbara Read is Professor in the School of Education, University of Glasgow, Scotland. A sociologist of education, she has published widely on gender issues in higher education in the UK and internationally, particularly in relation to educational cultures and knowledges, student experience, academic work, inequalities of experience and the issue of casualisation. Recent research, in collaboration with Professor Carole Leathwood, includes a focus on the precarity of higher education lecturers and implications for teaching. She is currently principal investigator for Gendered Journeys: The Trajectories of STEM Students through Higher Education and into Employment in India and Rwanda, a project funded by UK Research and Innovation.

Lambros Roumbanis is Associate Professor in Sociology and a researcher at Stockholm Centre for Organizational Research (SCORE), Stockholm University, Sweden, and at the Institute for Futures Studies. His research interests are primarily focused on the organisation of expert judgements, evaluation technologies, selection mechanisms and complex decision-making processes. Currently, he is conducting two different projects: (a) the social dynamics of academic peer review and (b) the new emerging forms of human–artificial intelligence interaction effects in job recruitment processes. In addition, he also has a long-term interest in sociological theory and is for the moment especially occupied by theorising the problem of mediation.

Tiina Suopajärvi is University Lecturer of Cultural Anthropology at the University of Oulu Finland. Her ethnographic research ranges from ageing and nature–culture analyses to studies of gender and academic work in which she is interested in the everyday practices and experiences of researchers and academic affects. She is currently the principal investigator of projects titled Designing, Experiencing and Sensing the Socio-Materiality of Linnakaupunki Neighbourhood in Turku; and Ageing with Nature: Sensory Ethnographic Study on Ageing in Sparsely Populated Areas in Finland.

Dawn Sutherland is Professor and Associate Dean (Social Studies and Humanities) in the Faculty of Graduate Studies at the University of Manitoba, Canada. She held a Canada Research Chair in Science Education in Cultural Contexts (2006–2016) at the University of Winnipeg. More recently she has been involved in research programmes focused on interprofessional collaboration that supports the educational outcomes of children in care, graduate school admissions through the lens of EDI (equity, diversity and inclusion) and historical inequities in access to federal research funding. She teaches undergraduate and graduate courses and advises graduate students in the Faculty of Education at the University of Manitoba. She is often called upon to be an external PhD examiner in Canada and internationally.

Merli Tamtik is Associate Professor of Educational Administration in the Faculty of Education, University of Manitoba, Canada. Her research interests are in multi-level governance, internationalisation of (higher) education and education policy. She is a recipient of several federal (Social Sciences and Humanities Research Council of Canada) and institutional grants for her research projects. In 2019 she was the recipient of a merit award for research from the University of Manitoba and its faculty association. In 2020 she was awarded the Canadian Bureau of International Education (CBIE) Catalyst Award for the co-edited book *International Education as Public Policy in Canada*. She is an active member of the Canadian Society for the Study of Higher Education (CSSHE).

Shirley Anne Tate is Professor and Canada Research Chair Tier 1 in Feminism and Intersectionality, Department of Sociology, University of Alberta, and Honorary Professor in the Chair for Critical Studies in Higher Education Transformation, Nelson Mandela University, South Africa. Her intersectional research areas span Black diaspora studies, institutional racism, critical mixed-race studies and decolonial thought.

Marie A. Vander Kloet is Associate Professor in the Department of Education in the Program for University Pedagogy at the University of Bergen, Norway. Prior to joining the University of Bergen, she worked as an academic developer in Canada at McMaster University and the University of Toronto. Her current research interests focus on equity and accessibility in university teaching and on difference and power in academic work.

Marja Vehviläinen is a visiting researcher and retired University Lecturer in Gender Studies, in the Faculty of Social Sciences, Tampere University,

Finland. She has studied and worked in Sweden and Canada, in addition to Finland, and has researched gender, science and technology, gendered work, and everyday practices of nature–culture. Her most recent research includes the Nordic Centre of Excellence Beyond the Gender Paradox (2017–2022), funded by NordForsk, which investigated gender equality and women's career opportunities in research and innovation inside and outside academe.

Oili-Helena Ylijoki is Senior Research Fellow at the Research Centre for Knowledge, Science, Technology and Innovation Studies (TaSTI), Faculty of Social Sciences, Tampere University, Finland. She has investigated and published on transformations of academic work, identities and careers, temporalities of knowledge production, disciplinary cultures and gender in academia. She was a member of the NordForsk-funded Nordic Centre of Excellence Beyond the Gender Paradox (2017–2022). Her most recent projects include Changing University Institution and Equalities in the Academy; and Academic Affects – Research Strategies as Emotional Hotspots.

EDITORS' ACKNOWLEDGEMENTS

Sandra Acker, Oili-Helena Ylijoki and Michelle K. McGinn would like to thank everyone who has helped in the shaping of this book for their feedback and support. We are grateful to the series editors, Rachel Brooks and Sarah O'Shea, and the Director of the Society for Research into Higher Education, Clare Loughlin-Chow, for encouraging us in the book proposal and book writing stages. We also want to acknowledge the Routledge editorial and production teams, especially Sarah Hyde and Lauren Redhead, for assisting us in myriad ways, answering our questions and displaying commendable patience. We thank our talented indexer, Patti Phillips. Victoria Kannen and Caitlin Campisi participated helpfully in the administrative work for the book. As well, we owe a considerable debt to our contributing authors, who kindly absorbed and responded to our tracked changes and explained their country's research particularities to us when required.

We would like to acknowledge the core team of the project Academic Researchers in Challenging Times, which includes Sandra and Michelle as well as Caitlin Campisi, Pushpa Hamal, Marie Vander Kloet and Anne Wagner. The book arises from the work of the project, which was funded by the Social Sciences and Humanities Research Council of Canada (SSHRC), grant number 435-2017-0104.

Sandra would also like to thank her family for moral support and helpful discussions, and the Department of Social Justice in Education of the University of Toronto for two small SSHRC Institutional Grants that secured research assistance for the book in its early stages.

Oili-Helena wants to thank the Faculty of Social Sciences of Tampere University for flexible working conditions and her colleagues and family for intellectual, emotional and practical support and inspiration throughout the editing process.

Michelle expresses gratitude to Brock University for granting an administrative leave that cleared her calendar at just the right time to pull together the final text.

SERIES EDITORS' INTRODUCTION

This series, co-published by the Society for Research into Higher Education and Routledge Books, addresses key issues in higher education relevant to a wider international audience. Drawing upon innovative and empirically based scholarly thinking, the series aims to provide cross-cutting analysis that can inform policy and practice across the field.

Internationally focused, the Research in Higher Education series provides an opportunity for scholars and thought leaders to showcase recent research and insights relevant to the higher education environment. Each book in the series is unique but shares the common objective of meeting at least one of the principal aims of the Society: to advance knowledge; to enhance practice; and to inform policy.

In this book, the editors have successfully combined the research and perspectives of researchers from several countries and higher education settings to critically reflect on the intersections of gender and research funding. The result is a collection of diverse and thought-provoking contributions, which delve into the ways that gender, funding policies and procedures interact with the very nature of research, shedding light on the challenges faced by scholars across Canada, Finland, Sweden and the United Kingdom and by extension in many other sites. There are pervasive gender disparities that persist across academia, and while some of this is captured by large datasets and bibliometric explorations, the contributors in this book point to the need for a more nuanced understanding of these dilemmas. A series of qualitative studies is presented that illustrates the often oblique and subtle ways that gender interacts with the research funding process, including the deeply embodied and emotional nature of this work. The result is both deeply personal and public accounts of the social production of research, including the broader implications for innovation, knowledge production and societal progress.

Rachel Brooks
Sarah O'Shea

PART 1

Introduction

1
EDITORS' INTRODUCTION

Sandra Acker, Oili-Helena Ylijoki and Michelle K. McGinn

Today's universities operate within a neoliberal climate in which accounting and accountability are central, and managerial practices are expected to ensure that research and publishing productivity are kept at peak levels (Leišytė, 2016; Olssen, 2016; Shore & Wright, 2000). Granting structures and cultures appear in the shadows of higher education literature (Polster, 2007), yet they greatly influence academic lives and careers. In this context, universities compete for government funding and academics compete for external grants to support their research (Laudel, 2006). Academics require funding as both a means and an end. As a means, funding allows them to do research in order to publish in approved outlets and keep or progress in their positions. As an end, gaining funding counts in performance reviews as an achievement. And to be fair, not all motives are utilitarian: many, perhaps most, academics enjoy the research work that funding makes possible. Regardless of motive, researchers frequently find themselves in uncomfortable situations where funding is elusive and success rates low. They are 'faced with an increasingly complex and changing environment affected by the behavior of external funders and by national university policies' (Luukkonen & Thomas, 2016, p. 100).

This volume draws attention to gendered dimensions within the current neoliberal research funding context. Our rationale behind this effort is that the two important topics of gender and research funding have not usually been considered together. It is not that there is a scarcity of work on gender in the academy nor even on research funding. However, linkages between gender (and other intersecting social divisions) and research funding are less common.

A growing scholarly trend involves bibliometric and other explorations of large datasets, some of which consider the relationship of gender to funding success, citations and/or research productivity (e.g. Ceci et al., 2023; Kozlowski et al., 2022; Larivière et al., 2013; Sá et al., 2020; Sugimoto & Larivière,

DOI: 10.4324/9781003330431-2

4   Sandra Acker, Oili-Helena Ylijoki and Michelle K. McGinn

2023). These approaches are useful in identifying broad patterns and have become increasingly sophisticated, revealing information about issues such as the gendered nature of authorship and credit during research collaborations (Ni et al., 2021; Ross et al., 2022).

A complementary approach involves smaller scale, usually qualitative studies that focus on the aspects that the quantitative studies cannot reach: how it feels to search for funding, the gatekeeping operations of networking, and the everyday gendered and racialised practices that sustain and often mask inequalities in research work (e.g. Acker & McGinn, 2021; Grant & Elizabeth, 2015; Griffin, 2022; Leberman et al., 2016; Murgia & Poggio, 2019; O'Connor & Fauve-Chamoux, 2016; Rollock, 2013; Steinþórsdóttir et al., 2020). Chapters in this volume follow this second path by exploring the social production of research. Contributors investigate personal and group experience with research funding; funding-body, institutional and country contexts; and the impact on the research ecosystem and the careers of academics of sudden changes such as the COVID-19 pandemic or the United Kingdom's withdrawal from the European Union. The chapters provide nuanced accounts of the social, emotional and political conditions in which research is produced and the ways that academics enact, shape, negotiate and resist these conditions in their everyday practice. Authors draw on a wide variety of qualitative methods: in-depth interviews, ethnography, diary-interview methods, media analysis, email questionnaires, vignettes, focus groups and policy critique. Overall, the chapters provide critical perspectives on the research funding imperative and its gendered repercussions.

The book differs from many collections on aspects of higher education in multiple nations. Although we take an international approach, we focus on a limited selection of countries: Canada, Finland, Sweden and the United Kingdom (UK). (Although the UK is an amalgam of four countries, we treat it collectively as a 'country' for convenience and comparability.) We believe that this smaller scope involving a limited set of countries enables a deeper analysis, leaving room to include details of each country's higher education and research ecosystem essential to understanding individuals' actions and sense-making, while still exploring a range of themes across chapters that are relevant beyond the four countries. In the next section, we introduce the four countries, after which we provide an account of how the book came to be written and an overview of the contributions that follow.

Countries: similarities and differences

Our four countries look very different from one another when we consider area and population, although their research ecosystems have much in common. In terms of area, we have from largest to smallest: Canada, Sweden, Finland, UK. For population, the order is different with the UK leading, followed by Canada, Sweden and Finland (Worldometer, n.d.). All four countries are welfare states to a degree, but with elements of capitalism as well. Gosta Esping-Andersen's (1990) three types of welfare states (conservative, liberal and social democratic) seem at least partially apposite. The Nordic countries have been well-known as social democratic states, where social services are widely available and usually free, although recent governments have moved towards market orientations in different sectors, including higher education. Canada and the UK are mixed systems, generally falling under the liberal umbrella where market solutions play a role, while medical, social and educational services remain largely accessible but may be means-tested. All four countries offer free elementary and secondary education and have all or mostly public universities and robust research ecosystems. There are important variations in academic career structures, explored to an extent in the following discussion and in chapters of this book. The next sections consider the four countries' gender equality frameworks and the place of their research funding systems within neoliberal higher education.

Gender equality frameworks

All four countries have gender equality (or equity[1]) policies for higher education, yet gender gaps in research funding as well as more broadly in academic career-building persist in each of them (see Acker, this volume).

The Nordic countries, including Finland and Sweden, are known for both gender equality and investment in innovation (Griffin & Vehviläinen, 2021). Still, writers (e.g. Helgesson & Sjögren, 2019; Silander et al., 2022, p. 73) point to a 'Nordic gender paradox' wherein certain gendered inequalities remain stubbornly resistant to change. In Sweden and Finland, and also in the UK and Canada, the representation of academic women in senior promoted positions, top leadership roles and STEM (science, technology, engineering, mathematics) disciplines falls behind that of men. Despite comprehensive legislation prohibiting discrimination and years of gender mainstreaming[2] (Silander, 2023, p. 47), the Swedish Research Council is quoted as saying, 'It is expected that achieving gender balance among professors will take another 25 years' (Myklebust, 2021). In a review of journal articles from Nordic countries published between 2003 and 2018, Silander and colleagues (2022) stress the importance of the early post-PhD years in gaining access to career-building networks, with men holding a cumulative advantage that begins early (Angervall et al., 2015) and grows over time. Griffin and Vehviläinen (2021) point to cases in their data where old boys' networks operated to offer posts to young men, bypassing formal job searches. Our chapter authors dig deeper into some of the sources and consequences of gender inequality. For example, when research funding becomes scarce, as began in Finland in 2008 (see Aarrevaara & Pietiläinen, 2021), men have a greater chance of survival as male-dominated hierarchies (re)assert themselves (see Griffin, this volume; Vehviläinen et al., this volume; and Ylijoki, this volume).

Gender equality policies have been applied to higher education institutions that receive government funding and to research funding bodies themselves and developed with increasing force over time, yet as Tamtik and Sutherland (this volume) point out, 'targets are not enough'. Following Ahmed (2012), Griffin and Vehviläinen (2021) comment that sometimes the creation of a policy is taken as a signal of action and no effort is put towards the real work of implementation: 'nothing is done *because* a policy is in place' (p. 7, emphasis added). The UK's Athena Swan[3] charter programme is a well-known and imitated intervention in which universities work towards awards at different levels for their gender equality policies and practices. Critics point to the emphasis on performativity rather than the reality of change, the extra labour for women who usually do the work of preparing submissions, and metrics that insufficiently prioritise intersectionality (Bhopal & Henderson, 2021; Tzanakou, 2019). The UK has more recently developed a Race Equality Charter, which Bhopal and Henderson (2021) regard as showing potential but suffering from institutions' reluctance to add more work beyond their Athena Swan applications.

Canada's research funding agencies have launched a pilot of their own version of Athena Swan, named 'Dimensions' and encompassing a broad sweep of considerations under the umbrella of 'equity, diversity and inclusion' (EDI). 'Best practices' guidelines for a funding stream initiated in 2018, titled the New Frontiers in Research Fund (NFRF), contain detailed requirements to demonstrate EDI practices in grant applications, including research team composition, research environment and project details (Government of Canada, 2023). Interestingly, the NFRF funds 'interdisciplinary, high-risk/high-reward, transformative research' intended 'to support world-leading innovation and enhance Canada's competitiveness and expertise in the global, knowledge-based economy' (Government of Canada, 2022, para. 1), the type of rhetoric often thought to be implicitly masculinised (see Read & Leathwood, this volume). EDI requirements have also been added to evaluation criteria for other funding streams and to institutional processes associated with the Canada Research Chairs Program, the latter detailed in this volume by Tamtik and Sutherland.

These Canadian initiatives are informed by contemporary feminist writing that emphasises intersectional approaches, i.e. acknowledges the intersecting categories that cut across gender. While race and class are the most frequently cited such categories, others such as age, disability, indigeneity, sexual orientation and ethnicity also feature prominently. How intersectionality is approached tends to vary across countries. Hübinette and Mählck (2015) write that 'in the English-speaking world, racial discrimination is a well established research area and an integral part of the equality and quality work of the university sector' (p. 67). Yet Tate (this volume) draws attention to the difficult climate for Black women academics in the UK who wish to conduct funded research. In contrast, the focus in Nordic scholarship has been more directly on gender or gender and class than on the intersections of gender and race or ethnicity (e.g. Hübinette & Mählck, 2015; Lund, 2019). The intersecting social divisions considered in this volume's chapters depend on the historical and demographic composition of each country, local area and institutional profile (Hvenegård-Lassen et al., 2020).

Research and the neoliberal university

In recent years, the higher education sectors in all four countries have been subject to competition, rankings, differentiation among institutions, increased accountability and other aspects of neoliberalism. The neoliberal turn in academe (also called 'corporatisation' and 'academic capitalism') has consequences, such as a market orientation guiding decisions, emphasis on competition both within and between institutions, strategic planning and managerialism (Croucher & Lacy, 2020; Olssen, 2016). Two topics that have implications for research work are often mentioned in chapters in this volume: *performance management through selective funding* and *security of academic positions.*

Performance management through selective funding

Government funding is of two main types: core funding for universities; and competitive funding for individuals and sometimes for institutions through public funding agencies, especially research councils. Competitive funding for individual research projects or research programmes has become increasingly prominent in the lives of academics and is analysed in various chapters of this volume. One key reason for the increased emphasis is said to be that universities increasingly depend on external funding for financial survival (Pelkonen et al., 2014; Sugimoto & Larivière, 2023, p. 93). In research council and similar awards, there are systems of peer review that consider the quality of the research proposal and often the track record of the proposer(s) (see Husu & Peterson, this volume; Roumbanis, this volume). Peer review is necessarily subjective, at least in part, and review systems become characterised as unfair and 'a lottery' (Perez Velazquez, 2019), especially when award rates are low. The question that animates our contributors is whether there are gendered patterns to the processes of grant application, review and acquisition, and if so, how they operate (see also Sato et al., 2021; Steinþórsdóttir et al., 2020).

Core funding for universities is increasingly performance-based, though differently determined from country to country. Governments are actively altering these systems and their investments in research and development (R&D) so that it is difficult to describe a situation that is forever in flux.

For individual universities, selective government funding is like an investment, intended to give greater support to research programmes with outstanding promise or better records, or direct the energies of individual institutions into areas that appear to build on their strengths and sometimes would-be strengths. Thus one university might have a stronger emphasis on science and technology, while another will be shaped around contributions to its local community. This is the 'strategic planning and profiling' discussed by Silander and Haake (2017) for Sweden and in this volume's chapter by Hokka et al. for Finland. Differentiation among institutions and the concentration of resources across and within them are likely to have unanticipated consequences. Silander and Haake (2017) write, 'In Sweden, the state-funded investment in excellence has resulted in an unintended concentration of research resources going to a few universities, certain research areas and to men' (p. 2010).

Sweden is not the only country that features elements of performance management related to core research funding. The UK's Research Excellence Framework (REF) stands out as a key example, one that appears to shape everything that happens in the UK research world (see Carruthers Thomas, this volume; Lucas, this volume). Periodic peer-review judgements of submissions to the REF from 'Units of Assessment' lead to core research funding differentials among universities.

Finland has moved over time to a sharp focus on competition for both core government research funding and external research grants (Hokka et al., this volume; Ylijoki, this volume). Publications in Finland are rated by a system known as 'JuFo' (an acronym for *Julkaisufoorumi*, meaning 'publication forum') and operated by the Federation of Finnish Learned Societies. JuFo is one indicator in the Finnish Ministry of Education and Culture's funding formula for universities. Although not meant to be used in evaluating research outputs of individuals (as opposed to aggregates), in practice it often has a role in hiring and promotion.

Canada has no federal department of education and gives its provinces the responsibility for regulating education and distributing core funding, although the federal government retains the major role in providing competitive research funding and scholarships through its agencies (research councils), as well as some competitive infrastructure funding. Although a system like the UK's Research Excellence Framework could not be implemented at a national level in Canada, certain individual provinces are beginning to distribute some of the core funding to institutions according to performance on metrics agreed with each university (Peters, 2021). Despite its strong commitments to equity, Canada has been criticised for inadequate federal funding for research (Innovation, Science and Economic Development Canada, 2023; U15 Canada, 2023).

Security of academic positions

Two superficially different phenomena but with oddly similar aspects are *tenure systems* and *precarity*. Finland and Sweden have introduced new tenure-track systems for some academics, whereas the UK abolished its former tenure system in 1988 and offers a variety of contracts and statuses, some more secure than others. Canada has a well-established tenure system (Acker et al., 2012). Being hired into a tenure-track position (the potential pathway to permanence) is an accomplishment, and obtaining tenure after performing at a high enough level is even more so. Whereas in Canada, details vary from one institution to another and candidates complain that the rules are unclear (Acker & Webber, 2016), in Sweden, criteria seem to be formalised and metricised. In a case study, Helgesson and Sjögren (2019) conclude that several of the highly specific metrics used to determine tenure and promotion in the newly initiated Swedish tenure system were disadvantageous to women. Their title phrase 'no finish line' implies that there is no way to be 'good enough',[4] the sentiment echoed in Finland, where, according to Pietilä (2019), academics on the tenure track are 'encouraged to present themselves as a particular kind of academic: as productive, collaborative tireless selves who are capable of performing multiple tasks and reaching the high standards set for new assistant professors' (p. 935; for Canada, see Acker & McGinn, 2021; Acker & Webber, 2016).

The flip side of the security implied by tenure is *precarity*. All four countries have responded to the shortage of government funding that accompanies neoliberalism by increasing the numbers of staff in precarious positions, whether teaching- or research-oriented (or both), characterised by a lack of job security and often a short-term commitment with few institutional supports (Griffin, this volume; Read & Leathwood, this volume). There are different ways to experience precarity, depending on the ways that research in a particular country is configured in universities. Finland appears to have the highest level of precarity, where 70% of researchers lack permanent contracts, including many who are advanced and successful in their careers (Ylijoki, this volume). Whereas Finland's precarious academics are predominantly researchers, Canada's precarious academics are usually teachers (Pasma & Shaker, 2018; Vander Kloet & Campisi, this volume) and the UK has examples of both. A huge rise in reliance on short-term contract academics for teaching in Canada has consequences for doctoral graduates who cannot find tenure-track positions. The two phenomena of precarity and tenure are linked together: if there are fewer permanent academics, they have more work to do to maintain the institution ('service') and keep up its research record.

Developing and organising the book

Discussions on the need for this book arose in conversation with members of the Academic Researchers in Challenging Times research project. The project, funded by the Social Sciences and Humanities Research Council of Canada, 2017–2021, with an unfunded extension to 2024, focused on the experience of leading academic research projects in the social sciences. Its overall aim was to explore the academic experience of the social production of research in the current context of Ontario, Canada (Acker & McGinn, 2021; Acker et al.,

2019; McGinn et al., 2019; Vander Kloet & Campisi, 2023; Vander Kloet & Wagner, 2023; Wagner & Acker, 2024). Early in the project, Sandra Acker and Oili-Helena Ylijoki delivered a joint paper to the International Sociological Association annual conference comparing experiences in seeking grant funding in the different contexts of Finland and Canada (Acker & Ylijoki, 2018). For example, both the Academy of Finland (AF; in 2023 renamed the Research Council of Finland) and the Social Sciences and Humanities Research Council of Canada (SSHRC) set up panels to evaluate grant proposals. AF panellists were predominantly international experts and proposals were written in English. Panel members for SSHRC's flagship Insight Grants programme came mostly from Canadian universities and were expected to be able to read submissions in the two official languages of English and French. We began to realise that the effort to find research funding would take different forms in different nations, belying any taken-for-granted assumptions located in our own histories, and that it would make interesting reading to compare experiences of funding from several countries. To Canada and Finland, we added the United Kingdom and Sweden. Michelle McGinn became our third editor.[5] In terms of finding a publisher, the Society for Research into Higher Education's series on Research into Higher Education, published with Routledge, seemed ideal from the start and we were encouraged by the series editors to produce a proposal, which was ultimately accepted.

Each chapter went through several revisions, and we attempted to be as consistent as possible across contributions. Perhaps what was most difficult for authors was 'knowing what they didn't know'. Through the work of compiling this volume, the editors have learned repeatedly that not only are nations different in their research structures and practices, in both obvious and subtle ways, but they are also subject to frequent change from multiple directions and for a variety of reasons, not least changes of government. The rapidity of change posed a problem for us: how could we keep the volume up to date? We have combed through the chapters, making efforts, along with the contributors, to update references to statistics and documents whenever possible, while recognising that there are limits.

Individual chapters in this volume explain the situations that frame the contributors' research. We opted to allow some overlap (e.g. explanations of the UK's Research Excellence Framework) so that a chapter would be self-sufficient and readers would not need to flip to an introduction or glossary to grasp a concept or system. We asked each set of contributors to provide sufficient background information to make their research comprehensible to others not from that country. This effort extends to descriptions of acronyms, organisations and so forth. We edited for consistency across chapters, yet we did not wish to erase any author's voice, so some variations (e.g. 'equality' and 'equity', 'women' and 'female') remain.

More broadly, in terms of language, there are many cases where the same or a similar word might mean something different. 'Professor' is one example.

As indicated in the chapter in this volume by Tate, there is a rough comparability between the UK's 'professor' with North American 'full professor', but the proportions of (full) professors in Canada and the US are much larger than in the UK. Confusingly, 'professor' is also used colloquially in North America for almost anyone teaching at a post-secondary institution. Even among European countries, there may be subtle variations in the meaning of professor. Salminen-Karlsson (2023) points out that the percentage of academics who are professors varies and when it is smaller, the status is higher, as in Germany compared with Italy (p. 94).

Even 'researcher', a term used throughout this volume, has its ambiguities. Some of the chapters (Griffin, this volume; Vehviläinen, this volume) refer to the European four-stage model which, although varying in actual practice, gives a framework of (1) doctoral researcher, (2) postdoctoral researcher, (3) lecturer or senior researcher, and (4) professor. As Griffin points out, in Sweden and Finland the fourth stage is reached only relatively late in a career, and many in the other stages, even stage three, work without permanent contracts. She notes that in Norway, in contrast, there is usually a permanent contract in stages three and four. In Canadian writing on higher education, the term 'researcher' typically means an academic who conducts research, teaches and performs service (administration), often with teaching and research in equal proportions.

Across all four countries, though, there are gender issues, with women, having improved their position in the research economy over time, still at a disadvantage compared to men colleagues. Whatever the lower-ranked category is (such as insecure teaching or research positions), we find women overrepresented.

Previewing the book

There were several ways that the main body of the book could have been structured. We decided against organising by country, as we thought that might provide less incentive to read across nations. Of course, a reader might select chapters from a particular national context if that is their interest. The chapter titles cue the country location to enable such an approach. We decided to organise by broad themes: introduction, stability and change, care and conflict, and funding and defunding. Next, we briefly summarise these main themes and introduce the individual chapters.

Part 1: Introduction

After this chapter's introductory opening, the second chapter, by Sandra Acker, reviews selectively what is known about research funding and how it intersects with gender. Acker develops a three-part structure within which approaches to the topic fit: the experiences of individual grant-seekers, the institutional frameworks, and the practices of government and funding bodies.

12 Sandra Acker, Oili-Helena Ylijoki and Michelle K. McGinn

Part 2: Stability and change

The chapters in Part 2 emphasise the contrasts of coexisting stability (long-standing arrangements, including persistent inequalities) and change (new subject fields, policies, research environments, structures, cultures, government decisions, health crises). Some elements like 'precarity' (job insecurity) are not new but have intensified in the era of neoliberalism/academic capitalism: all four chapters refer to precarious situations or precarity. Women researchers may be in especially precarious positions trying to return to research after parental leave or when an unexpected situation like COVID-19 arises, or when funding for research declines and male-dominated networks assert their privilege.

In Chapter 3, Gabriele Griffin writes about a newly developing interdisciplinary field, digital humanities, that is struggling to establish itself in Sweden in an era of uncertain funding and precarity of researcher positions. It brings together traditionally feminised domains like the humanities with masculinised ones like technology. The interview-based research takes place in centres where funding is uncertain and researchers find themselves taking on multiple projects with restrictions around how to account for their time, ending up with both precarity and work overload. Compared to the men, women in the study found themselves in more vulnerable positions when funding declined.

The theme of precarity arises strongly in Chapter 4, by Barbara Read and Carole Leathwood. The authors undertake a media analysis of articles published over an 18-month period in the *Times Higher Education* that concerned the UK's withdrawal from the European Union (Brexit) and the COVID-19 pandemic. The authors relate these episodes to 'changing configurations in the research landscape', highlighting gendered and racialised consequences of the relevant discourses and the implications for knowledge production.

Chapter 5, by Marja Vehviläinen, Hanna-Mari Ikonen and Päivi Korvajärvi, takes us to Finland and another new field, health technology. Like digital humanities, health technology crosses the boundaries of traditional disciplines for men and for women. The chapter focuses on academic mothers who took parental leave, a feature of Nordic countries that is believed to be supportive of gender equality. Coming back to work was often problematic: if the project was supported by the Academy of Finland, there was a good chance that there was a place for the mother to return; in other cases, they were unable to do so. As in Griffin's analysis, the combination of male-dominated workplaces and funding shortages was especially harmful to women researchers. The authors argue that funding agencies and employing institutions could work together to avoid these deleterious conditions.

In Chapter 6, Kate Carruthers Thomas addresses the effects of the COVID-19 pandemic in the UK. Many articles in the popular press have argued that women's research productivity suffered during the pandemic, as they so often had children at home when schools were closed and their own teaching responsibilities shifted precipitously to unfamiliar online methods. Carruthers Thomas uses an unusual method of combining diary entries at two points in time with interviews to get an in-depth sense of what actually happened to the career prospects of these academics and considers what the long-term result is likely to be. The dominant response was struggle, but there were some women in the study who flourished under the conditions, formulating new long-distance collaborations through videoconferencing or finding the writing of grant applications easier than producing high-quality journal articles.

Part 3: Care and conflict

In Part 3, the chapters highlight the differing and sometimes conflicting perspectives of persons positioned differently within academe. Care or lack of care for others in the research ecosystem is evident across the chapters and affects people's sense of themselves and connections to others. Managers defend university strategies, while lower placed academics fret about the impact on their futures. Black women academics in the UK are rarely positioned as research leaders, especially when compared with White men. When circumstances dictate, men may close ranks against their women colleagues, some of whom can only rise above their situations through superperforming by raising grant funding. In a sense, those who are threatened must care for themselves.

Chapter 7, by Oili-Helena Ylijoki, goes deeply into two career stories from a study of researchers in health technology in Finland. The stories of Sara and Heidi are atypical in their combination of successes and setbacks. By detailing their ups and downs, Ylijoki shows that their ability to raise external research funding is what saves them not only financially but also socially and emotionally and allows them to continue in academic career paths.

In Chapter 8, Marie A. Vander Kloet and Caitlin Campisi analyse data from a Canadian study of professional staff (research administrators) and academic women with strong research records and social justice themes in their work. Neither group wants to be associated with lower level 'administration'. They covet thinking work instead. This chapter considers the role of care for each other and for the work, and it conveys the unease with which academics and 'non-academics' (often with PhDs) interact with each other.

The sense of group identities in tension within academe is continued in another study from Finland described in Chapter 9 by Johanna Hokka, Elisa Kurtti, Pia Olsson and Tiina Suopajärvi. Drawing on a combination of focus groups ('affect cafes') and interviews, the authors show how emotions are attached to the ways researchers and university leaders see various university and funding practices, such as 'strategies' that are meant to be complied with by all levels of the university. The university's gendered affective economy is experienced differently depending on one's position in it.

The final chapter in Part 3, Chapter 10, is by Shirley Anne Tate and is a strong critique of the ways in which misogynoir – racism against Black women – operates in the UK university sector. Statistics support the argument that Black women academics are a tiny fraction of those enabled to become principal investigators or fellows in the research funding ecosystem. Thirteen Black women academics from the UK share their experiences of being downgraded and disregarded in a system that lacks care and requires drastic reform. Conflict is evident in this critique of the status quo.

Part 4: Funding and defunding

Chapters in Part 4 focus closely on the operation of research funding organisations (RFOs) and the consequences of exercises such as the UK's Research Excellence Framework. The outcomes of RFO procedures and eventual decisions and of assessment exercises are that some grant-seekers are funded and some are not, producing emotional responses, repeated efforts and a cynicism about the process. Nevertheless, RFOs continue efforts to improve procedures and to instil gender equality into all aspects of funding practices.

Chapter 11 is an unusual study by Lambros Roumbanis, who was allowed to observe as an ethnographer in a series of science and engineering assessment panels of the Swedish Research Council. In this chapter, he conveys the intensity of debate in two such panels, not because they were typical but because they illustrate the ways in which status can impact the interactions and ultimately the decisions. Younger men and women of all ages tend to defer to older, experienced, high-status men, and efforts to interrupt this male dominance are often unsuccessful.

Merli Tamtik and Dawn Sutherland, in Chapter 12, tell the story of the origins and development of the Canada Research Chairs Program, an initiative launched in 2000 by the federal government to fund and fill around 2,000 additional university positions with leading researchers. At the start, the programme paid little attention to gender balance, but over time, efforts of equity-seeking groups and greater awareness of how inequity operates for a range of minoritised groups eventually changed the system, moving through monitoring to targets to actual consequences for non-compliance, although excellence is still defined rather narrowly in the programme.

Chapter 13 by Lisa Lucas builds on her earlier work on the UK's Research Assessment Exercise (RAE) and Research Excellence Framework (REF). Two sets of interviews conducted with women academics prior to different iterations of the RAE/REF are revisited to show the levels of anxiety and hard work funnelled into each of these reviews. She pays particular attention to the changes in the framework over time and its impact on women's careers and speculates as to what lies ahead.

Finally, in Chapter 14, Liisa Husu and Helen Peterson, like Roumbanis, analyse the Swedish Research Council (SRC) but with a different methodology, and like Tamtik and Sutherland, chart the changes over time. They propose that an RFO can be conceptualised as a change agent. Through document analysis and interviews with employees, panel members and reviewers, the authors critically explore policies and practices related to gender equality in research funding and the dilemmas faced in implementation. This chapter is one that raises the issue of the Nordic paradox: how a country can be so strongly focused on gender equality yet remain unequal in many areas. Its detailed examination of changes in the SRC suggests progress is possible.

Final thoughts

Throughout this volume, the authors take seriously the contention that research is a social production that emerges through the confluence of social, emotional and political considerations that shape the context and actions of academics. Complexity and change are the abiding lessons we drew from the work of compiling this volume and trying to explain variations from place to place. For example, one helpful comparison of Finland and the UK's project funding by Pelkonen and colleagues was written in 2014; ten years later, many details are no longer accurate and the names of funding and government bodies have nearly all changed. Complexity and change are relevant to how gender is interpreted and interpolated in research funding arrangements, the social relations of higher education and the expanding grants culture in academe. We hope that this volume will stimulate more thought and work on these vital issues.

Notes

1 Canada tends to use 'equity' while the European countries and the UK more often use 'equality'. In Canada, a distinction is sometimes made between equality (treating people the same) and equity (removing barriers and allocating resources to support comparable outcomes).
2 Gender mainstreaming is a European Commission policy, based on systemic interventions in all policies and stages, applying extensively but nevertheless considered rather vague (Silander, 2023, pp. 48–49).
3 Originally, SWAN was an acronym and often spelled with all capital letters. More recent usage, which we follow, is to capitalise only the 'S'.
4 In a similar vein, McGinn (2012) used the metaphor of Procrustes's bed to describe the ever-changing and unattainable standards perceived by Canadian academics.
5 In the early stages of organising the book and securing the publisher, Caitlin Campisi was engaged as an additional editor; our thanks to Caitlin for her contributions.

References

Aarrevaara, T., & Pietiläinen, V. (2021). The role of Finnish higher education in the innovation and research system. In T. Aarrevaara, M. Finkelstein, G. A. Jones, & J. Jung (Eds.), *Universities in the knowledge society: the nexus of national systems of innovation and higher education* (pp. 277–295). Springer. https://doi.org/10.1007/978-3-030-76579-8_16

Acker, S., & McGinn, M. K. (2021). Fast professors, research funding, and the figured worlds of mid-career Ontario academics. *Brock Education Journal, 30*(2), 79–98. https://doi.org/10.26522/brocked.v30i2.864

Acker, S., McGinn, M. K., & Campisi, C. (2019). The work of university research administrators: praxis and professionalization. *Journal of Praxis in Higher Education, 1*(1), 61–85. https://doi.org/10.47989/kpdc67

Acker, S., & Webber, M. (2016). Discipline and publish: the tenure review process in Ontario universities. In L. Shultz & M. Viczko (Eds.), *Assembling and governing the higher education institution* (pp. 233–255). Palgrave Macmillan.

Acker, S., Webber, M., & Smyth, E. (2012). Tenure troubles and equity matters in Canadian academe. *British Journal of Sociology of Education, 33*(5), 743–761. https://doi.org/10.1080/01425692.2012.674784

Acker, S., & Ylijoki, O.-H. (2018, July 20). *Grant hunting in corporatized universities: experiences from Canada and Finland.* Paper presented at the International Sociological Association Conference, Toronto, Canada.

Ahmed, S. (2012). *On being included: racism and diversity in institutional life.* Duke University Press.

Angervall, P., Beach, D., & Gustafsson, J. (2015). The unacknowledged value of female academic labour power for male research careers. *Higher Education Research & Development, 34*(5), 815–827. https://doi.org/10.1080/07294360.2015.1011092

Bhopal, K., & Henderson, H. (2021). Competing inequalities: gender versus race in higher education institutions in the UK. *Educational Review (Birmingham), 73*(2), 153–169. https://doi.org/10.1080/00131911.2019.1642305

Ceci, S. J., Kahn, S., & Williams, W. (2023). Exploring gender bias in six key domains of academic science: an adversarial collaboration. *Psychological Science in the Public Interest, 24*(1), 15–73. https://doi.org/10.1177/15291006231163179

Croucher, G., & Lacy, W. B. (2020). The emergence of academic capitalism and university neoliberalism: perspectives of Australian higher education leadership. *Higher Education, 83*(2), 279–295. https://doi.org/10.1007/s10734-020-00655-7

Esping-Andersen, G. (1990). *The three worlds of welfare capitalism.* Polity Press.

Government of Canada. (2022, January 7). *About the New Frontiers in Research Fund.* https://www.sshrc-crsh.gc.ca/funding-financement/nfrf-fnfr/about-au_sujet-eng.aspx

Government of Canada. (2023, July 7). *Best practices in equity, diversity and inclusion in research practice and design.* https://www.sshrc-crsh.gc.ca/funding-financement/nfrf-fnfr/edi-eng.aspx

Grant, B. M., & Elizabeth, V. (2015). Unpredictable feelings: academic women under research audit. *British Educational Research Journal, 41*(2), 287–302. https://doi.org/10.1002/berj.3145

Griffin, G. (Ed.). (2022). *Gender inequalities in tech-driven research and innovation: living the contradiction.* Bristol University Press.

Griffin, G., & Vehviläinen, M. (2021). The persistence of gender struggles in Nordic research and innovation. *Feminist Encounters: A Journal of Critical Studies in Culture and Politics, 5*(2), Article 28. https://doi.org/10.20897/femenc/11165

Helgesson, K. S., & Sjögren, E. (2019). No finish line: how formalization of academic assessment can undermine clarity and increase secrecy. *Gender, Work, & Organization, 26*(4), 558–581. https://doi.org/10.1111/gwao.12355

Hübinette, T., & Mählck, P. (2015). The racial grammar of Swedish higher education and research policy: the limits and conditions of researching race in a colour-blind context. In R. Andreassen & K. Vitus (Eds.), *Affectivity and race: studies from Northern contexts* (pp. 59–73). Routledge.

Hvenegård-Lassen, K., Staunæs, D., & Lund, R. (2020). Intersectionality, yes, but how? Approaches and conceptualizations in Nordic feminist research and activism. *NORA – Nordic Journal of Feminist and Gender Research, 28*(3), 173–182. https://doi.org/10.1080/08038740.2020.1790826

Innovation, Science and Economic Development Canada. (2023). *Report of the Advisory Panel on the Federal Research Support System.* https://ised-isde.canada.ca/site/panel-federal-research-support/en/report-advisory-panel-federal-research-support-system

Kozlowski, D., Larivière, V., Sugimoto, C. R., & Monroe-White, T. (2022). Intersectional inequalities in science. *Proceedings of the National Academy of Sciences, 119*(2), Article e2113067119. https://doi.org/10.1073/pnas.2113067119

Larivière, V., Ni, C., Gingras, Y., Cronin, B., & Sugimoto, C. R. (2013). Bibliometrics: global gender disparities in science. *Nature News, 504*(7479), 211–213. https://doi.org/10.1038/504211a

Laudel, G. (2006). The 'quality myth': promoting and hindering conditions for acquiring research funds. *Higher Education, 52*(3), 375–403. https://doi.org/10.1007/s10734-004-6414-5

Leberman, S. I., Eames, B., & Barnett, S. (2016). 'Unless you are collaborating with a big name successful professor, you are unlikely to receive funding.' *Gender and Education, 28*(5), 644–661. https://doi.org/10.1080/09540253.2015.1093102

Leišytė, L. (2016). New public management and research productivity – A precarious state of affairs of academic work in the Netherlands. *Studies in Higher Education, 41*(5), 828–846. https://doi.org/10.1080/03075079.2016.1147721

Lund, R. W. B. (2019). Exploring "whiteness" as ideology and work knowledge. In R. W. B. Lund & A. C. E. Nilsen (Eds.), *Institutional ethnography in the Nordic region* (pp. 101–113). Routledge.

Luukkonen, T., & Thomas, D. A. (2016). The 'negotiated space' of university researchers' pursuit of a research agenda. *Minerva, 54*(1), 99–127. https://doi.org/10.1007/s11024-016-9291-z

McGinn, M. K. (with Manley-Casimir, M., Fenton, N. E., & Shields, C.). (2012). Fitting Procrustes' bed: a shifting reality. *Workplace: A Journal for Academic Labor, 19*, 65–79. https://doi.org/10.14288/workplace.v0i19.182372

McGinn, M. K., Acker, S., Vander Kloet, M., & Wagner, A. (2019). Dear SSHRC, what do you want? An epistolary narrative of expertise, identity, and time in grant writing. *Forum Qualitative Sozialforschung / Forum: Qualitative Social Research, 20*(1). https://doi.org/10.17169/fqs-20.1.3128

Murgia, A., & Poggio, B. (Eds.). (2019). *Gender and precarious research careers: a comparative analysis.* Routledge. https://doi.org/10.4324/9781315201245

Myklebust, J. P. (2021, July 7). Gender balance of Swedish professors will take 25 years. *University World News.* https://www.universityworldnews.com/post.php?story=20210707135517278

Ni, C., Smith, E., Yuan, H., Larivière, V., & Sugimoto, C. R. (2021). The gendered nature of authorship. *Science Advances, 7*(36), Article eabe4639. https://doi.org/10.1126/sciadv.abe4639

O'Connor, P., & Fauve-Chamoux, A. (2016). European policies and research funding: a case study of gender inequality and lack of diversity in a Nordic research programme. *Policy & Politics, 44*(4), 627–643. https://doi.org/10.1332/030557315X14501227093917

Olssen, M. (2016). Neoliberal competition in higher education today: research, accountability and impact. *British Journal of Sociology of Education, 37*(1), 129–148. https://doi.org/10.1080/01425692.2015.1100530

Pasma, C., & Shaker, E. (2018). *Contract U: contract faculty appointments at Canadian universities.* Canadian Centre for Policy Alternatives. https://policyalterna tives.ca/sites/default/files/uploads/publications/National%20Office/2018/11/Contract%20U.pdf

Pelkonen, A., Thomas, D. A., & Luukkonen, T. (2014). *Project-based funding and novelty in university research: findings from Finland and the UK* (ETLA Report No. 29). The Research Institute of the Finnish Economy (ETLA). http://pub.etla.fi/ETLA-Raportit-Reports-29.pdf

Perez Velazquez, J. L. (2019). The tragicomedy of peer review – the publication game and the lottery of grants. In *The rise of the scientist-bureaucrat: survival guide for researchers in the 21st century* (pp. 67–83). Springer.

Peters, D. (2021, February 22). *Performance-based funding comes to the Canadian post-secondary sector.* University Affairs. https://www.universityaffairs.ca/news/news-arti cle/performance-based-funding-comes-to-the-canadian-postsecondary-sector/

Pietilä, M. (2019). Incentivising academics: experiences and expectations of the tenure track in Finland. *Studies in Higher Education, 44*(6), 932–945. https://doi.org/10.1080/03075079.2017.1405250

Polster, C. (2007). The nature and implications of the growing importance of research grants to Canadian universities and academics. *Higher Education, 53*(5), 599–622. https://doi.org/10.1007/s10734-005-1118-z

Rollock, N. (2013). A political investment: revisiting race and racism in the research process. *Discourse, 34*(4), 492–509. https://doi.org/10.1080/01596306.2013.822617

Ross, M. B., Glennon, B. M., Murciano-Goroff, R., Berkes, E. G., Weinberg, B. A., & Lane, J. I. (2022). Women are credited less in science than men. *Nature, 608* (7921), 135–145. https://doi.org/10.1038/s41586-022-04966-w

Sá, C., Cowley, S., Martinez, M., Kachynska, N., & Sabzalieva, E. (2020). Gender gaps in research productivity and recognition among elite scientists in the U.S., Canada, and South Africa. *PloS ONE, 15*(10), Article e0240903. https://doi.org/10.1371/journal.pone.0240903

Salminen-Karlsson, M. (2023). The FESTA project: doing gender equality work in STEM faculties in Europe. In E. M. Trauth & J. L. Quesenberry (Eds.), *Handbook of gender and technology: environment, identity, individual* (pp. 90–105). Edward Elgar.

Sato, S., Gygax, P. M., Randall, J., & Schmid Mast, M. (2021). The leaky pipeline in research grant peer review and funding decisions: challenges and future directions. *Higher Education, 82*(1), 145–162. https://doi.org/10.1007/s10734-020-00626-y

Shore, C., & Wright, S. (2000). Coercive accountability: the rise of audit culture in higher education. In M. Strathern (Ed.), *Audit cultures: anthropological studies in accountability, ethics and the academy* (pp. 57–89). Taylor & Francis.

Silander, C. (2023). Gender equality in Swedish academia: unpacking the toolbox. *Journal of Praxis in Higher Education, 5*(1), 45–68. https://doi.org/10.47989/kpdc372

Silander, C., & Haake, U. (2017). Gold-diggers, supporters and inclusive profilers: strategies for profiling research in Swedish higher education. *Studies in Higher Education, 42*(11), 2009–2025. https://doi.org/10.1080/03075079.2015.1130031

Silander, C., Haake, U., Lindberg, L., & Riis, U. (2022). Nordic research on gender equality in academic careers: a literature review. *European Journal of Higher Education, 12*(1), 72–97. https://doi.org/10.1080/21568235.2021.1895858

Steinþórsdóttir, F. S., Einarsdóttir, Þ., Pétursdóttir, G. M., & Himmelweit, S. (2020). Gendered inequalities in competitive grant funding: an overlooked dimension of gendered power relations in academia. *Higher Education Research & Development*, *39*(2), 362–375. https://doi.org/10.1080/07294360.2019.1666257

Sugimoto, C. R., & Larivière, V. (2023). *Equity for women in science: dismantling systemic barriers to advancement*. Harvard University Press.

Tzanakou, C. (2019). Unintended consequences of gender-equality plans. *Nature*, *570*(7761), 277–277. https://doi.org/10.1038/d41586-019-01904-1

U15 Canada. (2023). *U15 Canada proposals for Budget 2024*. https://u15.ca/wp-content/uploads/2023/08/U15-Budget-2024-Proposals-EN.pdf

Vander Kloet, M., & Campisi, C. (2023). Becoming legitimate academic subjects: doing meaningful work in research administration. *Journal of Higher Education Policy and Management*, *45*(6), 658–673. https://doi.org/10.1080/1360080X.2023.2222446

Vander Kloet, M., & Wagner, A. (2023). Accountability, ethics and knowledge production: racialised academic staff navigating competing expectations in the social production of research with marginalised communities. *Higher Education Research & Development*. Advance online publication. https://doi.org/10.1080/07294360.2023.2291058

Wagner, A., & Acker, S. (2024). Women's research leadership in the academy. In B. Momani & R. Johnstone (Eds.), *Glass ceilings and ivory towers: gender inequality in the Canadian academy*. University of British Columbia Press.

Worldometer. (n.d.). *Population*. Retrieved on 12 January 2024 from https://www.worldometers.info/population/

2

RESEARCH FUNDING AND GENDER

Insights from the literature

Sandra Acker

My interest in this chapter is in the ways in which gender issues interconnect with the search for research funding that is taking over large parts of academic life (Morley, 2018). How these interconnections play out depends on many considerations, including subject field, gender, departmental cultures and national context (Deem & Lucas, 2007; Nokkala & Diogo, 2020).

I organise the discussion under three broad themes derived from the literature: individual experiences, institutional frameworks, and practices of government and funding bodies. These are analytical categories, useful for organisational purposes, but I do not claim that they are exhaustive or wholly independent of one another. There is no intent to provide a systematic review or to cover all relevant work; rather, by interweaving studies of gender issues and research funding, I create a basis for raising questions about this nascent field of 'gender and research funding' and a foundation for the chapters that follow.

Individual experiences

The first category features personal accounts and some research studies, often critical of aspects of the granting process and their impact on grant-seekers. A pervasive issue is the excessive workload and time involved in grant-writing (e.g. Herbert et al., 2013; Leberman et al., 2016). McGinn and colleagues (2019) describe in detail their experience of constructing a social science research proposal in Canada: 'I [the principal investigator] spent more than 300 hours during that almost three-month period. ... The summer was entirely devoted to writing, with few breaks, no holiday, and little attention paid to family or other work or leisure' (para. 19). Not everyone has a free summer to spend in this way, building inequalities into the granting process even before it formally begins (Bosch & Pondayi, 2022).

DOI: 10.4324/9781003330431-3

Time is relevant in another sense. Ylijoki (2015) points out that grant applications feature 'project time', which is decontextualised, with fixed beginnings, endings and milestones based on specific dates, while in actual research, 'process time' is the non-linear development and evolution of ideas. Thus one of the difficulties that grant-writers face is reducing complexity by shoehorning their ideas into a fixed application format that may bear little resemblance to their work style (Acker & McGinn, 2021).

Finding a way to embark on a successful research career presents challenges, different from country to country, reflecting the structure of doctoral and postdoctoral training, disciplinary cultures and local norms (Hakala, 2009). Maximising chances of success requires not only writing a good proposal but also mastering appropriate strategies (Laudel, 2023; Luukkonen & Thomas, 2016; Yousoubova & McAlpine, 2022). This kind of knowledge is often passed on informally to novices (Windsor & Kronsted, 2022). Salminen-Karlsson's (2023) study of STEM (science, technology, engineering and mathematics) departments in several European countries documents instances where such informal communication bypassed women and international students.

In situations where there is insecurity and uncertainty around continued employment for project researchers, emotions related to the search for funding run particularly high (Acker & Wagner, 2019; Bozzon et al., 2019). Even for those who occupy secure academic positions, rejection of a grant proposal can be disturbing. Chan et al. (2021), in Australia, consider the emotional consequences of frequent criticism and rejection, using imagery of 'the battle-hardened academic'. Leathwood (2017) reports a study of UK academics where 'the sense of not being good enough' (p. 237) was a sentiment expressed by women; failure in acquiring a grant tended to be ascribed to individual inadequacies and could be met by punitive consequences such as 'more marking or teaching' (p. 238; see also Lucas, this volume). Morley lists 'shame, fear, pride, guilt, desire and joy' (p. 23) as emotions associated with what she and others call an 'affective economy' in academe (Hokka et al., this volume).

Women's research productivity was interrupted in many cases by the COVID-19 pandemic. When, during lockdowns, 'working from home' became a necessity rather than a choice, academic mothers were said to be especially at risk (Bender et al., 2022; Oleschuk, 2020; Sala-Bubaré et al., 2023). Carruthers Thomas (this volume), however, reports a case where a UK participant claimed that writing a grant proposal during the pandemic was less stressful than the deep thinking that writing an article would require.

Institutional frameworks

The university as a gendered organisation shapes the micro-level academic activity discussed in the previous section. Paraphrasing Joan Acker (1992), Clavero and Galligan (2020) explain this terminology: 'To say that an institution is "gendered" means that gender is present in its process, practices, images, ideologies, and distributions of power' (p. 650). In a later publication, Acker (2006) expanded her focus to organisational 'inequality regimes' to incorporate the intersections of class, race and gender. These structures are usually thought to work to the disadvantage of minoritised[1] academics and may be found in hiring and promotion procedures, perceptions of leaders, divisions of labour, availability of secure positions, mobility expectations, family-(un) friendly policies and so on (S. Acker & Muzzin, 2019; Angervall et al., 2015; Bozzon et al., 2019; Mählck, 2013; Nikunen & Lempiäinen, 2020). Moreover, institutions vary in the extent to which policies and procedures have been implemented to counter these inequities and to assist researchers with research proposal writing and project administration (Murray et al., 2016). The confluence of institutional advantages and disadvantages, often seen as cumulative, also shapes research opportunities and careers (G. Griffin & Vehviläinen, 2021).

Conceptions of excellence and divisions of labour are two of the deeprooted ideas and practices that affect minoritised academics. Jenkins et al. (2022) describe the 'paradigm of excellence' as a 'governing discourse shaping ways of thinking about the purpose and values of academia' (p. 1). In an oftcited article, van den Brink and Benschop (2012) argue that assessments of academic excellence are 'subject to multiple cultural and political influences' (p. 509). Their scrutiny of documents and interviews with hiring committee members in searches for (full) professors in Dutch universities produced an array of comments confirming a pronounced, if indirect, disadvantage for women candidates. For example, anyone (usually women) with career interruptions or periods of part-time work that resulted in their being 'older' than the norm was usually counted out, demonstrating an intersection between gender and age (see also Søndergaard, 2005). As long as such judgements were considered neutral markers of merit, men continued to have greater chances of appointments and promotions. In turn, such positions facilitated access to funding and research time. Helgesson and Sjögren (2019) investigated a newly initiated tenure-track system in a private higher education institution in Sweden. They conclude that several metrics used to determine tenure and promotion disadvantaged women (e.g. student evaluations of teaching; publications in highly ranked journals), were unduly vague (e.g. 'leadership potential') and/or failed to reward the relational work women often do. Moreover, small groups of senior academics, mostly men, were charged with making the decisions.

Divisions of labour within the university reflect gender and other demographic characteristics. It is clearly more difficult to succeed in research when workloads, class size, administrative duties and lack of internal supports are not in harmony with research demands. Heavy teaching 'loads' – more often held by women – seem particularly inimical to research time (Angervall, 2018), while balanced teaching–research responsibilities improve research productivity (Leišytė, 2016). In at least some countries, it is increasingly difficult to find secure academic appointments after the doctorate. Family responsibilities often make it difficult for women to search for jobs beyond the local area or to take up grants that require geographical mobility (Bosch & Pondayi, 2022). Academics in precarious teaching positions are rarely encouraged by their institutions to pursue research interests (Vander Kloet et al., 2017) and those on project-based research contracts worry about what will happen when the contract ends (Archer, 2008).

Additionally, academic women often take responsibility for disproportionate amounts of caring and service (administration) work in the university (S. Acker et al., 2016; Guarino & Borden, 2017; Heijstra et al., 2017). During COVID-19, academic mothers' care responsibilities increased, most obviously in caring for children at home when schools and day care centres were closed, but also in providing assistance to students and colleagues. Studies from different parts of the world reported that the emotional labour of supporting students and colleagues through the pandemic was left to women academics (Bam et al., 2023; Górska et al., 2021).

Academics from racialised groups experience 'cultural taxation' or 'identity taxation', finding themselves with an extra workload as they counsel and mentor racialised students, serve on equity committees and take on diversity responsibilities (Ahmed, 2012; Hirshfield & Joseph, 2012; Mohamed & Beagan, 2019). As Tate (this volume) points out, Black women academics may be so stretched by other responsibilities that they have little time left to pursue research funding. Indigenous faculty in Canada often have community responsibilities that are not factored into workload or promotions (Mohamed & Beagan, 2019; Wagner & Acker, 2024). K. A. Griffin et al.'s (2013) study of Black faculty at two American universities reveals that women have more difficulty than men in refusing service requests (p. 503) and more often frame this extra work as exhausting and overwhelming (pp. 505–506).

Practices of government and funding bodies

We come now to the operations of research funding systems and the government and funding body decision-making that lies behind them. Where government support for universities has diminished, academics are encouraged to find sources of additional funding such as competitive research grants (Castro-Ceacero & Ion, 2019). Arguably, the 'spirit of research' has changed, moving from one that valued discovery to one 'expressed and evaluated almost exclusively in terms of publications, grant getting and doctoral completions' (Macfarlane, 2021, p. 737).

In addition to its effects on individual well-being and institutional priorities, heavy reliance on external funding exacerbates inequalities. Funding availability varies across disciplines and regions (Laudel, 2006). It is well-known that women and men academics tend to work in different subject areas, such that women are under-represented in technology-related fields and over-represented in care-related ones (Directorate-General for Research and Innovation, 2021). Technological fields have good access to industry and academic funding sources (Ylijoki et al., 2011), whereas 'social sciences and humanities areas in general [have] very few funding opportunities' (Luukkonen & Thomas, 2016, p. 119).

Peer review has an important role in determining which grant applications are funded. Sugimoto and Larivière (2023) point out that reviews of grant proposals differ from those for journal articles, as the former take place in a context of limited funding for distribution and recourse to ambiguous concepts like 'excellence' (p. 93). Judgements of such criteria become problematic when particular groups are systematically disadvantaged. Efforts have been made to institute gender equality in review panel processes and outcomes (Husu & Peterson, this volume; Tamtik & Sutherland, this volume), but it may be impossible to fully control all biases. For example, in an ethnographic study, Roumbanis (this volume) notes instances where review panel members deferred to other panellists with higher status, often older men.

Research evaluation exercises such as the UK's Research Excellence Framework are intended to distribute central government funding unequally under the assumption that higher performing researchers or institutions are more deserving than lower performing peers. These policies are said to have a range of unanticipated consequences, including narrowing the nature of research produced, and intensifying competition and performativity among academics and institutions. One result of rewarding success is a 'Matthew effect' (Merton, 1988) whereby 'the rich get richer' and 'the poor get poorer' (Hamann, 2016; Hoenig, 2018).

When we look at the intersection of gender and research funding, a logical question is whether there is a Matilda effect (Rossiter, 1993), i.e. evidence of a cumulative disadvantage working against women. The literature is ambiguous on this point. Sugimoto and Larivière (2023) indicate that conflicting results may arise from the use of different data sources, as there are no funding databases at a global level (p. 95). The general tendency is that women are less likely than men to apply for grant funding and that women who do apply receive on average smaller research grants than men receive (Stadmark et al., 2020; Sugimoto & Larivière, 2023, p. 94), but there are differences across disciplines (Brouns, 2000; Sugimoto & Larivière, 2023) and national contexts (Abramo et al., 2021; O'Connor & Fauve-Chamoux, 2016; Salminen-Karlsson, 2023). In a meta-analysis including 39 studies containing over two million grant applications as data, Ceci et al. (2023) conclude that their overall results do not support gender bias in success rates in the United States, but they concede that factors not included in their research (e.g. sexual harassment, chilly climates and deeper systemic biases) may still work against women researchers.

The mechanisms and reasons behind these varied findings are manifold and disputed. Women academics may be engaged in topics and fields that are not a priority for funders (Tamblyn et al., 2018). Although women often collaborate, their collaborations appear less likely to be international (Sugimoto & Larivière, 2023, p. 55; Uhly et al., 2017), which may give their profiles a less impressive appearance. Several studies find that women are more successful when only the strength of the proposal is evaluated, rather than cases where the calibre or track record of the principal investigator is included in the assessment (van der Lee & Ellemers, 2015; Witteman et al., 2019). More broadly, the research economy under neoliberal governance tends to value and reward research areas where men have traditionally dominated (Morley, 2018); the convention of funding natural sciences far more generously than social sciences and humanities goes almost unnoticed (Advisory Panel on Federal Support for Fundamental Science, 2017, p. 82). Taking an unusual approach, Bosch and Pondayi (2022) analyse the details of 270 research grants directed at early-career researchers, finding that a number of what they call grant conditions (such as age cut-offs and requirements for geographical mobility without providing a family allowance) could discourage women in the 'invisible' pre-application stage. They argue that what appears to be 'gender neutrality' – treating everyone the same – actually operates as gender inequality.

There are many difficulties encountered in efforts to study gender differences in research funding. In some large-scale, quantitative research, gender is seen to be relatively unproblematic, binary, rarely intersectional and often deduced from names. Interpretations are frequently speculative. For example, women's lower amounts of funding have been ascribed to their being less ambitious (Bedi et al., 2012) or less competitive (Ginther et al., 2016, p. 1105). Steinþórsdóttir et al. (2020) criticise simplistic descriptions that make women 'the ones whose behaviour needs to be improved' (p. 366). Stadmark et al. (2020) write that women's lower 'application behaviour' could reflect many factors, including

> the support from their Institutions, such as who are allowed to apply, who gets institutional support, support from national contact points and grant offices to apply, or who has collegial support to apply or someone to polish the application before it is actually submitted.
>
> (p. 111)

Despite the neoliberal influences on what funding bodies expect and reward and the often pessimistic tone of the literature, there are also counter-influences such as efforts to promote gender equality via European research funding (European Research Council, n.d.); awards for gender equality work to UK universities through the Athena Swan programme (Tzanakou & Pearce, 2019); gender equality plans in Nordic universities (Silander, 2023); and requirements that equity, diversity and inclusion, including Indigenous perspectives, be integrated into research proposals submitted to Canadian funding agencies (Canada Research Coordinating Committee, 2021). As Cruz-Castro and Sanz-Menéndez (2020) comment, progress in overcoming bias within the research funding ecosystem requires studying the interactions among research funding organisations, grant-seekers and their employing institutions (pp. 63–64). Sources of research funding other than government funding bodies, such as foundations and industry, should also receive equivalent scrutiny.

Conclusion

This chapter has juxtaposed the two themes of the book: research funding and gender. My three-layer organising approach helped to make sense of different aspects of the literature. With regard to individual experiences, grant-writing requires allocating extensive time, foregoing self-care and coping with emotions associated with success and failure. Concerning institutional frameworks, inequality regimes privilege some researchers over others: for example, women and racialised scholars tend to do more institutional service and more care-related activities, which reduces the time available for research. Finally, the practices of government and funding bodies result in researchers facing complex challenges in a competitive environment. A number of questions and thoughts about future research arise from this exercise.

Despite extensive analyses of gender equity in academe in the past four decades, why are there so few sources that focus on research funding? One part of the answer may be that it has only been in recent times that securing external funding has become so crucial to an academic career (Edlund & Lammi, 2022; Polster, 2007). The expectation would then be that future studies will increasingly incorporate a perspective on funding.

If we accept that there is more to discover about gender and research funding, what is the best way to go about incorporating such a perspective? We noted that when authors do think about the connection between gender and funding, they often turn to quantitative, sometimes bibliometric, studies where sex or gender is one variable among others. The main thrust of such studies is to understand how women and men compare on indicators such as publication productivity, citations, grant success rates or amounts of funding and to explain any observed differences. Technological developments have made possible the search for trends among enormous numbers of publications or grant applications. Sato and colleagues (2021) conclude that studies where results show no discrimination in grant funding tend to have 'large sample sizes ... and typically include control variables' (p. 155). In contrast, it is mostly qualitative studies that go deeper into perspectives, understandings and organisational cultures and more often identify disadvantages for women seeking research funding. It appears that methodological choices influence research results, a finding that needs further investigation.

Regardless of method, and despite feminism's engagement with intersectionality (Hvenegård-Lassen et al., 2020), few of the identified studies about research funding take an intersectional approach to gender. Explorations of the experiences of racialised women academics, which could be considered intersectional, rarely focus on research funding. Moreover, most of the studies are located in the Global North; accessing research funding elsewhere encounters further tensions and disadvantages, less often documented (Connell et al., 2018). There is much work still to be done.

Another area with limited literature concerns the inner workings of funding bodies themselves (Peterson & Husu, 2023). What are the variations between government funding bodies and other funding sources with regard to equity (see Vehviläinen et al., this volume)? How have the policy changes that have mandated attention to equity issues in so many settings affected the operations of these agencies and the outcomes for researchers? How might the political backlash against equity, diversity and inclusion found in certain jurisdictions, such as some parts of the United States, influence the nexus of gender and funding? What were, and continue to be, the consequences of the transition to online peer-review meetings necessitated by COVID-19 (Peterson & Husu, 2023)?

The three layers of analysis overlap in various ways, making it complicated to analyse any given situation (Stadmark et al., 2020). For instance, if applicants whose proposals are rejected by research funding bodies become demoralised, their departments and institutions might also suffer and their research cultures may be impacted. This point suggests a need for more longitudinal studies, something almost unknown in work on gender and research funding. More comparative research is also needed. For example, what are the consequences for equity of more generous research funding in Germany as compared to Australia (Laudel, 2006) or Canada (Innovation, Science and Economic Development Canada, 2023)?

Finally, my review and most of the literature take for granted the importance and 'goodness' of competitive external research funding for research progress and academic careers. Yet the life of an academic is frequently portrayed as excessively stressful and lacking the satisfactions available in the past. Finding more equitable pathways to research funding in itself will not address this issue. Are there other ways to be a successful academic and should we be working to promote a more humane means to that end?

Acknowledgements

This chapter was developed while working as the principal investigator of Academic Researchers in Challenging Times, a project supported by the Social Sciences and Humanities Research Council of Canada (435-2017-0104). I am grateful to Michelle K. McGinn and Oili-Helena Ylijoki for improvements to the chapter.

Note

1 At times, the word 'minoritised' can substitute for the awkwardness of separating 'women' and 'racialised people' as the categories clearly overlap. Women academics may be a majority numerically in some fields but are minoritised (subject to numerical and power imbalances) in the university, as are 'faculty from racial, Indigenous, and sexual minorities and faculty with disabilities' (S. Acker & Muzzin, 2019, p. 178).

References

Abramo, G., Aksnes, D. W., & D'Angelo, C. A. (2021). Gender differences in research performance within and between countries: Italy vs Norway. *Journal of Informetrics*, *15*(2), Article 101144. https://doi.org/10.1016/j.joi.2021.101144

Acker, J. (1992). From sex roles to gendered institutions. *Contemporary Sociology*, *21* (5), 565–569. https://doi.org/10.2307/2075528

Acker, J. (2006). Inequality regimes: gender, class, and race in organizations. *Gender and Society*, *20*(4), 441–464. https://doi.org/10.1177/0891243205628949

Acker, S., & McGinn, M. K. (2021). Fast professors, research funding, and the figured worlds of mid-career Ontario academics. *Brock Education Journal*, *30*(2), 79–98. https://doi.org/10.26522/brocked.v30i2.864

Acker, S., & Muzzin, L. (2019). Minoritized faculty in Canada's universities and colleges: gender, power, and academic work. In L. Nichols (Ed.), *Working women in Canada: an intersectional approach* (pp. 177–201). Women's Press.

Acker, S., & Wagner, A. (2019). Feminist scholars working around the neoliberal university. *Gender and Education*, *31*(1), 62–81. https://doi.org/10.1080/09540253.2017.1296117

Acker, S., Webber, M., & Smyth, E. (2016). Continuity or change? Gender, family, and academic work for junior faculty in Ontario universities. *NASPA Journal About Women in Higher Education*, *9*(1), 1–20. https://doi.org/10.1080/19407882.2015.1114954

Advisory Panel on Federal Support for Fundamental Science. (2017). *Investing in Canada's future: strengthening the foundations of Canadian research*. https://ised-isde.canada.ca/site/canada-fundamental-science-review

Ahmed, S. (2012). *On being included: racism and diversity in institutional life*. Duke University Press.

Angervall, P. (2018). The academic career: a study of subjectivity, gender and movement among women university lecturers. *Gender and Education*, *30*(1), 105–118. https://doi.org/10.1080/09540253.2016.1184234

Angervall, P., Beach, D., & Gustafsson, J. (2015). The unacknowledged value of female academic labour power for male research careers. *Higher Education Research & Development*, *34*(5), 815–827. https://doi.org/10.1080/07294360.2015.1011092

Archer, L. (2008). Younger academics' constructions of 'authenticity', 'success' and professional identity. *Studies in Higher Education*, *33*(4), 385–403. https://doi.org/10.1080/03075070802211729

Bam, A., Walters, C., & Jansen, J. (2023). Care and academic work in a pandemic lockdown: a study of women academics in South Africa. *Higher Education*. Advance online publication. https://doi.org/10.1007/s10734-023-01091-z

Bedi, G., Van Dam, N. T., & Munafo, M. (2012). Gender inequality in awarded research grants. *The Lancet*, *380*(9840), 474. https://doi.org/10.1016/S0140-6736(12)61292-6

Bender, S., Brown, K. S., Hensley Kasitz, D. L., & Vega, O. (2022). Academic women and their children: parenting during COVID-19 and the impact on scholarly productivity. *Family Relations, 71*(1), 46–67. https://doi.org/10.1111/fare.12632

Bosch, A., & Pondayi, G. (2022). Gendered research grant conditions and their effect on women's application (dis)engagement. *Journal for Transdisciplinary Research in Southern Africa, 18*(1), Article a1281. https://doi.org/10.4102/td.v18i1.1281

Bozzon, R., Murgia, A., & Poggio, B. (2019). Gender and precarious careers in academia and research. In A. Murgia & B. Poggio (Eds.), *Gender and precarious research careers: a comparative analysis* (pp. 15–49). Routledge.

Brouns, M. (2000). The gendered nature of assessment procedures in scientific research funding: the Dutch case. *Higher Education in Europe, 25*(2), 193–199. https://doi.org/10.1080/713669261

Canada Research Coordinating Committee. (2021). *Tri-agency equity, diversity and inclusion action plan (2018–2025)*. https://www.nserc-crsng.gc.ca/NSERC-CRSNG/EDI-EDI/Action-Plan_Plan-dAction_eng.asp

Castro-Ceacero, D., & Ion, G. (2019). Changes in the university research approach: challenges for academics' scientific productivity. *Higher Education Policy, 32*(4), 681–699. https://doi.org/10.1057/s41307-018-0101-0

Ceci, S. J., Kahn, S., & Williams, W. M. (2023). Exploring gender bias in six key domains of academic science: an adversarial collaboration. *Psychological Science in the Public Interest, 24*(1), 15–73. https://doi.org/10.1177/15291006231163179

Chan, H., Mazzucchelli, T. G., & Rees, C. S. (2021). The battle-hardened academic: an exploration of the resilience of university academics in the face of ongoing criticism and rejection of their research. *Higher Education Research & Development, 40*(3), 446–460. https://doi.org/10.1080/07294360.2020.1765743

Clavero, S., & Galligan, Y. (2020). Analysing gender and institutional change in academia: evaluating the utility of feminist institutionalist approaches. *Journal of Higher Education Policy and Management, 42*(6), 650–666. https://doi.org/10.1080/1360080X.2020.1733736

Connell, R., Pearse, R., Collyer, F., Maia, J., & Morrell, R. (2018). Re-making the global economy of knowledge: do new fields of research change the structure of North–South relations? *The British Journal of Sociology, 69*(3), 738–757. https://doi.org/10.1111/1468-4446.12294

Cruz-Castro, L., & Sanz-Menéndez, L. (2020). *Grant allocation disparities from a gender perspective: literature review* (GRANteD Project D1.1). https://doi.org/10.20350/digitalCSIC/10548

Deem, R., & Lucas, L. (2007). Research and teaching cultures in two contrasting UK policy contexts: Academic life in education departments in five English and Scottish universities. *Higher Education, 54*(1), 115–133. https://doi.org/10.1007/s10734-006-9010-z

Directorate-General for Research and Innovation. (2021). *She figures 2021: gender in research and innovation statistics and indicators*. European Commission. https://doi.org/10.2777/06090

Edlund, P., & Lammi, I. (2022). Stress-inducing and anxiety-ridden: a practice-based approach to the construction of status-bestowing evaluations in research funding. *Minerva, 60*(3), 397–418. https://doi.org/10.1007/s11024-022-09466-9

European Research Council. (n.d.). *Working group on gender and diversity*. Retrieved on 12 January 2024 from https://erc.europa.eu/about-erc/thematic-working-groups/working-group-gender-and-diversity

Ginther, D. K., Kahn, S., & Schaffer, W. T. (2016). Gender, race/ethnicity, and National Institutes of Health R01 research awards: is there evidence of a double bind for women of color? *Academic Medicine, 91*(8), 1098–1107. https://doi.org/10.1097/ACM.0000000000001278

Górska, A. M., Kulicka, K., Staniszewska, Z., & Dobija, D. (2021). Deepening inequalities: what did COVID-19 reveal about the gendered nature of academic work? *Gender, Work & Organization, 28*(4), 1546–1561. https://doi.org/10.1111/gwao.12696

Griffin, G., & Vehviläinen, M. (2021). The persistence of gender struggles in Nordic research and innovation. *Feminist Encounters, 5*(2), Article 28. https://doi.org/10.20897/femenc/11165

Griffin, K. A., Bennett, J. C., & Harris, J. (2013). Marginalizing merit? Gender differences in Black faculty D/discourses on tenure, advancement, and professional success. *The Review of Higher Education, 36*(4), 489–512. https://doi.org/10.1353/rhe.2013.0040

Guarino, C. M., & Borden, V. M. H. (2017). Faculty service loads and gender: are women taking care of the academic family? *Research in Higher Education, 58*(6), 672–694. https://doi.org/10.1007/s11162-017-9454-2

Hakala, J. (2009). Socialization of junior researchers in new academic research environments: two case studies from Finland. *Studies in Higher Education, 34*(5), 501–516. https://doi.org/10.1080/03075070802597119

Hamann, J. (2016). The visible hand of research performance assessment. *Higher Education, 72*(6), 761–779. https://doi.org/10.1007/s10734-015-9974-7

Heijstra, T. M., Steinþorsdóttir, F. S., & Einarsdóttir, T. (2017). Academic career making and the double-edged role of academic housework. *Gender and Education, 29*(6), 764–780. https://doi.org/10.1080/09540253.2016.1171825

Helgesson, K. S., & Sjögren, E. (2019). No finish line: how formalization of academic assessment can undermine clarity and increase secrecy. *Gender, Work & Organization, 26*(4), 558–581. https://doi.org/10.1111/gwao.12355

Herbert, D. L., Barnett, A. G., Clarke, P., & Graves, N. (2013). On the time spent preparing grant proposals: an observational study of Australian researchers. *BMJ Open, 3*(5), Article e002800. https://doi.org/10.1136/bmjopen-2013-002800

Hirshfield, L. E., & Joseph, T. D. (2012). 'We need a woman, we need a black woman': gender, race, and identity taxation in the academy. *Gender and Education, 24*(2), 213–227. https://doi.org/10.1080/09540253.2011.606208

Hoenig, B. (2018). Structures, mechanisms and consequences of Europeanization in research: how European funding affects universities. *Innovation: the European Journal of Social Science Research, 31*(4), 504–522. https://doi.org/10.1080/13511610.2018.1497479

Hvenegård-Lassen, K., Staunæs, D., & Lund, R. (2020). Intersectionality, yes, but how? Approaches and conceptualizations in Nordic feminist research and activism. *NORA – Nordic Journal of Feminist and Gender Research, 28*(3), 173–182. https://doi.org/10.1080/08038740.2020.1790826

Innovation, Science and Economic Development Canada. (2023). *Report of the Advisory Panel on the Federal Research Support System.* https://ised-isde.canada.ca/site/panel-federal-research-support

Jenkins, F., Hoenig, B., Weber, S. M., & Wolffram, A. (2022). Introduction: inequalities and the paradigm of excellence. In F. Jenkins, B. Hoenig, S. M. Weber, & A. Wolffram (Eds.), *Inequalities and the paradigm of excellence in academia* (pp. 1–15). Routledge.

Laudel, G. (2006). The 'quality myth': promoting and hindering conditions for acquiring research funds. *Higher Education, 52*(3), 375–403. https://doi.org/10.1007/s10734-004-6414-5

Laudel, G. (2023). Researchers' responses to their funding situation. In B. Lepori, B. Jongbloed, & D. Hicks (Eds.), *Handbook of public funding of research* (pp. 261–278). Edward Elgar.

Leathwood, C. (2017). Women academic researchers: still interlopers in the UK academy? In H. Eggins (Ed.), *The changing role of women in higher education* (pp. 227–242). Springer. https://doi.org/10.1007/978-3-319-42436-1_12

Leberman, S. I., Eames, B., & Barnett, S. (2016). 'Unless you are collaborating with a big name successful professor, you are unlikely to receive funding'. *Gender and Education, 28*(5), 644–661. https://doi.org/10.1080/09540253.2015.1093102

Leišytė, L. (2016). New public management and research productivity – a precarious state of affairs of academic work in the Netherlands. *Studies in Higher Education, 41*(5), 828–846. https://doi.org/10.1080/03075079.2016.1147721

Luukkonen, T., & Thomas, D. A. (2016). The 'negotiated space' of university researchers' pursuit of a research agenda. *Minerva, 54*(1), 99–127. https://doi.org/10.1007/s11024-016-9291-z

Macfarlane, B. (2021). The spirit of research. *Oxford Review of Education, 47*(6), 737–751. https://doi.org/10.1080/03054985.2021.1884058

Mählck, P. (2013). Academic women with migrant background in the global knowledge economy: bodies, hierarchies and resistance. *Women's Studies International Forum, 36*, 65–74. https://doi.org/10.1016/j.wsif.2012.09.007

McGinn, M. K., Acker, S., Vander Kloet, M., & Wagner, A. (2019). Dear SSHRC, what do you want? An epistolary narrative of expertise, identity, and time in grant writing. *Forum Qualitative Sozialforschung / Forum: Qualitative Social Research, 20*(1). https://doi.org/10.17169/fqs-20.1.3128

Merton, R. K. (1988). The Matthew Effect in science, II: cumulative advantage and the symbolism of intellectual property. *Isis, 79*(4), 606–623. http://www.jstor.org/stable/234750

Mohamed, T., & Beagan, B. L. (2019). 'Strange faces' in the academy: experiences of racialized and Indigenous faculty in Canadian universities. *Race Ethnicity and Education, 22*(3), 338–354. https://doi.org/10.1080/13613324.2018.1511532

Morley, L. (2018). Gender in the neo-liberal research economy: an enervating and exclusionary entanglement? In H. Kahlert (Ed.), *Gender studies and the new academic governance* (pp. 15–40). Springer.

Murray, D. L., Morris, D., Lavoie, C., Leavitt, P. R., MacIsaac, H., Masson, M. E., & Villard, M. A. (2016). Bias in research grant evaluation has dire consequences for small universities. *PloS One, 11*(6), e0155876. https://doi.org/10.1371/journal.pone.0155876

Nikunen, M., & Lempiäinen, K. (2020). Gendered strategies of mobility and academic career. *Gender and Education, 32*(4), 554–571. https://doi.org/10.1080/09540253.2018.1533917

Nokkala, T., & Diogo, S. (2020). Institutional perspectives in transition: research groups' profiles and embeddedness in organisational and national context. *Higher Education, 79*(3), 515–532. https://doi.org/10.1007/s10734-019-00421-4

O'Connor, P., & Fauve-Chamoux, A. (2016). European policies and research funding: a case study of gender inequality and lack of diversity in a Nordic research programme. *Policy & Politics, 44*(4), 627–643. https://doi.org/10.1332/030557315X14501227093917

Oleschuk, M. (2020). Gender equity considerations for tenure and promotion during COVID-19. *The Canadian Review of Sociology*, *57*(3), 502–515. https://doi.org/10.1111/cars.12295

Peterson, H., & Husu, L. (2023). Online panel work through a gender lens: implications of digital peer review meetings. *Science & Public Policy*, *50*(3), 371–381. https://doi.org/10.1093/scipol/scac075

Polster, C. (2007). The nature and implications of the growing importance of research grants to Canadian universities and academics. *Higher Education*, *53*(5), 599–622. https://doi.org/10.1007/s10734-005-1118-z

Rossiter, M. W. (1993). The Matthew Matilda effect in science. *Social Studies of Science*, *23*(2), 325–341. https://doi.org/10.1177/030631293023002004

Sala-Bubaré, A., Castelló, M., Corcelles, M., & Suñé-Soler, N. (2023). Researchers' strategies to cope with the COVID-19 impact on their activity. *Current Psychology*. Advance online publication. https://doi.org/10.1007/s12144-023-04601-5

Salminen-Karlsson, M. (2023). The FESTA project: doing gender equality work in STEM faculties in Europe. In E. M. Trauth & J. L. Quesenberry (Eds.), *Handbook of gender and technology: environment, identity, individual* (pp. 90–105). Edward Elgar.

Sato, S., Gygax, P. M., Randall, J., & Schmid Mast, M. (2021). The leaky pipeline in research grant peer review and funding decisions: challenges and future directions. *Higher Education*, *82*(1), 145–162. https://doi.org/10.1007/s10734-020-00626-y

Silander, C. (2023). Gender equality in Swedish academia: unpacking the toolbox. *Journal of Praxis in Higher Education*, *5*(1), 45–68. https://doi.org/10.47989/kpdc372

Søndergaard, D. M. (2005). Making sense of gender, age, power and disciplinary position: intersecting discourses in the academy. *Feminism & Psychology*, *15*(2), 189–208. https://doi.org/10.1177/0959353505051728

Stadmark, J., Jesus-Rydin, C., & Conley, D. J. (2020). Success in grant applications for women and men. *Advances in Geosciences*, *53*, 107–115. https://doi.org/10.5194/adgeo-53-107-2020

Steinþórsdóttir, F. S., Einarsdóttir, Þ., Pétursdóttir, G. M., & Himmelweit, S. (2020). Gendered inequalities in competitive grant funding: an overlooked dimension of gendered power relations in academia. *Higher Education Research & Development*, *39*(2), 362–375. https://doi.org/10.1080/07294360.2019.1666257

Sugimoto, C. R., & Larivière, V. (2023). *Equity for women in science: dismantling systemic barriers to advancement*. Harvard University Press.

Tamblyn, R., Girard, N., Qian, C. J., & Hanley, J. (2018). Assessment of potential bias in research grant peer review in Canada. *Canadian Medical Association Journal*, *190*(16), E489–E499. https://doi.org/10.1503/cmaj.170901

Tzanakou, C., & Pearce, R. (2019). Moderate feminism within or against the neoliberal university? The example of Athena SWAN. *Gender, Work & Organization*, *26*(8), 1191–1211. https://doi.org/10.1111/gwao.12336

Uhly, K. M., Visser, L. M., & Zippel, K. S. (2017). Gendered patterns in international research collaborations in academia. *Studies in Higher Education*, *42*(4), 760–782. https://doi.org/10.1080/03075079.2015.1072151

van den Brink, M., & Benschop, Y. (2012). Gender practices in the construction of academic excellence: sheep with five legs. *Organization*, *19*(4), 507–524. https://doi.org/10.1177/1350508411414293

van der Lee, R., & Ellemers, N. (2015). Gender contributes to personal research funding success in The Netherlands. *Proceedings of the National Academy of Sciences of the United States of America*, *112*(40), 12349–12353. http://www.jstor.org/stable/26465358

Vander Kloet, M., Frake-Mistak, M., McGinn, M. K., Caldecott, M., Aspenlieder, E. D, Beres, J. L., Fukuzawa, S., Cassidy, A., & Gill, A. (2017). Conditions for contingent instructors engaged in the scholarship of teaching and learning. *Canadian Journal for the Scholarship of Teaching and Learning, 8*(2). https://doi.org/10.5206/cjsotl-rcacea.2017.2.9

Wagner, A., & Acker, S. (2024). Women's research leadership in the academy. In B. Momani & R. Johnstone (Eds.), *Glass ceilings and ivory towers: gender inequality in the Canadian academy.* University of British Columbia Press.

Windsor, L. C., & Kronsted, C. (2022). Grant writing and the hidden curriculum: mentoring and collaborating across disciplines. *PS: Political Science & Politics, 55*(2), 313–323. https://doi.org/10.1017/S1049096521001827

Witteman, H. O., Hendricks, M., Straus, S., & Tannenbaum, C. (2019). Are gender gaps due to evaluations of the applicant or the science? A natural experiment at a national funding agency. *The Lancet, 393*(10171), 531–540. https://doi.org/10.1016/S0140-6736(18)32611-4

Ylijoki, O.-H. (2015). Conquered by project time? Conflicting temporalities in university research. In P. Gibbs, O.-H. Ylijoki, C. Guzmán-Valenzuela, & R. Barnett (Eds.), *Universities in the flux of time* (pp. 94–107). Routledge.

Ylijoki, O.-H., Lyytinen, A., & Marttila, L. (2011). Different research markets: a disciplinary perspective. *Higher Education, 62*(6), 721–740. https://doi.org/10.1007/s10734-011-9414-2

Yousoubova, L., & McAlpine, L. (2022). Developing as a post-PhD researcher: agency and feedback in construction of grant funding success. *Infancia y Aprendizaje, 45*(1), 1–36. https://doi.org/10.1080/02103702.2021.1928950

PART 2
Stability and change

3

HERE TODAY, GONE TOMORROW

The vicissitudes of funding in gendered higher education contexts – a view from Sweden

Gabriele Griffin

This chapter centres on the vicissitudes of funding encountered in a context where a newly emerging discipline with specific gendered contours, in this instance digital humanities (DH), seeks to establish itself within the university at a time of shifting funding regimes. Drawing on interviews conducted with 30 DH practitioners in Sweden, Norway and Finland in 2017–2018, but focusing on the Swedish context, I explore how gendered staffing structures ('all the researchers are women; all the techies are men'), newness of discipline and changing funding regimes conjoin to create precarious work conditions for those embarking on work in DH. I explore the particular forms of precarity this conjunction takes in a country that publicly professes gender equality and has strong histories of worker protection.

The issue of changing funding regimes for higher education over the past four decades or so has been the object of much comment (e.g. Chowdry et al., 2012; Deem, 1998; Deem et al., 2007; Kwiek, 2012; Liefner, 2003). Many factors have produced a higher education and research culture of rapid change. They include the introduction of fees for 'home' as well as 'international' students in public higher education in some European countries, notably in the UK but not, at least for 'home' students, in the Nordic countries; the gradual reduction of public funding for higher education, in particular of block grants, in favour of competitive and external funding (Vehviläinen et al., 2022); and more general changes in higher education such as the global convergence of research agendas (Bach et al., 2020; Marginson & Sawir, 2005; Marginson & van der Wende, 2007), the rise of audit cultures (Strathern, 2000) and the marketisation and general neoliberalisation of research and/in higher education (del Cerro Santamaría, 2020; Ingleby, 2015). Many higher education institutions (HEIs) have engaged with these changes by in turn making repeated and significant changes in their work regimes, their internal funding allocation

DOI: 10.4324/9781003330431-5

mechanisms, the structures of their organisational units, the contracts they give to researchers, and the processualising and technologising of their practices. These developments have also entailed the precarisation of academic work (Standing, 2011) and of researchers (Murgia & Poggio, 2019).

The precarisation has partly been influenced by external economic factors which have affected university and research funding regimes. Among these factors, there were ones that impacted higher education in many countries and particular ones that have been especially important for research funding in the Nordic context. By Nordic context I mean the five countries that make up the Nordic region, i.e. Denmark, Finland, Iceland, Norway and Sweden, and their associated territories. However, in this chapter, I shall mainly refer to Sweden, although the research was carried out in Finland, Norway and Sweden. Nonetheless, it is worth noting that Finland, for example, was hard hit by one of its main research funders, the mobile phone company Nokia, losing market share to Microsoft and Apple in the 2010s, and having to sell its initially very successful mobile phone division to Microsoft in 2014. But there were also several iterations of changing (research) funding regimes within universities that precarised research and led to its abolishment in some contexts. Histories of requiring researchers to bring in their own funding and associated restructurings are only too familiar to academics of the late 20th and early 21st century. And these histories can and do repeat themselves. They provide object lessons for newly emerging academic fields as to what their future trajectory might be – though, of course, this is not inevitable.

DH has emerged as a new academic field within this increasingly precarious context of higher education and research. It bears all the hallmarks of that context. To date, in Europe, this field exists mostly not in 'traditional' academic structures such as departments and faculties but as centres, forums, laboratories, networks, projects and other similar, provisional entities. As I have suggested elsewhere (Griffin, 2019, 2022), as an academic field, DH is characterised by certain core traits, most particularly its interdisciplinarity, its institutionalisation in atypical formations such as centres, and its uncertain funding structures.

With regard to many of these traits, DH has much in common with other newly emerging academic fields. But it also has specificities not necessarily replicated elsewhere, such as the fact that it brings together academic domains from the humanities and technology (in their various incarnations) that conventionally are significantly gendered: humanities disciplines frequently have significant numbers of women students and staff, while technology subjects tend to be male-dominated. Further, given that potentially all disciplines in the humanities and all disciplines dealing with technology and technologisation (e.g. human–computer interaction, information studies, information and technology studies, computer sciences) can be involved in DH, DH can emerge as a pan-organisational academic field where it is simultaneously seemingly everywhere and hence nowhere. Its importance, not just for the humanities as an academic domain but also for the major challenges facing contemporary societies, is unquestionable: increasingly, governments and transnational bodies such as the Organisation for Economic Co-operation and Development (OECD) have begun to plan and account for the digitalisation and technologisation of the societies and cultures they serve (e.g. Directorate for Science, Technology and Innovation, n.d.; Directorate-General for Communications Networks, Content and Technology, n.d.; Directorate-General for Research and Innovation, n.d.; OECD, 2017). But the funding stories of the DH practitioners I interviewed tell a somewhat different story, one of precarisation and struggle in a work environment, HEIs, that is only partly supportive.

In the following, I briefly discuss the theoretical framing of this chapter, and higher education and research funding, before describing the methods used in this study and the research participants, then presenting the results with their attendant discussion and finally arriving at some conclusions.

Theoretical framing

This chapter draws on four theoretical frames: organisational history and in particular Henry Etzkowitz and Carol Kemelgor's (1998) work on research centres; Fiona Mackay's (2014) concept of 'nested newness' and its relevance to institutional innovation and change; Joan Acker's (2006) account of 'inequality regimes' in organisations; and Guy Standing's (2011) notion of precarity and the precariat, here used to characterise certain sections of academe in the Nordic countries. Etzkowitz and Kemelgor's work provides a sophisticated account of the history of research centres within the post-World War II US academy. It makes clear the extent to which the establishment and maintenance of such centres, including DH ones, is tied to obtaining, investing and harvesting funds (p. 274). It also highlights the provisionality, hence precarity, of such structures given that 'centres are temporary bodies that may close if funds run out' (p. 277). Accordingly, 'centres represent less of an institutional commitment than departments: they need no permanent staff' (p. 272). 'Here today, gone tomorrow' thus applies to the shifting and unstable fiscal landscape that accompanies the research funding regimes of the past four decades, to the precarisation of staff positions and to the organisational structures such as centres that have come to the fore during this period.

Part of the issue for centres is that they are inserted into existing HEIs with their already established customs, practices and regulations. Fiona Mackay (2014) theorises this in terms of 'nested newness' to analyse the ways in which innovations such as the establishment of a new academic field are contoured by 'past institutional legacies and … by initial and ongoing interactions with already existing institutions (formal structures and rules, informal rules, practices, and norms) within which they are "nested" and interconnected' (p. 567). This nestedness is operationalised through two mechanisms: 'remembering the old' and 'forgetting the new'. Mackay links these two mechanisms of resistance to newness to 'the liability of newness': 'the liability of newness relates to the vulnerability of fledgling organizations ... as they face multiple challenges that relate to their newness' (p. 556). Seeking to reduce unfamiliarity and uncertainty, institutional actors may 'remember the old', i.e. fall back onto existing ways of doing things, and 'forget the new', thus countering the potential liability of newness. Mackay suggests that 'in most cases, institutional innovation comprises bounded change within an existing system' (p. 567). This, indeed, could be said to be the case for DH as a discipline as it is currently set up in Nordic HEIs: bounded change.

Joan Acker (2006) roots her discussion of inequality regimes and bounded change both in 'inequality in the surrounding society, its politics, history, and culture' (p. 443) and, importantly, in 'economic decision making' (p. 442). Her emphasis on the economic dimension of this decision-making, as imbricated with gender, is what differentiates her position from Mackay's. Acker views inequality in organisations as 'systematic disparities between participants in power and control over goals, resources, and outcomes; workplace decisions such as how to organize work; opportunities for promotion ...; security in employment and benefits; pay and other monetary rewards' (p. 443). In discussing how inequality regimes operate, she invokes both questions of visibility (how evident are inequalities?) and legitimacy (how okay is it to engage in unequal practices?) to explain what factors may facilitate or hinder change of unequal working conditions. Her analysis of inequality regimes is significant for this chapter because it links economic disparities with gender and other inequalities, and because it explains how funding and gender issues interrelate to produce inequalities. This is the situation of DH researchers in Nordic academe in the 21st century who are labouring under conditions of job insecurity, reorganisation and the marketisation of higher education.

Increases in job insecurity are at the heart of Guy Standing's (2011) work on the precariat. Standing discusses how increasing labour market flexibility – for instance, through greater variation in types of contracts, e.g. more short-term and time-delimited – leads to 'precariousness of residency, of labour and work and social protection' (p. 5). This precariousness finds its expression in how researchers experience their working conditions (Murgia & Poggio, 2019). And it was evident in how the DH practitioners I interviewed articulated their work experiences in a climate of changing funding regimes.

Higher education and research funding in the Nordic countries

To understand the interviewees' work experiences, it is useful to know a little about how higher education and research funding operate in the Nordic countries. As Griffin and Vehviläinen (2021, pp. 5–6) discuss, higher education in the Nordic countries, though broadly in line with the European Science Foundation four-stage researcher career model (Scholz et al., 2009), has some differences regarding the funding and the relative job security of the four stages. In all Nordic countries, the first stage of doctoral researcher involves fixed-term contracts and is dependent on external funding, usually obtained by applying competitively for advertised studentships. In Sweden, these are almost all full-time and involve a decent living wage. The second stage, postdoctoral researcher ('postdoc'), in all Nordic countries also involves fixed-term contracts of varying lengths and percentages of full-time jobs. This stage can be quite extensive, with years of moving from one contract to another, sometimes having multiple contracts at the same time or in over-lapping periods. It is very common to have several successive postdoc positions, each lasting anywhere from two to five years. Stage three is the most differentiated of the four stages; here one is an independent researcher or a university lecturer. In Norway, these are mostly permanent positions, so some degree of stability is achieved. But in Finland and Sweden, stage three researcher posts are largely fixed-term, often fractional rather than full-time and dependent on external funding, whereas lecturer posts are funded from the university's teaching grant and may be either fixed-term or permanent. Only at stage four, the full professor or senior researcher stage, are staff mostly on full-time permanent contracts, often funded from a combination of insti-tutional and external funding. The upshot of all this is that while Norwegian researchers can begin to feel less precarious once they reach stage three, for all others this sense of security is only really achieved at stage four, in other words, quite late in their career. And, as Griffin and Vehviläinen (2021, p. 5) show, stage four is also the hardest to enter and the proportions of women drop from nearly 50% at stage three, to on average 30% at stage four (for Finland, Norway and Sweden averaged; see Directorate-General for Research and Innovation, 2021, p. 184). Significantly, across genders:

> The employment category that has seen the highest percentage increase is 'postdoc'. The employment category 'postdoc' was introduced in 2008, and increased greatly over the first ten years, to then slow down in the last few years. Instead, researcher employment has increased.
>
> (Swedish Research Council, 2021b, p. 42)

This statement means that personnel at stages two and three, the most inse-cure forms of researcher employment, have increased significantly, whilst the increase in the most stable position, that of professor, has been 'marginal' (Swedish Research Council, 2021b, p. 42).

An additional and significant factor here is that the funding parameters for much research funding are set at certain percentages of full-time work, so that when one applies for funding from, for example, the Swedish Research Council, one can only ask for between 20% and 70% of one's full working time. Often, especially when the research requires collaboration involving multiple researchers, the overall envelope of the funding (i.e. the maximum one can apply for) does not allow one to claim for more than 10% to 20% of one's working time. For the large numbers of people stuck at stages two and three, this restriction means that in order to make a living wage they have to be involved in multiple projects or combine project work with other work. This situation is detrimental to the research and also to the researcher, as I have discussed elsewhere (Griffin, 2022). It creates precarity as well as work overload as researchers struggle to get enough projects to sustain themselves and cope with the workload of doing multiple projects, and also attend multiple meetings, often in different sites, etc. Researchers here are doubly precarised: through the temporariness of their employment and through the fragmentedness that results from the limited percentages of full-time work that they can apply for when trying to gain funded projects.

Methods and research participants

This chapter draws on research involving 30 semi-structured, one-on-one interviews with DH practitioners from Finland, Norway and Sweden, conducted in 2017–2018, pre-COVID-19. The interviews were either done in person face-to-face (18) or by Skype (12), depending on participant availability. They lasted between 50 and 75 minutes. The interviewees were purposively sampled, with the key criterion being that they were working in DH. Websites of university DH centres or labs in the three Nordic countries were searched for potential interviewees, as were research funder sites, to identify DH practitioners involved in funded projects in DH. Altogether 17 women and 13 men were interviewed: 17 Swedes (11 women, six men), seven Finns (three women, four men) and six Norwegians (three women, three men). Their mean ages were 44.7 years (range 29–62) for the women and 44.3 years (range 39–50) for the men. They occupied many different positions within DH, sometimes concurrently, such as being a half-time director of a centre and working half-time for another organisation, for example (Griffin, 2022).

Note that for the purposes of this chapter, the Swedish interviewees are in focus. In selecting these interviewees the idea was not to achieve representativeness which, in any event, is not the aim of qualitative research, but to gain in-depth information about the interviewees' work experiences and to achieve saturation, a point where similar information recurred in interviewees' accounts or certain patterns occurred in the responses. The intention was to create a bottom-up account of the interviewees' gendered DH work experiences and to understand, inter alia, how funding issues influenced these experiences. An interview guide was used, focusing on questions regarding the interviewees' familial and educational background, their technology-based education, their working lives and career trajectories, their experiences of mentorship, support for DH within their institution, and their sense of how gender operated in their academic field. These questions produced the themes that emerged in the later analysis of the interview data. Prior to the interviews, all participants were given or sent information sheets about the project and asked to sign consent forms allowing the use of their pseudonymised data in subsequent publications. The study itself was approved by the relevant ethics review boards in Finland, Norway and Sweden.

The interview data were transcribed verbatim and uploaded into the qualitative data analysis software NVivo 11 for a thematic analysis (Braun & Clarke, 2006, 2021). This involved repeated close readings of the interview texts and coding them according to the themes that emerged as a function of what the interviewees had been asked about and how they responded. More than 30 different themes emerged. Of these, the most pertinent for this chapter were DH and funding, DH and resources, career, closing courses or centres, gender, and collaboration.

Results and discussion

The first thing to say is that all interviewees were strongly aware of the need to get external funding in order to have a place in the academy. However, junior researchers (stage one and two) often could not apply for funding in their own right but instead depended on being invited into projects by more senior staff members. As Lena, a Swedish postdoc on successive temporary contracts for a number of years following her PhD, put it:

> Everything is about securing funding, and the only way to do that is through external funding and like, knowing people and being asked to, I mean applying for money yourself but that is difficult as long as you are a junior researcher, and so the only option seems to be to know the right people and get invited to be part of their projects, because otherwise you would lose your position.

Lena considered herself lucky because, according to her, 'why I have been able to stay in academia for this long after doing my PhD is that I have been invited to be part on several projects so ... that has really helped my career and it's all because of these male project leaders'. The necessity to have someone invite you into a project rather than being able to apply in your own right immediately created gender and power asymmetries since the senior people the interviewees depended on for invitations were usually men. Here connections and networks were vital, and women, unlike Lena in this instance, tended to lose out relative to men. Junior men were frequently better networked than the women and, as part of the tendency to reproduce the same in recruitment contexts (Lamont, 2009), were more likely – because they were men – to be selected for inclusion in a project (Angervall et al., 2015).

Centres often need to finance themselves, at least in part, through external funding. Nils, a Swedish interviewee, described the psychosocial dynamics of applying for funding:

44   Gabriele Griffin

> Everybody knows this is the condition for being here [in the DH centre] ... competing about financing, but you are not supposed to talk about it that way. ... You also try to uphold some kind of idea of that you are actually part of this organisation for different reasons.

Interviewees repeated again and again in different ways the institutional imperative to generate funding which, if successful, maintained their jobs and furthered their careers, but if unsuccessful threatened their livelihoods and jobs. This situation must be seen in a context where, in Sweden for example, approval rates for research funding applications amount to 13% for the humanities and social sciences, with applications by women being on average 1% less likely to be funded than men's (Swedish Research Council, 2023). The success rates for Formas, another Swedish research funder, amount to 14%–15% for open calls, research projects and research projects for early-career researchers (Formas, 2022). In other words, around 85% or more of research funding applications are unsuccessful.

Further, three funding conditions in particular created problems for the researchers: provisions for overhead expenses, the amount of funded research time as a percentage of one's working time one could apply for and the funding requirements of DH as a discipline. The problem of overhead costs is well established among academics across Europe, in relation to both European Commission funding and, in the Nordic countries, foundations that often pay no overheads. Nina, a postdoc working in Sweden, said:

> The money that the Swedish Research Council gives to the Swedish organisations is so little that ... we have to negotiate whether or not my job environment can sponsor my overhead ... and [my project partners] are ready to go and I am still waiting to hear from my work environment. Because they haven't planned for next year yet.

This clash between limited research funder provision and institutional fiscal requirements puts researchers in a difficult position, causing work stress as they scrabbled around trying to knit the different and often incompatible demands together.

This stressful situation was exacerbated by the fact that, as already discussed, in most research funding applications researchers can apply for only a limited percentage of their actual work time, anything from 10% to 50% across the various funding bodies. This is both because some funders specify salary caps at a particular percentage of full-time employment and because research funding schemes have funding limits (e.g. applying for up to 3 million Swedish kronor – around £220,000 – for a two- or three-year project), which automatically restrict the amount of funding that one can allocate for researcher time, given that other research expenses and an overhead of anything between 25% to 60% comes off that money. One consequence of this restriction is that researchers frequently work on multiple projects, for varying percentages of their time, a situation that invariably leads to overwork and problems with balancing the demands made by the various projects on the researchers' time and energies (see Griffin, 2022). In Sweden, 10% involvement in a research project equals four hours per week. That time can be taken up just through attending meetings or participating in writing an article. It does not allow time to do the actual research. Researchers in the Nordic countries who work to time schedules are very clear about their work time parameters. In this respect, Sweden, like the other Nordic countries, has articulated concerns for worker welfare, and it is not considered acceptable, for example, to send emails on the weekend. But, these concerns do not translate into properly accounting for researchers' time when funding is awarded or projects are taken on. Nina, quoted earlier, talked of having 'maybe 15 collaborations', that is, projects she was involved with. Even at only 10% of her time per project, one can see that this would add up to much more than a full-time workload; in fact, it is not doable. She, like other interviewees, also talked about projects not working out, meaning that the projects had been abandoned or not completed.

Faced with working simultaneously on multiple projects, a function of the very small amount of actual researcher time awarded in most research projects, or with other forms of irreconcilable work demands (Griffin, 2022), interviewees admitted that they had to abandon, short-change or re-distribute work in order to be able to manage. Malin, a Swedish postdoc, for example, described how a project 'got stopped. No publication came out of it, after data collection. But it was a very big project.' This situation of lack of research time and leading a distributed working life across multiple projects with possibilities of non-completion reinforced the sense of precarity the interviewees felt. As Lena put it, 'I mean the future seems quite insecure in a way. … I have a position right now and I know that I have funding for a couple more years, but after that I don't know what happens.'

Another major issue for DH researchers in relation to funding was the matter of DH's infrastructure requirements. In many instances, DH infrastructure, the technologies through which DH operates, such as eye-movement tracking devices or visualisation platforms, are bought with external funding. As Dirk, a Swedish 'techie', described it: 'Lots of equipment that we have has been paid for by the funder. So it's not the university who provided that.' Indeed, it was quite clear that universities were not ready for this equipment need. Once DH equipment is in place, it needs to be operated, maintained and updated. As Nina put it, 'so you have, for example, an expensive screen. The question is, can you use it or do you need a technician for it? Which means technicians become part of the infrastructure and then when you apply for money you need the cost to maintain that big bullshit.' In other words, DH infrastructure was not just a matter of hardware, bought as a one-off expense, but also generated ongoing expenses both in labour and material costs. This meant budgeting for potential additional staff (technicians) and for upgrades and repairs. But, again, universities were not really prepared for this. Several interviewees talked about this problem. There were repeated narratives about infrastructure that had become unusable because it had broken down and the university had not been able or willing to pay for its repair. One consequence of this, of course, was that no further research could be undertaken that depended on that infrastructure, and institutions were thus, inter alia, limiting the research potential of their researchers.

Indeed, there seemed to be little medium- to long-term planning regarding the building up of DH infrastructure and centres that was based on a realistic assessment of the necessary funding. This situation is, of course, fully in line with Etzkowitz and Kemelgor's (1998) assessment of the provisionality of such centres. But it also derives from a conventional ('how we've always done it') understanding of humanities disciplines in line with Mackay's concept of 'nested newness' whereby remembering the old, e.g. using pen and paper only, also entails sidelining the new, e.g. failing to consider the new infrastructure needs of DH. The interviewees stressed that there was no continuity of funding. Helena, talking about Sweden, linked her DH experiences to the prevailing funding and priority structures: 'I guess money is one aspect. But it is not an explanation because it is also about priorities … our [centre] is funded on the Faculty level so that means three years and then we have to apply for a new period, and it's not a lot of money.'

Changing funding and changing priorities meant turbulence in every respect. The constant shifts in name, and reorganisations, meant that it was difficult for such centres to establish a brand identity and to flourish. One might argue that these shifts indicate institutional flexibility and agility, qualities supposedly necessary to survive in a marketised higher education system. But they also unsettle and undermine the possibility of building something up as opposed to creating temporary precarious structures.

The effects of this provisionality were predictable. Problems invariably arose when funding ran out. Sven, a Swedish interviewee and director of a DH centre, described how a reduction in funding meant that staff had to be 'laid off or fired': 'It struck harder on the support side and on the research side than on the technology side, which had to do with funding.' The distinction between 'support side' and 'research side' here hides the fact that the 'research side' was mainly women, while the 'support (technology) side' referred to men. In other words, when the money became tight, women tended to lose out. Vehviläinen et al. (2022) have discussed how reductions in research funding in the Finnish system led to men's networks drawing closer together and supporting each other, while women found themselves sidelined, out of a job, or having their research project taken away from them and given to a male colleague. This finding suggests that funding crises or periods of austerity in research funding foster conservatism, the remembering of the old, including gender conservatism. Vehviläinen et al. also show how pinpointing the exact reasons for or processes leading to this treatment of women was very difficult, leaving the women in doubt as to what exactly they had experienced. (See also Vehviläinen et al., this volume.) As Joan Acker (2006) put it, 'The interaction practices that re-create gender and racial inequalities are often subtle and unspoken, thus difficult to document' (p. 451).

This state of affairs links to the wider problem of informal processes and practices within organisations that promote inequality regimes (Acker, 2006), making redress a thing that is difficult to achieve. Ultimately, centres died if they remained starved of funds, or staff moved on, unwilling to tolerate any longer the precarity that accompanied working in such centres. The investments made in human and material resources along the way were rendered obsolescent, and in some instances, interviewees embarked on significant career changes. Again, it may be that this turbulence is simply part of the innovation and renewal that should be an integral aspect of knowledge production, but, given that DH is here to stay in the contemporary technologising world, thinking in this way may also just be part of the problematic short-termism that characterises contemporary research funding regimes.

Conclusion

In this chapter, I have explored the working and research funding conditions under which DH higher education practitioners in Sweden labour. I showed how the establishment of emerging disciplines in centres, in line with Etzkowitz and Kemelgor's (1998) analysis, creates a precarious work environment that is reinforced by changing research funding regimes and by the conflict between the conventional requirements for an academic career (Mackay's 'the old') and the income-generating focused proclivities of new public management-oriented higher education institutions (one aspect of Mackay's 'the new'). In this, Sweden is no exception.

In thinking through the vicissitudes of funding in gendered higher education contexts, I am struck by the fact that among my interviewees the men talked much more about funding regimes, their consequences and impacts, whilst the women talked much more about how all this impacted on their work situation and careers. Women's careers seemed in some respects much more directly affected by changes in funding regimes than men's; men responded to, and with, accounts of institutional measures and structures, whilst the women were more preoccupied with how they as researchers were situated by the context, fiscal and otherwise, in which they worked.

Women and men become more exploitable under precarious working conditions, but that exploitation may take gender-specific forms. It was noticeable to me that the men I interviewed, even when they occupied precarious positions, were not inclined to see themselves as strongly endangered in those positions. They seemed able to move from post to post, able to find employment through their networks and opportunities that these afforded them (see

48 Gabriele Griffin

also Griffin, 2019). This could not be said for the women. And it led in some cases, eventually, to a 'leakage' of women leaving higher education (Swedish Research Council, 2021a, p. 81). Such leakage but also the fact of the uncompleted research, the demotivation of researchers and the attendant waste of public money cannot be in the interests of any of the actors involved here: researchers, funders or higher education institutions. It is time that there was a serious overhaul of the system.

Acknowledgements

The chapter was supported by funding from NordForsk as part of the Nordic Centre of Excellence Beyond the Gender Paradox (2017–2022; No. 81520) and in part through a Marie Curie Fellowship (749218) held by the Fellow Doris Leibetseder I supervised.

References

Acker, J. (2006). Inequality regimes: gender, class, and race in organizations. *Gender & Society, 20*(4), 441–464. https://doi.org/10.1177/0891243206289499

Angervall, P., Beach, D., & Gustafsson, J. (2015). The unacknowledged value of female academic labour power for male research careers. *Higher Education Research & Development, 34*(5), 815–827. https://doi.org/10.1080/07294360.2015.1011092

Bach, T., Meyer-Sahling, J. H., & Staroňová, K. (2020). Top officials in turbulent times: converging research agendas in Europe East and West. *The NISPAcee Journal of Public Administration and Policy, 13*(2), 25–34. https://doi.org/10.2478/nispa-2020-0012

Braun, V., & Clarke, V. (2006). Using thematic analysis in psychology. *Qualitative Research in Psychology, 3*(2), 77–101. https://doi.org/10.1191/1478088706qp063oa

Braun, V., & Clarke, V. (2021). Can I use TA? Should I use TA? Should I not use TA? Comparing reflexive thematic analysis and other pattern-based qualitative analytic approaches. *Counselling and Psychotherapy Research, 21*(1), 37–47. https://doi.org/10.1002/capr.12360

Chowdry, H., Dearden, L., Jin, W., & Lloyd, B. (2012). *Fees and student support under the new higher education funding regime: what are different universities doing?* (IFS Briefing Note BN134). Institute of Fiscal Studies. https://dera.ioe.ac.uk/33191/1/bn134.pdf

Deem, R. (1998). New managerialism and higher education: the management of performances and cultures in universities in the United Kingdom. *International Studies in Sociology of Education, 8*(1), 47–70. https://doi.org/10.1080/0962021980020014

Deem, R., Hillyard, S., & Reed, M. (2007). *Knowledge, higher education, and the new managerialism: the changing management of UK universities.* Oxford University Press.

del Cerro Santamaría, G. (2020). Challenges and drawbacks in the marketisation of higher education within neoliberalism. *Review of European Studies, 12*(1), 22–38. https://doi.org/10.5539/res.v12n1p22

Directorate for Science, Technology and Innovation. (n.d.). *OECD science, technology and industry scoreboard.* Organisation for Economic Co-operation and Development. https://www.oecd.org/sti/scoreboard.htm

Directorate-General for Communications Networks, Content and Technology. (n.d.). *Digital economy and society index.* European Commission. https://digital-strategy. ec.europa.eu/en/policies/desi

Directorate-General for Research and Innovation. (n.d.). *European innovation scoreboard 2021.* European Commission. https://ec.europa.eu/info/research-and-in novation/statistics/performance-indicators/european-innovation-scoreboard

Directorate-General for Research and Innovation. (2021). *She figures 2021: gender in research and innovation statistics and indicators.* European Commission. https:// doi.org/10.2777/06090

Etzkowitz, H., & Kemelgor, C. (1998). The role of research centres in the collectivisation of academic science. *Minerva, 36*(3), 271–288. https://doi.org/10.1023/A: 1004348123030

Formas. (2022, November 23). *Statistics: success rates and administrating organizations.* https://formas.se/en/start-page/applying-for-funding/different-types-of-financing/ formas-annual-open-call/statistics-success-rates-and-administrating-organisations.html

Griffin, G. (2019). Intersectionalized professional identities and gender in the digital humanities in the Nordic Countries. *Work, Employment and Society, 33*(6), 966–982. https://doi.org/10.1177/0950017019856821

Griffin, G. (2022). The 'work–work balance' in higher education: between over-work, falling short and the pleasures of multiplicity. *Studies in Higher Education, 47*(11), 2190–2203. https://www.tandfonline.com/doi/full/10.1080/03075079.2021.2020750

Griffin, G., & Vehviläinen, M. (2021). The persistence of gender struggles in Nordic research and innovation. *Feminist Encounters, 5*(2), Article 28. https://doi.org/10. 20897/femenc/11165

Ingleby, E. (2015). The house that Jack built: neoliberalism, teaching in higher education and the moral objections. *Teaching in Higher Education, 20*(5), 518–529. https://doi.org/10.1080/13562517.2015.1036729

Kwiek, M. (2012). Higher education reforms and their socio-economic contexts: shifting funding regimes and competing social narratives. In M. Kwiek & P. Maassen (Eds.), *National higher education reforms in a European context: comparative reflections on Poland and Norway* (pp. 155–178). Peter Lang.

Lamont, M. (2009). *How professors think: inside the curious world of academic judgment.* Harvard University Press.

Liefner, I. (2003). Funding, resource allocation, and performance in higher education systems. *Higher Education, 46*(4), 469–489. https://doi.org/10.1023/A: 1027381906977

Mackay, F. (2014). Nested newness, institutional innovation, and the gendered limits of change. *Politics & Gender, 10*(4), 549–571. https://doi.org/10.1017/ S1743923X14000415

Marginson, S., & Sawir, E. (2005). Interrogating global flows in higher education. *Globalisation, Societies and Education, 3*(3), 281–309. https://doi.org/10.1080/ 14767720500166878

Marginson, S., & van der Wende, M. (2007). *Globalisation and higher education* (Education Working Paper No. 8). Organisation for Economic Co-operation and Development. https://doi.org/10.1787/173831738240

Murgia, A., & Poggio., B. (Eds.). (2019). *Gender and precarious research careers: a comparative analysis.* Routledge.

Scholz, B., Vuorio, E., Matuschek, S., & Cameron, I. (2009). *Research careers in Europe: landscapes and horizons.* European Science Foundation. http://archives.esf. org/fileadmin/Public_documents/Publications/moforum_research_careers.pdf

Standing, G. (2011). *The precariat: the new dangerous class*. Bloomsbury.
Strathern, M. (Ed.). (2000). *Audit cultures: anthropological studies in accountability, ethics and the academy*. Routledge.
Swedish Research Council. (2021a). *How gender-equal is higher education? Women's and men's preconditions for conducting research*. https://www.vr.se/english/analysis/reports/our-reports/2021-12-21-how-gender-equal-is-higher-education-womens-and-mens-preconditions-for-conducting-research.html
Swedish Research Council. (2021b). *Swedish research barometer*. https://www.vr.se/english/analysis/swedish-research-in-figures/the-swedish-research-barometer.html
Swedish Research Council. (2023, February 16). *Statistics 2022*. https://www.vr.se/english/analysis/swedish-research-in-figures/overall-decision-statistics/statistics-2022.html
Vehviläinen, M., Ikonen, H.-M., & Korvajärvi, P. (2022). Changes in funding and the intensification of gender inequalities in research and innovation. In G. Griffin (Ed.), *Gender inequalities in tech-driven research and innovation: living the contradiction* (pp. 76–92). Bristol University Press. https://doi.org/10.51952/9781529219494.ch005

4

DISCOURSES OF UNIVERSITY RESEARCH IN PRECARIOUS TIMES

A spatial/temporal analysis from the United Kingdom

Barbara Read and Carole Leathwood

In this chapter, we explore how the landscape of research funding in UK higher education has been impacted by two extraordinary events: Brexit (the withdrawal of the United Kingdom [UK] from the European Union [EU], officially on 31 January 2020) and the onset of the COVID-19 pandemic, which took hold in the UK in January 2020, with the first lockdown two months later. Based on a media analysis of articles in the UK's leading higher education publication, *Times Higher Education* (THE), from January 2020 to June 2021, and associated policy texts, we conduct a feminist intersectional analysis of relevant academic and government discourses. We utilise theorisations of spatiality, temporality and precarity to explore changing geometries of power in the UK research arena during this period, with a particular focus on gender, and consider the equity implications in relation to research and researchers.

In the UK, government research funding is split between a quality-related block grant allocation to individual universities based on the outcomes of a periodic research audit (the Research Excellence Framework, or REF), and competitive grants and programmes administered by discipline-based research councils under the auspices of UK Research and Innovation (UKRI). Additional research funding opportunities come from charitable bodies and commercial organisations, as well as from EU research programmes. The research arena has long been a highly gendered and racialised field, not only in terms of employment and access to the more prestigious and senior research posts, but also in research grant applications and funding success (Sato et al., 2021). Although data show that applications and successful outcomes for UKRI grants increased for women between 2014–2015 and 2019–2020, around two thirds of all research grant applications are still from men, the majority of whom are White (UKRI, 2021). These inequalities continue to be sustained by a neoliberal research economy, which, as we shall discuss, tends to value

DOI: 10.4324/9781003330431-6

most highly the fields and activities in which men have historically dominated (Morley, 2018).

Recent decades have seen an increase in the precarity of research funding and employment in parts of the world where neoliberalism is a dominant influence in the higher education (HE) sector (Chattarji, 2016; Read & Leathwood, 2020). In the UK, research relies increasingly on the precarious labour of academics on short- and fixed-term (i.e. casualised) contracts. According to the University and College Union (UCU, 2021), drawing on 2019–2020 data from the UK's Higher Education Statistical Agency, women are more likely than men to be on fixed-term, hourly-paid or zero-hours[1] contracts. In addition, these data show that 'teaching-only' contracts, with no allocated research time, are disproportionately held by women. As well, almost one in five Black academics are on hourly-paid contracts, compared to just 12% of White academics (UCU, 2021). As a group, Black and minority ethnic[2] academic staff are more likely than White academic staff to be on fixed-term contracts. More specifically, Black women and Asian background women are much more likely to hold this type of contract, 40% and 44%, respectively, than White women (32%) and White men (28%) (UCU, 2021, p. 16).

Butler (2004, 2009) uses the term 'social precarity' to refer to precariousness that is not simply the product of accident but is connected to, or indeed induced by, wider socio-political policies and practices. Of particular concern to Butler is that the ability to cushion oneself from the worst effects of precarity is greatly mediated and constrained by the advantages and disadvantages of particular social positionings. Those in less advantaged positions are far more likely to experience insecurity and precarity in the first place and to experience it more severely (Butler, 2009). Academics without ongoing contracts, and those on teaching-only contracts, are less able to apply for grant funding or to produce the publications that contribute to high scores in the REF and to the funding that such scores generate. Identities and positionings (e.g. gender, social class/ socio-economic background, race, ethnicity, disability, sexuality and age, as well as discipline and university status) thus influence who is able to conduct research and apply for research funding as well as what knowledge is produced.

In exploring these issues, it is imperative to note their fluidity and contextual specificity, for which a temporal/spatial lens can be helpful. A temporal perspective can denaturalise and problematise particular structures, cultures and practices that may seem natural and 'timeless' (Clegg, 2010; Leathwood & Read, 2022; Ylijoki, 2015). A spatial lens can also help emphasise the specificity of particular dynamics and the nuance of context (Alzeer, 2018). Indeed, theorists of temporality such as Adam (2004) and of spatiality such as Massey (1994, 2005) are keen to emphasise the need to look at time and space in conjunction. We draw in particular on Massey's (2009) concept of power geometries – which articulates the ways in which particular spaces and spatial connections are imbued with power relations – to explore the changing configurations of power at play in relation to the grant funding landscape in these precarious times.

The majority of this chapter utilises articles from THE archives (and related government policy texts) published between 1 January 2020 and 30 June 2021: the time span chosen in order to chart the issues arising during the period immediately after the UK's withdrawal from the EU, combined with the onset of the COVID-19 pandemic. The end point is somewhat arbitrary and practical in order for us to complete this chapter for publication – the impacts of these two events will be felt for many years to come (see Carruthers Thomas, this volume, for COVID-19 effects) – but is able to capture some of the short-term, immediate discussions, concerns and projections of the future in these articles. In order to choose which articles to review, we firstly checked the title, and if it looked potentially relevant, we then skimmed the content, finally including in our dataset any article that mentioned Brexit or COVID-19 and/or discussed research funding or social inequalities in the sector. Overall, 540 articles were chosen from the 'News' and 'Opinion' sections of the online edition of the paper.

Both thematic (Braun & Clarke, 2006) and Foucauldian discourse analyses (Khan & MacEachen, 2021) were applied to elucidate key issues and dynamics and to chart the influence of particular discourses and narratives. Our focus here is not, therefore, on the epistemological status of the articles (e.g. reflecting, or not, a 'true' account of events), but on an analysis of the ways in which the discourses in play construct and frame the research funding landscape in relation to both Brexit and COVID-19. In the sections to follow, we consider how Brexit (or its anticipation) and COVID-19 (or its potential threat) complicated research power dynamics. We finish by looking at some of the consequences and impacts of these events for social inequalities in the academy in the UK and further afield, particularly in relation to gender and race/ethnicity.

Changing configurations in the research landscape (1): Brexit

The 2016 referendum decision that the UK should leave the EU produced shock waves throughout the UK HE sector and beyond. Universities are international endeavours, relying not only on academic and student mobility for teaching and research, but also on cross-border networks, grant funding and collaborations, all of which were feared by HE sector leaders to be at risk following the Brexit vote. As Massey (1994) argues, when looking at the spatial connections among students, academics and institutions, physical spaces and points of travel cannot be separated from the social construction of these relations, establishing and perpetuating particular geometries of power.

In relation to Brexit, the temporal aspect of these dynamics can be seen in the ways UK government discourse attempts to establish the timepoint of departure from the EU as allowing for future UK HE prosperity and indeed dominance of the research landscape, as long as individuals and institutions take advantage of what is being offered. UK government discourse in relation to university-based research and Brexit tended to be optimistic, reassuring and expansionist, with visions of 'Global Britain'[3] leading the world in research excellence and innovation. Such imagery is epitomised by the UK Research and Development Roadmap which, despite very little explicit reference to the UK leaving the EU, articulates 'a once-in-a-generation opportunity to strengthen our global position in research, unleash a new wave of innovation, enhance our national security and revitalise our international ties' (HM Government, 2020, p. 4). The discourse is positive and confident, insisting on the importance of global research collaborations and partnerships 'regardless of borders', with an acknowledgement that such 'international collaborations lead to new advances and discoveries, pushing the frontiers of knowledge faster and further' (p. 39). 'Global Britain' can be seen as a signifier of all that is good – positive, open and future-focused – working to dissimulate negative representations of the past (including imperialism and colonialism) and the present (such as the economic, social and prestige costs of Brexit for UK universities).

This positive and optimistic government discourse contrasts sharply with the anticipations of academics and leaders in the HE sector in the UK and in the EU, who frequently challenge the UK government's construction of the future. The dominant themes in THE articles in relation to Brexit have been uncertainty and anxiety, affective responses that have been evident since the referendum in 2016 (Brusenbauch Meislová, 2021). Concerns about UK membership in the Horizon Europe programme (a seven-year EU-funded academic research initiative) persisted throughout the time frame of this study. In June 2021, it was reported that ongoing uncertainty in relation to membership meant that the UK had lost almost £1.5 billion in Horizon 2020 funding in the years after the Brexit vote (Baker, 2021b). Problems foreseen related not only to the loss of research funding but also to the 'networks of collaboration' that Horizon membership brought and that the UK 'simply could not do as a single nation' (Morgan, 2020b).

Collaboration still seemed possible when the UK was expected to become an associate member of Horizon Europe in December 2020, retaining many of the rights and obligations within the scheme. Nevertheless, uncertainty continued due to ongoing and often fraught negotiations between the UK and the EU. Issues of tension included the UK government's threat to renege on the Northern Ireland Protocol, one part of the Withdrawal Agreement designed to ensure that there is no border on the island of Ireland. As a result, one research body in Austria suggested that the UK was considered a risky partner for Horizon 2020 grant applications (Riedl & Staubmann, 2021). During this period of uncertainty, some recipients were forced to relocate within the EU to keep their funds or stay in the UK and hope that the backup scheme promised by the UK government would come to fruition (Matthews, 2022). Fully associated membership for the UK was finalised in September 2023 (UKRI, 2023).

Government discourse, however, remained relentlessly dynamic and positive, perpetuating a 'bright, uncomplicated future' (Brusenbauch Meislová, 2021, p. 43). UK research promises 'to pursue ambitious new goals – the "moonshots" that will define the next decade and beyond' (HM Government, 2020, p. 4), alongside a commitment to attracting 'top talent' and the prioritisation of science and innovation, with a clear emphasis on lab-based sciences, technology and engineering. Although Dame Ottoline Leyser, appointed as head of UKRI in 2020, argued for changes that moved away from the masculinised 'lone genius' model of academic knowledge production (Grove, 2020d), a contrasting discourse was being established in the promotion of a UK research agency that would lie outside UKRI. The new agency, ARIA (Advanced Research and Innovation Agency), was said to reduce the 'red tape' – or accountability – couched as 'hampering' scientists applying for EU funding. The goal is 'high-risk, high-reward scientific research', 'led by prominent, world-leading scientists who will be given the freedom to identify and fund transformational science and technology at speed', helping 'to cement the UK's position as a global science superpower' (Department for Business, Energy and Industrial Strategy [DBEIS], 2021a, para. 1). Although ARIA is to be funded as part of the UK government's commitment to increase the proportion of GDP spent on research and development (with £800 million initially), there are concerns that the diversity of the UK's research ecosystem may be compromised if existing research funds are diverted to ARIA (Bennett, 2022).

The projected future envisioned by ARIA can be seen to be gendered, with the masculinist/phallic imagery of ejaculatory 'moonshots' and the focus on 'high risk', with riskiness often culturally associated with the masculine (Mellström & Erickson, 2014), whilst the eulogising of the discourses of science, technology, engineering and mathematics (STEM) ensures that men, who predominate in these disciplines, are likely to secure the majority of research funding. The focus on high-prestige 'risky' research was reinforced with the introduction of the government's 'Global Talent Route', designed to attract 'world-leading' scientists (Prime Minister's Office, 2020). Such rhetoric is not simply about recognising scientific expertise, but also insisting that the UK is 'world-leading', 'at the forefront of innovation' and 'a science superpower' (DBEIS, 2021b). So, despite references to internationalism, partnership and collaboration, the discourse remains nationalistic, with 'Global Britain' not simply collaborating with others but leading the world.

Instead, Brexit has so far ended up reducing cross-border collaboration and research funding opportunities. The fears that Brexit would negatively affect researcher mobility and the diversity of the academic workforce appear to have been borne out, with an 11% rise in the number of EU academics leaving UK universities between 2015–2016 and 2016–2017 (Russell Group, 2019), including a disproportionately high percentage of academics in biosciences, physics, chemistry and engineering – i.e. disciplines with a higher proportion of men. In addition, there has been a decline in younger EU academics coming to the UK (Baker, 2020b). Another article (Matthews, 2021) reported that many EU academics have lost interest in applying for UK research posts, with Brexit and the associated visa, health costs and bureaucracy being cited as reasons. The gender implications of these mobility trends are unclear, but research suggests that women academics tend to be less mobile than men due to caring commitments and various forms of sexism (Morley et al., 2018), whilst Sang and Calvard's (2019) study indicates a complex pattern of privilege and disadvantage in international academic staff mobility that overall tends to favour White men, who are more likely to be sponsored and mentored by other senior White men. It seems unlikely, therefore, that these changes to cross-border research collaboration opportunities and the decline in EU academics working in UK universities will lead to any rebalancing in terms of equity in research funding opportunities.

In addition, the government's aims of being 'world-leading' in the research arena have been significantly affected by the COVID-19 pandemic from early 2020 onwards, our next topic.

Changing configurations in the research landscape (2): COVID-19

The effects of the COVID-19 pandemic have exacerbated academic and university concerns about access to research funding opportunities and the impact on international research collaborations that were already prevalent in the HE sector as a result of Brexit. A THE article in March 2020 predicted that the emerging pandemic would have a significant negative effect on the quality and quantity of research due to academics' inability to attend conferences and network face-to-face, with particular hardships for early-career researchers relying on these contacts (Bothwell, 2020). Again, we can see the temporal dimension of these constructions of the changing dynamics among students, academics and institutions in this period, with concerns and anxieties over the future – and their relation to changing geometries of power – dominating discussion.

Some HE sector leaders utilised the government's earlier stated enthusiasm for academic research to push the government to support the sector through the combined impact of COVID-19 and Brexit. The UK government provided £280 million in 'COVID relief' money to universities and offered long-term, low-interest loans to research-active universities (as defined through the REF), a practice that favoured more prestigious institutions (Havergal, 2020).

In the context of COVID-19, forms of support and forms of jeopardy varied from discipline to discipline in this period. Although THE articles addressing these dynamics did not explicitly discuss gender, we can see that the socially 'masculinised' STEM disciplines were advantaged over their 'feminised' counterparts such as the social sciences and humanities. As we noted earlier, it was particularly the sciences that the UK government was keen to champion in the wake of Brexit. And with the rise of COVID-19, it was the sciences that were singled out by many commentators as key areas that needed support (although interestingly, a prominent STEM disciplinary area championed was medicine, including the 'feminised' area of nursing). A survey commissioned by University Alliance, a group of UK universities that provide specialist technical and professional education, somewhat conveniently found that the public considered applied subjects such as medicine most important and valued STEM as a whole far more highly (50%) than the social sciences (24%), languages (13%) or the arts (12%) (Grove, 2020c).

The argument for the prioritisation of STEM and applied subjects was echoed in numerous THE articles arguing that research needs to be 'useful' and 'tackle the most critical questions' (Basken, 2020; Grove, 2020a; Morgan, 2020a). The rhetoric of non-applied research as socially irrelevant feeds into a discourse where (non-applied) social sciences and especially the arts and humanities are less valued and become more vulnerable in terms of funding support. These dynamics have specifically gendered and racialised consequences, as explored in the next section.

With COVID-19 as well as Brexit, we can see that discourses of shifting spatial power relations also have a temporal dimension – of projected constructions of potential power relations in the future. As discussed earlier, the UK government attempted to construct a somewhat imperial image of a risk-taking, entrepreneurial UK as a 'world leader' after becoming 'free' from the restrictions of the EU. Countering this projection, many academics and sector leaders saw future visions of UK research as reduced in status and power, and the onset of the pandemic led many in the sector worldwide to fear future consequences for research quality and international collaboration. Arguably, the UK government has been able to sidestep some of the negative consequences of Brexit on research by publicly focusing on the impact of the pandemic, and it is difficult to disentangle the specific effects of one or the other on the HE sector. What is becoming clear, however, are consequences for equity in academia, particularly in relation to gender and race inequalities. Consistent with Butler's (2004, 2009) notion of social precarity, the uncertainty of Brexit and the pandemic has only deepened existing patterns of social inequality in the sector.

Gendered and racialised consequences of Brexit and COVID-19 for university research

Both Brexit and COVID-19 have exacerbated inequalities, with a number of reports highlighting actual and potential negative socio-economic consequences for women and other marginalised and disadvantaged groups (Hepburn, 2020; Women's Budget Group, 2018). Women were largely excluded from the Brexit debate (Galpin, 2018), the Brexit negotiations (Barr, 2017) and the COVID-19 committees set up to advise the government

(Marren & Bazeley, 2022), with the lack of diversity of voices advising the government during the pandemic noted by the campaign group Scientists for EU (Baker, 2020a). A group of women scientists of diverse ethnicities, mostly from the United States, collectively wrote in THE in May 2020 of a range of ways the pandemic was disadvantaging women in the field of science, especially women of colour, including the bypassing of their expertise by policymakers and the media (Buckee et al., 2020). Noting additional inequities in relation to care responsibilities and in job vulnerability, the collective stated that despite 'lifelong battles for a place in science', they were nevertheless

> unprepared for the gendered and racial inequalities we have experienced in the response to the Covid-19 pandemic. ... What is surprising and demoralising is seeing the fault lines of sexism that define our unequal footing with men crack into gaping chasms under the pressure of the pandemic.
>
> (para. 2)

One aspect of inequity that the group referenced is the proportion of academics on short-term, part-time and zero-hours casualised contracts. Although most research about the precarity of job contracts in HE has focused on the Global North, universities across the globe have been affected by this trend (Chattarji, 2016). In the UK context, as described earlier, there are gendered and racialised patterns in relation to contract status in HE, and it is potentially those who are already in precarious situations in academia who are at most risk of further cuts and job losses post-Brexit and post-COVID-19 (Watermeyer et al., 2020). As we argued, such precarity impacts knowledge production in the academy. Those with the stability to lead research projects are much more likely to be on full-time contracts and in senior positions, and White men are disproportionately represented in such positions (Morris et al., 2022). In addition, a UK survey of new principal investigators found that women were significantly less likely than men to have secured grant funding, and particularly funding in excess of £1 million, within the first five years of their careers (Acton et al., 2019).

Brexit and especially the COVID-19 pandemic seem to have intensified these pre-existing gendered and racialised patterns of inequality in relation to grant funding and knowledge production (Gill, 2020). A plethora of THE articles during the period focused on fears and uncertainties over job losses in the sector, with both Brexit (Conlon et al., 2021) and COVID-19 affecting university income. Consequently, many universities drastically reduced the number of casualised staff on their books during this period, thus adding to the precarity of women and Black or minority ethnic academics (UCU, 2021). Interviewed in THE in June 2020, Simon Marginson, professor of higher education at the University of Oxford, argued that this practice will result in a turndown in overall research output and a loss of opportunities for a generation of would-be researchers (Baker, 2020d).

Pay and hiring freezes as well as job losses began to be reported in the UK from May 2020, seemingly skewed towards disciplinary fields that employ more women. The first UK university to announce permanent job cuts – the University of Roehampton – established a voluntary redundancy scheme particularly focused on education, dance, drama, media culture and languages, and the humanities (McKie, 2020). The University of Liverpool was said to be earmarking staff for compulsory redundancy in health and life sciences based on research income and citation impact scores (Havergal, 2021a), a move later rescinded following protests (Havergal, 2021b). In addition to threatening a 'feminised' science field, the concept of linking redundancy to such metrics has potentially gendered consequences due to gender disparities in attracting research income (Acton et al., 2019), in publishing – especially during COVID-19 (Orchard et al., 2022; see also Carruthers Thomas, this volume), and in achieving citations in high-impact journals (Chatterjee & Werner, 2021).

Other articles looked at the working conditions of academics since the beginning of the pandemic and especially during periods of lockdown. Commentators anticipated that the loss of fixed-term teaching staff would have a knock-on effect of creating greater workloads for remaining permanent staff, undermining their ability to conduct research (Watermeyer et al., 2020). Another UK study found that the workloads of junior academics increased an average of approximately five per cent more than that of their senior colleagues, which has gendered and racialised implications due to the disproportionate number of White men in senior positions in academia (Walker et al., 2020).

In contrast, work was drying up for those on research-only contracts. Many research projects reported delays – sometimes severe – to research that could not easily be conducted online (Walker et al., 2020). Research-only fixed-term staff were considered especially vulnerable.

A particularly gendered issue is the unequal burden on those with caring commitments. Academics in all disciplines raised concerns over the difficulties of combining work with care, especially during lockdowns when education shifted to the home (Baker, 2021a; Walker et al., 2020). An article in May 2020 focused on the fears of PhD students and early-career researchers who were struggling to deal with increased childcare burdens in the present and anticipating a 'funding cliff edge' in terms of available opportunities in the future (Baker, 2020c). Sector leaders acknowledged the inequities in relation to research output but without a clear conception of how to ameliorate them. One early article noted that principal investigators would need to 'make allowances' for project researchers with young children; the same article noted that others – presumably without caring commitments – were finding lockdown a time for increased productivity (Grove, 2020b). Research England, the government's research audit body responsible for the REF for the whole of the UK, announced a postponement of the assessment regime for 2020 and stated that the effects of COVID-19 on researchers' outputs would be taken into account in the next audit.

Finally, the imposition of post-Brexit visa requirements for EU academics coming to work at UK universities after the end of the transition period had significant personal consequences for some academics, compounded by delays brought on by the pandemic. According to one University of Cambridge academic writing in THE (Islam, 2020), this situation raised questions about 'the value and treatment of global researchers in the UK, and the UK's reputation as an academic leader in the post-Brexit world'. She noted that the discriminatory 'hostile environment' that non-EU migrants have long faced in the UK is now also impacting academics from the EU, raising serious questions 'about the future of academia in the UK' – a statement that stands in marked contrast to the UK government's stated goal of becoming a global research 'superpower'.

Conclusion

In this chapter, we have explored the impact of Brexit and COVID-19 on inequalities in the research landscape in the UK HE sector through an analysis of articles published in THE over an 18-month period. We concentrated on one specific geographical space – the UK – although, as we have seen, complex 'power geometries' (Massey, 2009) continue to link the UK inextricably with countries within and beyond the EU, as much as the UK government wished for a separation. We also focused on a particular snapshot in time, one where projections of the future and evocations of an imperial past featured almost as strongly as accounts of contemporary events. Both Brexit and COVID-19 were constructed as, or assumed to be, one-off events, with the UK government promising to 'Get Brexit Done' with the signing of the Withdrawal Agreement in January 2020, and COVID-19, at least initially, expected to be largely over by the summer of the same year. Yet in 2023 considerable uncertainties persist with regard to both.

In many ways, COVID-19 has eclipsed Brexit, making it harder to untangle the impact of Brexit on academic work from the more immediate effects of lockdowns (Foster, 2021), and it was COVID-19 that generated most of the concerns about inequalities in the articles we examined. The UK government has also downplayed any negative impacts of Brexit, with challenges in the UK Research and Development Roadmap (HM Government, 2020) almost entirely framed as a consequence of COVID-19 rather than Brexit. It is clear, however, that both events have reshaped the research landscape. Common themes emerged in relation to the geopolitics of research, including a reconfiguration of borders and boundaries, impacting cross-national research projects, funding opportunities and researcher mobility, and generating insecurities for researchers and universities. Butler's (2004, 2009) conception of social precarity as differentially experienced and exacerbating already existing dynamics of inequality is reflected in our analysis. The effects of the pandemic have served to widen pre-existing aspects of inequality in the research funding landscape and within academia more broadly, especially in relation to career stage, gender and race/ethnicity. As we have argued, the shifting configurations of power among researchers, students and institutions need to be explored through a temporal as well as a spatial analysis, highlighting especially that much discourse in this period involved competing projected hopes, concerns, fears and anxieties over the future of the HE sector post-Brexit and post-pandemic. By 2024, it is far from clear which projections are more likely to be realised.

Notes

1 'Zero-hours' contracts are those where the employer is not obliged to provide regular (or any) hours of work.
2 We recognise the limitations of amalgamating Black and minority ethnic scholars or Black, Asian and minority ethnic scholars, but follow the practice of Advance HE (2019) 'to identify patterns of marginalisation and segregation' (p. 9) in relation to ethnicity in reporting statistical data in higher education. Limitations include the grouping together of non-homogeneous subgroups and potential confusion and inconsistencies around which subgroups are or are not included. Also, when encountering statements about 'women and minority ethnic academics', readers should keep in mind that these two categories intersect but are often presented separately in statistical publications.
3 'Global Britain' is a term that has been used by the UK Government since the 2016 Brexit referendum (see Robinson, 2021). The term 'Britain' or 'Great Britain' applies specifically to the island comprising England, Scotland and Wales, rather than to the UK as a whole, which also includes Northern Ireland. Its usage in this context can be seen to evoke the mythology of the supposed greatness and benevolence of the British Empire.

References

Acton, S. E., Bell, A. J. D., Toseland, C. P., & Twelvetrees, A. (2019). Research culture: a survey of new PIs in the UK. *eLife*, *8*, Article e46827. https://doi.org/10.7554/eLife.46827

Adam, B. (2004). *Time*. Polity Press.

Advance HE. (2019). *Equality + higher education: staff statistical report 2019*. https://www.advance-he.ac.uk/knowledge-hub/equality-higher-education-statistical-report-2019

Alzeer, G. (2018). A perspective on women's spatial experiences in higher education: between modernity and tradition. *British Journal of Sociology of Education*, *39*(8), 1175–1194. https://doi.org/10.1080/01425692.2018.1478278

Baker, S. (2020a, March 26). Coronavirus shines spotlight on science advice system in UK. *Times Higher Education*. https://www.timeshighereducation.com/news/coronavirus-shines-spotlight-science-advice-system-inuk

Baker, S. (2020b, March 28). Half of academics leaving UK are EU citizens. *Times Higher Education*. https://www.timeshighereducation.com/news/half-academics-leaving-uk-are-eu-citizens

Baker, S. (2020c, May 18). Most early career academics face funding cliff edge, survey suggests. *Times Higher Education*. https://www.timeshighereducation.com/news/most-early-career-academics-face-funding-cliff-edge-survey-suggests

Baker, S. (2020d, June 11). HE financial crisis risks 'lost generation of researchers'. *Times Higher Education*. https://www.timeshighereducation.com/news/he-financial-crisis-risks-lost-generation-researchers

Baker, S. (2021a, January 15). Higher education and the pandemic: key trends to watch in 2021. *Times Higher Education*. https://www.timeshighereducation.com/news/higher-education-and-pandemic-key-trends-watch-2021

Baker, S. (2021b, June 24). UK 'lost £1.5 billion' Horizon 2020 funding after Brexit vote. *Times Higher Education*. https://www.timeshighereducation.com/news/uk-lost-ps15-billion-horizon-2020-funding-after-brexit-vote

Barr, H. (2017, June 21). Brexit without women: lack of female voices as UK negotiations with EU begin. *Human Rights Watch*. https://www.hrw.org/news/2017/06/21/brexit-without-women

Basken, P. (2020, March 23). US research labs closing down for everything but coronavirus. *Times Higher Education*. https://www.timeshighereducation.com/news/us-research-labs-closing-down-everything-coronavirus

Bennett, N. (2022, January 12). ARIA: what is it and what is it good for? *Green World*. https://greenworld.org.uk/article/aria-what-it-and-what-it-good

Bothwell, E. (2020, March 11). Conference cancellations could have 'big impact' on research. *Times Higher Education*. https://www.timeshighereducation.com/news/conference-cancellations-could-have-big-impact-research

Braun, V., & Clarke, V. (2006). Using thematic analysis in psychology. *Qualitative Research in Psychology*, *3*(2), 77–101. https://doi.org/10.1191/1478088706qp063oa

Brusenbauch Meislová, M. (2021). Lost in the noise? Narrative (re)presentation of higher education and research during the Brexit process in the UK. *European Journal of English Studies*, *25*(1), 34–48. https://doi.org/10.1080/13825577.2021.1918835

Buckee, C., Hedt-Gauthier, B., Mahmud, A., Martinez, P., Tedijanto, C., Murray, M., Khan, R., Menkir, T., Li, R., Suliman, S., Fosdick, B., Cobey, S., Rasmussen, A., Popescu, S., Cevik, M., Dada, S., Jenkins, H., Clapham, H., Mordecai, E., ... Dhatt, R. (2020, May 15). Women in science are battling both COVID-19 and the patriarchy. *Times Higher Education*. https://www.timeshighereducation.com/blog/women-science-are-battling-both-COVID-19-and-patriarchy

Butler, J. (2004). *Precarious life*. Verso.

Butler, J. (2009). *Frames of war: when is life grievable?* Verso.

Chattarji, S. (2016). Labor, precarity and the university: thinking about Indian higher education. *English Language Notes*, *54*(2), 167–174. https://doi.org/10.1215/00138282-54.2.167

Chatterjee, P., & Werner, R. (2021) Gender disparity in citations in high-impact journal articles. *JAMA Network Open*, *4*(7). https://doi.org/10.1001/jamanetworkopen.2021.14509

Clegg, S. (2010). Time future – the dominant discourse of higher education. *Time & Society*, *19*(3), 345–364. https://doi.org/10.1177/0961463X10381528

Conlon, G., Lader, R., Halterbeck, M., & Hedges, S. (2021). *EU exit: estimating the impact on UK higher education*. Department for Education. https://www.gov.uk/government/publications/estimating-the-impact-of-eu-exit-on-uk-higher-education

Department for Business, Energy and Industrial Strategy. (2021a, February 19). *UK to launch new research agency to support high risk, high reward science* [Press release]. https://www.gov.uk/government/news/uk-to-launch-new-research-agency-to-support-high-risk-high-reward-science

Department for Business, Energy and Industrial Strategy. (2021b, March 19). *Advanced Research and Invention Agency (ARIA): policy statement.* https://www.gov.uk/government/publications/advanced-research-and-invention-agency-aria-statement-of-policy-intent/advanced-research-and-invention-agency-aria-policy-statement

Foster, B. (2021). Brexit and scientific research? *European Journal of English Studies, 25*(1), 11–18. https://doi.org/10.1080/13825577.2021.1918831

Galpin, C. (2018, October 8). Women have been excluded from the Brexit debate. *UK in a changing Europe.* https://ukandeu.ac.uk/women-have-been-excluded-from-the-brexit-debate/

Gill, J. (2020, September 17). The burden of privilege. *Times Higher Education.* https://www.timeshighereducation.com/opinion/burden-privilege

Grove, J. (2020a, March 27). UK researchers redeploy to fight coronavirus. *Times Higher Education.* https://www.timeshighereducation.com/news/uk-researchers-redeploy-fight-coronavirus

Grove, J. (2020b, March 31). Research intelligence: how to run a research team remotely. *Times Higher Education.* https://www.timeshighereducation.com/career/research-intelligence-how-run-research-team-remotely

Grove, J. (2020c, June 10). 'Prioritise professional subjects in COVID-19 recovery', says poll. *Times Higher Education.* https://www.timeshighereducation.com/news/prioritise-professional-subjects-COVID-19-recovery-says-poll

Grove, J. (2020d, August 11). Ottoline Leyser: 'I'm not going to pussyfoot about'. *Times Higher Education.* https://www.timeshighereducation.com/news/ottoline-leyser-im-not-going-pussyfoot-about

Havergal, C. (2020, June 29). Unions unconvinced by UK's research rescue package. *Times Higher Education.* https://www.timeshighereducation.com/news/unions-unconvinced-uks-research-rescue-package

Havergal, C. (2021a, April 26). Work to rule at Liverpool over 'rank and yank' cuts. *Times Higher Education.* https://www.timeshighereducation.com/news/work-rule-liverpool-over-rank-and-yank-cuts

Havergal, C. (2021b, October 1). Liverpool strikes off as compulsory redundancies averted. *Times Higher Education.* https://www.timeshighereducation.com/news/liverpool-strikes-compulsory-redundancies-averted

Hepburn, E. (2020). *Social and equality impacts of Brexit.* Report for The Scottish Government. https://www.gov.scot/publications/social-equality-impacts-brexit/documents/

HM Government. (2020). *UK research and development roadmap.* https://www.gov.uk/government/publications/uk-research-and-development-roadmap

Islam, A. (2020, January 15). My experience with the Home Office doesn't bode well for foreign academics. *Times Higher Education.* https://www.timeshighereducation.com/blog/my-experience-home-office-doesnt-bode-well-foreign-academics

Khan, T. H., & MacEachen, E. (2021). Foucauldian discourse analysis: moving beyond a social constructionist analytic. *International Journal of Qualitative Methods, 20.* https://doi.org/10.1177/16094069211018009

Leathwood, C., & Read, B. (2022). Short-term, short-changed? A temporal perspective on the implications of academic casualisation for teaching in higher education. *Teaching in Higher Education, 27*(6), 756–771. https://doi.org/10.1080/13562517.2020.1742681

Marren, C., & Bazeley, A. (2022). *Sex and power 2022.* The Fawcett Society. https://www.fawcettsociety.org.uk/sex-power-2022

Massey, D. (1994). *Space, place and gender.* University of Minnesota Press.

Massey, D. (2005). *For space.* Sage.

Massey, D. (2009). Concepts of space and power in theory and in political practice. *Documents d'Anàlisa Geogràfica*, *55*, 15–26. https://raco.cat/index.php/Docum entsAnalisi/article/view/171747

Matthews, D. (2021, May 27). Cross-border universities initiative 'could extend far beyond EU'. *Times Higher Education*. https://www.timeshighereducation.com/news/cross-border-universities-initiative-could-extend-far-beyond-eu

Matthews, D. (2022, June 30). European Research Council withdraws the grants of 115 researchers based in the UK, as 19 scientists decide to relocate. *Science Business*. https://sciencebusiness.net/news/european-research-council-withdraws-grants-115-researchers-based-uk-19-scientists-decide

McKie, A. (2020, May 6). SOAS faces 'viability problems' amid pandemic crisis, director warns. *Times Higher Education*. https://www.timeshighereducation.com/news/soas-faces-viability-problems-amid-pandemic-crisis-director-warns

Mellström, U., & Erickson, M. (2014). Masculinity at risk. *Norma: International Journal of Masculinity Studies*, *9*(3), 147–150. https://doi.org/10.1080/18902138.2014.951181

Morgan, J. (2020a, July 8). Rothwell: Covid crisis puts UK research 'under huge threat'. *Times Higher Education*. https://www.timeshighereducation.com/news/rothwell-covid-crisis-puts-uk-research-under-huge-threat

Morgan, J. (2020b, September 9). Russell Group 'assuming' UK will not join Horizon Europe. *Times Higher Education*. https://www.timeshighereducation.com/news/russell-group-assuming-uk-will-not-join-horizon-europe

Morley, L. (2018). Gender in the neo-liberal research economy: an enervating and exclusionary entanglement? In H. Kahlert (Ed.), *Gender studies and the new academic governance: global challenges, glocal dynamics and local impacts* (pp. 15–40). Springer.

Morley, L., Alexiadou, N., Garaz, S., Gonzalez-Monteagudo, J., & Taba, M. (2018). Internationalisation and migrant academics: the hidden narratives of mobility. *Higher Education*, *76*, 537–554. https://doi.org/10.1007/s10734-017-0224-z

Morris, C., Hinton-Smith, T., Marvell, R., & Brayson, K. (2022). Gender back on the agenda in higher education: perspectives of academic staff in a contemporary UK case study. *Journal of Gender Studies*, *31*(1), 101–113. https://doi.org/10.1080/09589236.2021.1952064

Orchard, C., Smith, P. M., & Kromhout, H. (2022). Gender differences in authorship prior to and during the COVID-19 pandemic in research submissions to *Occupational and Environmental Medicine* (2017–2021). *Occupational and Environmental Medicine*, *79*(6), 361–364. https://doi.org/10.1136/oemed-2021-107915

Prime Minister's Office. (2020, January 27). *Boost for UK science with unlimited visa offer to world's brightest and best* [Press release]. https://www.gov.uk/government/news/boost-for-uk-science-with-unlimited-visa-offer-to-worlds-brightest-and-best

Read, B., & Leathwood, C. (2020). Casualised academic staff and the lecturer–student relationship: shame, (im)permanence and (il)legitimacy. *British Journal of Sociology of Education*, *41*(4), 539–554. https://doi.org/10.1080/01425692.2020.1748570

Riedl, V., & Staubmann, H. (2021). Internationalisation, Brexit, and the EU academic system: a case study in Austria. *European Journal of English Studies*, *25*(1), 65–79. https://doi.org/10.1080/13825577.2021.1918860

Robinson, T. (2021). *Global Britain* (Debate pack No. CDP 002). https://commonslibrary.parliament.uk/research-briefings/cdp-2021-0002/

Russell Group. (2019, August 8). *Brexit and EU academics*. https://russellgroup.ac.uk/news/brexit-and-eu-academics/

Sang, K. J. C., & Calvard, T. (2019). 'I'm a migrant, but the right sort of migrant': hegemonic masculinity, whiteness and intersectional privilege and (dis)advantage in migratory academic careers. *Gender, Work & Organization, 26*(10), 1506–1525. https://doi.org/10.1111/gwao.12382

Sato, S., Gygax, P. M., Randall, J., & Schmid Mast, M. (2021). The leaky pipeline in research grant peer review and funding decisions: challenges and future directions. *Higher Education, 82*(1), 145–162. https://doi.org/10.1007/s10734-020-00626-y

UK Research and Innovation. (2021, March 30). *Diversity results for UKRI funding data 2014–15 to 2019–20.* https://www.ukri.org/publications/diversity-results-analysis-for-ukri-funding-data-financial-years-2014-15-to-2019-20/

UK Research and Innovation. (2023, September 7). *Horizon Europe: help for UK applicants.* https://www.ukri.org/apply-for-funding/horizon-europe/

University and College Union. (2021). *Precarious work in higher education: insecure contracts and how they have changed over time. October 2021 update.* https://www.ucu.org.uk/media/10899/Precarious-work-in-higher-education-Oct-21/pdf/UCU_precarity-in-HE_Oct21.pdf

Walker, J., Brewster, C., Fontinha, R., & Haak-Saheem, W. (2020, June 12). Three challenges facing academic research during the Covid-19 crisis. *Times Higher Education.* https://www.timeshighereducation.com/blog/three-challenges-facing-academic-research-during-covid-19-crisis

Watermeyer, R., Courtois, A., & Lauder, H. (2020, April 3). Reacting to Covid-19 by slashing fixed-term staff would be a disaster. *Times Higher Education.* https://www.timeshighereducation.com/opinion/reacting-covid-19-slashing-fixed-term-staff-would-be-adisaster

Women's Budget Group. (2018). *Exploring the economic impact of Brexit on women.* https://wbg.org.uk/analysis/new-report-exploring-the-economic-impact-of-brexit-on-women/

Ylijoki, O.-H. (2015). Conquered by project time? Conflicting temporalities in university research. In P. Gibbs, O.-H. Ylijoki, C. Guzmán-Valenzuela, & R. Barnett (Eds.), *Universities in the flux of time: an exploration of time and temporality in university life* (pp. 94–107). Routledge.

5

GENDER INEQUALITIES, RESEARCH FUNDING AND ORGANISATIONAL PRACTICES

Academic mothers in Finnish universities

Marja Vehviläinen, Hanna-Mari Ikonen and Päivi Korvajärvi

Mothers who work in academia face gender inequalities across the globe (S. Acker & Armenti, 2004; Toffoletti & Starr, 2016) including in Nordic countries such as Finland, which for many decades have provided good care services for all children and relatively long parental leave to be shared between parents (Nikunen, 2014; Thun, 2020). However, academic institutions and their organisational practices play a key role in gender inequalities, and the improvement of state welfare services has not been able to change the trend (Krilic et al., 2019; Thun, 2020). In Finland, as elsewhere, the question of motherhood has remained one of the key concerns of gender equality in academic work and careers (Eren, 2022; Ollilainen, 2019; Thun, 2020), intertwined with other inequalities in academia such as gender bias in recruitment and promotion (Nielsen, 2016), male-dominated work cultures and networks (Case & Richley, 2013; van den Brink & Benschop, 2014), and the persistent under-representation of women in sciences and engineering (Directorate-General for Research and Innovation, 2021).

Universities have increasingly functioned under academic capitalism and with competitive external funding. Following Slaughter and Leslie (1997), Ylijoki (2003) explains that academic capitalism refers to 'actions intended to attract external revenue for higher education institutions as well as for individual university researchers' (p. 308) and includes both direct market activity, such as developing patents for profit, and market-like behaviour, such as competitively seeking grants, research contracts and donations. In Finland, the importance of external funding has meant that work at universities consists not only of traditional research and teaching, but also includes the production of applications for competitive funding, reports on funding for auditors and evaluators, and commercialisation. The managerial practices embedded in academic capitalism offer flexibility but simultaneously force individual academics to work more hours to

DOI: 10.4324/9781003330431-7

meet all the demands. For academic mothers, flexibility can be useful, yet individual mothers are often left to coordinate the differing logics of endless working hours in greedy academia and the need for their presence in childcare (Gaudet et al., 2022; Krilic et al., 2019; Thun, 2020; Toffoletti & Starr, 2016). Universities have done too little for gender equality generally (Griffin & Vehviläinen, 2021) and for the support of mothers' and other parents' careers in particular (Nikunen, 2014; Thun, 2020).

Additionally, funding agencies and instruments shape academic work and organisational practices (Drew, 2022; Rosa et al., 2021). Many funding agencies aim to promote gender equality as required by the national legislation for gender equality and mainstreaming in Finland and by European Union regulations (Directorate-General for Research and Innovation, 2021, p. 171). For example, they establish gender-balanced boards for decision-making to deliver grants in equal proportion to women and men (relative to the share of applicants) (Academy of Finland [AF], 2019, p. 8; Directorate-General for Research and Innovation, 2021, p. 259). However, the use of gender equality measures varies from funding agency to funding agency, as it varies from country to country (Husu & de Cheveigné, 2010). Some agencies grant funding to individuals, while others grant it to institutions. The former provides more autonomy and flexibility for individual researchers with grants and the latter gives more power to the universities.

In this chapter, we focus on gender (in)equality in academic work and careers by exploring the support and disadvantages that funding and (funded) research work in academic organisations produce in women academics' careers, with motherhood in academic work being a lens for illuminating the dynamics. By analysing researchers' experiences, reported in 30 career interviews with women working in health technology in Finland, we interrogate how gender equality in academic work and careers is (not) supported at the interplay of funding agency and university practices in the context of academic capitalism in Finland. More specifically, we trace how this (non)support affects the careers of academic mothers having parental leave and caring for young children.

We examine how gender equality and inequalities in academia are performed within organisational practices (J. Acker, 1990; Smith, 2005) by analysing the experiences of women researchers and how they are organised through societal orders of academic capitalism, structures of funding and welfare provisions for care. We understand gender inequalities as intersecting social inequalities that are more often experienced by women than men, causing disadvantages for women 'both born and made' (Evans, 2017, p. 9). Intersections of social conditions include class, race and age, with the significant conditions varying from one context to another (Evans, 2017; Rosa & Clavero, 2021). Here the main intersecting condition is career stage, somewhat relating to age, ranging from doctoral student and postdoctoral researcher to independent senior researchers and professors. Within the broad range of gender (in)equalities, the focus is on motherhood in academic work and careers, and on the supports and disadvantages that the interplay of funding agencies and academic organisations generates for mothers' careers in academia.

Before moving to the results of our empirical study, we briefly review elements of the literature on gender equality in academe, and describe the Finnish higher education and research and innovation (RI) funding landscape. After a discussion of data and methods, we present our findings. We argue that even though funding agencies can contribute significantly to gender equality, it is the combination of the practices of academic organisations and funding agencies that matters even more strongly and has the potential to support gender equality and women's careers.

Gender equality and persistent gender inequalities in academia

There is an extensive body of research on gender (in)equalities in academic careers over the decades and across countries (S. Acker & Armenti, 2004; Gaudet et al., 2022; Le Feuvre et al., 2019), including Finland and other Nordic nations (Griffin & Vehviläinen 2021; Husu, 2001; Thun, 2020). Women are known to suffer disproportionately from precarious work in the academy (Directorate-General for Research and Innovation, 2021, p. 155; Pereira, 2017; Rosa & Clavero, 2021), are unevenly represented across research fields (Directorate-General for Research and Innovation, 2021, pp. 120–121) and encounter bias in accessing professorships (Nielsen, 2016). In Finland, academics are located within four career stages: (1) doctoral researchers, (2) postdoctoral researchers, (3) university researchers and lecturers, and (4) professors. Women represent half of the academics at the first three career stages, but less than one third of the top stage, professors (Directorate-General for Research and Innovation, 2021, pp. 184, 324). Importantly, studies on academic motherhood (Eren, 2022; Nikunen, 2014) have shown how pregnancy and even the possibility of pregnancy construct women as 'unsuitable' academics (Huopalainen & Satama, 2019; Pecis, 2016), especially in male-dominated fields (Krilic et al., 2019), and how myths about motherhood have persistently caused disadvantages for academic women's careers (Husu, 2001; Luukkonen-Gronow, 1987; Pecis, 2016).

Gender equality in academia has been promoted through various measures in North America, Europe and beyond (Drew, 2022; Rosa et al., 2021). The European Union and European Commission have advanced gender mainstreaming approaches which focus on institutional and societal gender structures, involving 'the integration of a gender perspective into the preparation, design, implementation, monitoring and evaluation of policies, regulatory measures and spending programmes' (European Institute for Gender Equality, 2016, p. 5). In Finland, universities are obliged to prepare gender equality plans (GEPs) in collaboration with representatives appointed by their employees at least once every two years. These GEPs are typically produced by standing gender equality committees, and they consist of the assessment of the gender equality situation, necessary measures, and follow-up on previous measures (Ombudsman for Equality, n.d.). However, notoriously, the implementation of GEPs has often remained partial and even failed in Europe (Thomson et al., 2022). GEPs in Finnish universities often do not cover all aspects of Finnish gender equality legislation (Pietilä, 2021; Tanhua, 2020, p. 23). Concerning motherhood in academic work, GEPs name staff members' right to parental leave and flexible work arrangements. However, these rights are part of the Finnish legislation generally, and GEPs fail to address the specific structures of academia, for example, the different situations of academics in permanent (professor, lecturer) and in fixed-term (researcher working with external funding) positions, and the consequences of parental leave and flexible work arrangements for researchers' careers (Tanhua, 2020, pp. 30–31, 40).

Research and innovation funding in Finnish academia

Finnish higher education institutions include 13 universities and 22 universities of applied sciences, the latter offering more pragmatic education (Ministry of Education and Culture [MEC], n.d.). The focus of this chapter is on research universities, which consist of units with financial responsibility (faculties, departments, centres). These units employ researchers within the four career stages named earlier (MEC, 2016). According to Puhakka (2020), 79% of researchers with a PhD who work in Finnish universities do not have permanent positions. Excluding the recently inaugurated tenure-track system, researchers are not assumed to move from one career step to another but need to apply for vacancies at each stage. Universities function with competitive governmental and external funding; and universities, their units and individual researchers apply for the latter. The governmental core funding for universities is negotiated on a fixed schedule (based, for example, on the publications and degrees produced) between universities and the Ministry of Education and Culture. At the turn of the millennium, external funding exceeded the research part of the ministry's bulk funding (Oksanen et al., 2003, p. 24).

External research and innovation funding is delivered by a national research council, an innovation agency, ministries, private companies, non-profit organisations, the European Union, and international enterprises and funders (Oksanen et al., 2003, p. 24). The national research council, once called the Academy of Finland (AF), now the Research Council of Finland, funds individual researchers (postdoctoral researchers, senior researchers, professors), research projects, centres of excellence and universities developing new research profiles. The Finnish Funding Agency for Innovation (FAI) focused on financing research–industry collaborations involving university research units, private companies and/or public sector actors. A new entity, Business Finland, replaced the FAI in 2018, but with a different agenda and now mainly supports Finnish companies.

Many European funding agencies have aimed to counterbalance the notorious tendency of distributing smaller and fewer grants to women (Rosa et al., 2021; Steinþórsdóttir et al., 2020; van der Lee & Ellemers, 2015) by actively engaging in gender equality planning (AF, 2019; Doona, 2021; Drew, 2022; Husu & de Cheveigné, 2010). In Finland, the AF has systematically enacted GEPs since the 1980s (Husu, 2001, pp. 85–89; Husu & de Cheveigné, 2010, p. 58). The evaluation boards of the research councils in AF have gender parity (40%–60% of each sex) (AF, 2019; Directorate-General for Research and Innovation, 2021, p. 203) and measures for parental leave for researchers have been implemented (AF, 2019). In contrast, the FAI did not have a gender policy, nor did the private foundations (another funding source) have a systematic tradition of GEPs comparable to the AF. Furthermore, the private foundations' grants do not usually provide an employment contract to the university, making working conditions weaker compared even to fixed-term work contracts through other funders. In the following analysis, we shall examine how these different practices matter in the experiences of women researchers.

Data and method

The chapter analyses 30 career history interviews of women who have worked at universities in Finland.[1] Nearly all (28) had PhDs in multidisciplinary health technology centring on research and innovations for cures, health and well-being in life (and combining biological and health sciences, engineering, social sciences, humanities and business studies); and all had experience of doctoral studies and nearly all of postdoctoral research at a university. The health technology field was selected because it had a large population of women PhDs with potential research careers (Directorate-General for Research and Innovation, 2021, pp. 37–38, 41), and because of the field's relatively large external funding, reflecting academic capitalism (Nuutinen et al., 2016, p. 15; Slaughter & Leslie, 1997). About half of the interviewees worked in academia (at career stages two, three or four) and the other half in research institutes (as researchers and senior researchers), in private companies or in other organisations (as scientific experts and managers) at the time of the interviews. The 30 interviewees were White and born in Europe (two outside Finland). They ranged roughly from 30 to 60 years of age. The interview themes consisted of RI work histories, current work situations and future plans, gender in work, and work–life balance. The interviews, conducted in Finnish, lasted one to two hours and were transcribed verbatim. We used thematic analysis to identify interviewees' experiences of RI funding and motherhood during their careers. The interviewees were anonymised and the quotations were translated into English.

Findings

Although we did not specifically ask about RI funding, nearly all interviewees spoke about it when discussing the sources of funding throughout their careers. The interviewees typically referenced AF and FAI funding, even though both agencies have changed names. Of 26 interviewees who had children, 17 talked about motherhood or children in the context of their research careers and funding. These interviews allowed us to trace relationships among research funding, gendered organisational practices and careers intertwining with motherhood, and to further scrutinise mechanisms embedded in this interplay, giving support or causing disadvantages to women's research careers. We start the analysis from the support end and then continue with the practices that caused disadvantages to women's career paths.

Academy of Finland supported research careers through parental leave

Several interviewees noted that they were fortunate to have AF funding, as it meant that they could take parental leave. As only a few applicants (5%–15%) get the highly competitive AF grants awarded through international evaluation boards (AF, 2019, pp. 8–9), they were indeed privileged. AF has achieved gender parity in women's and men's success ratios, with slight variations between research fields (Directorate-General for Research and Innovation, 2021, pp. 259–260); thus, their applications had not faced any obvious gender bias in this phase, although there might be other structural gender disparities in academic funding processes (cf. Stadmark et al., 2020; Steinþórsdóttir et al., 2020). Additionally, they were fortunate because researchers with AF funding were able to take parental leave provided by the Finnish legislation (nearly one year to be shared by the parents, often mainly used by mothers) and, even more importantly, they were able to return to their research. As fixed-term contracts are common (Puhakka, 2020), the research contracts often finish before the leave ends. (Mother) researchers then are not self-evidently able to return to research work in the university, even though parental leave as such was available to all. One interviewee worked as a researcher in an AF project when her child was born:

> When I started the maternity leave … I happened to have a two-year work contract in an Academy [of Finland] project, and I then survived that phase. It could have meant a drop out from university, and it was clearly a lucky situation.
>
> *(Senior researcher, university)*

The interviewee recognised that the AF funding supported the continuity of her research career. Her part of the project work had been rescheduled to let her finish her research after the leave and saved her from dropping out.

Although she reflected on gender and gender inequalities elsewhere in the interview, parental leave was mentioned only briefly, as if it had a minor if any effect on her career path. The pattern of only briefly mentioning 'then I took a maternity or parental leave' and continuing with one's research work was especially common among the interviewees who had children during PhD studies or postdoctoral research. In addition to AF projects, many had funding from graduate schools, also committed to gender mainstreaming practices. In these cases, parental leave did not disrupt mother researchers' careers.

One interviewee explained that her AF research funding was extended by the length of the leave period:

> A girl was born ... and a boy was born [three years later]. They caused short interruptions in my career, but the Academy funding [allowed] nearly a year [including] the holidays in reserve. ... Then the funding period was extended until [mid-2010s].
>
> *(Associate professor, university)*

Highly educated women in Finland usually have parental leave of roughly one year (Salmi & Närvi, 2017), and this was the pattern that the latter interviewee with AF funding explicitly reported. However, researchers took leave in different ways depending on, for example, their career stages. One interviewee took a shorter parental leave and shared care work with the father and a nanny, as she was starting a new research group that required full-time supervision:

> I was not away from work for long, had just a four-month maternity leave. We had a six-hour system so that the father was responsible for six hours, I myself for six hours, and a nanny for six hours. ... When one is about to start a research group and starting a research career, one should stay there 24 hours to guard the group.
>
> *(Senior researcher, university)*

There was a consensus among interviewees that the AF funding, with its support of parental leave and the extension of grants enabling the return to research, had facilitated women's careers in academia, including those of single mothers. These examples show that the practices of funding agencies alone can significantly support gender equality in academia and research careers combined with motherhood. However, many times it is the practices of funding agencies and academic units together that matter, as we shall discuss in the following sections.

Innovation funding and university organisational practices (do not) support careers

The Funding Agency for Innovation funded RI projects in which research groups from universities collaborated with private industry. The funding agreements were made between institutions, with arrangements concerning research careers and leave depending on the university units and their organisational practices. The project timetables were fixed, as the industry partners needed quick results and could not be extended because of parental leave. Thus, although the researchers were allowed to take parental leave, the arrangements for parental leave in the funded projects varied significantly from organisation to organisation.

In some cases, there was support for researchers' careers, but it depended on the institution. One interviewee said that she had a nearly full-year leave, although she was head of the project, and then came back and continued to finish the project. Her unit worked collaboratively, the research group members took responsibility and a substitute was employed to cover the parental leave:

> We got a major Innovation Agency project then ... at the latter part of the following year, our child was born, and I was away from the project. ... We found a substitute for me in the department, doing the project work, and they understood very well, the project group.
>
> *(Professor, university)*

Organisational practices supporting gender equality, however, do not take place everywhere in academia (Thomson et al., 2022), and there were more instances where support was missing than where it was present. One interviewee related how she lost ownership of her innovation after her parental leave. The male-dominated unit did not support the continuity of her career:

> I've now sort of created a new field there, which would be worthwhile to research and they got the project and the money [from the FAI]. And I couldn't be a part of it because I was on maternity leave. And, basically, when I came back, it was – I wouldn't say far along, but it's that when you have a project you hire the people when you get the money, you can't wait like, let's wait a year for that person.
>
> *(Manager, private company)*

The FAI did not have a policy on gender equality, and it left the concerns about parental leave to the universities. Some units took care of the careers of their researchers, including those on parental leave, as the first example in this section showed. However, as Finnish universities do not fully implement the gender equality planning required in national gender equality legislation (Tanhua, 2020), and organisational practices causing disadvantages for women remain unsanctioned, there were also units that did not facilitate interviewees' return or consider their career trajectories. This non-support caused particularly nasty effects for the interviewee in the previous extract – who subsequently moved to a private company – as she could no longer work on the project that she herself had planned.

74 Marja Vehviläinen, Hanna-Mari Ikonen and Päivi Korvajärvi

Many interviewees continued career paths in private companies that worked on research-based innovations. These companies provided opportunities for several researchers as an alternative to academic career paths, including those who had not received support from the academic communities, those who wanted to work closer to clients in RI, and a rare case who felt that even leadership positions in private companies were more appropriate for a mother of several children than academia, with its endless working hours combined with commonly fixed-term contracts and continuous gendered struggles over grants and positions.

There was no (appropriate) place to return to academia after parental leave

Paid maternity and parental leaves are granted in academic work if a mother (or father) has a work contract when the leave starts. However, as noted earlier, fixed-term contracts often finish before the leave ends.

Consequently, some interviewees did not have a place to return to after parental leave, especially if they finished their doctoral degree simultaneously with the start of maternity leave, at the time when they could have become postdoctoral researchers. Although doctoral students are funded in research groups and graduate schools, postdoctoral researchers often need to secure funding for themselves. They cannot expect to get continued support. One interviewee had planned to work with private foundation grants after her parental leave, but those grants did not imply a work contract binding her to the university. Even worse, when the grant applications failed, the university unit had no formal obligations towards her. She became unemployed and detached from the previous community.

> [After parental leave] I defended my dissertation ... then, in about a month I was unemployed and alone, apart from the work community. ... I did not get support from there. ... The plans that we had made together were taken away ... and you did not have a clue about the future. And a small child.
>
> *(Scientific expert, private company)*

It is not easy to produce a competitive research plan in any circumstances (McGinn et al., 2019), and it is particularly demanding right after parental leave. Another interviewee said that she was supposed to write an application for competitive AF funding after her leave. She knew that the AF standards were high, requiring an excellent idea based on recent research, and she had been away from research for a year and just could not compose such a research plan. The opportunity to write a proposal for herself and a group turned into feelings of distress, and she moved to a private company:

When I got back from maternity leave, my husband stayed at home for the summer, so I could write the AF application. ... I kept agonising about the same thing, how on earth am I going to get that application done. ... You understand the high quality that is required. ... So, the despair sort of started to sink in.

(Scientific expert, private company)

Shrinking resources in male-dominated academic units excluded mothers

As Toffoletti and Starr (2016) also found in Australia, the interviewees did not report significant tensions in having both academic work and children. Some interviewees who worked in units with mostly women or a balance of men and women colleagues indicated that having children was common and taken kindly among colleagues.[2]

However, male-dominated academic units gave grounds for lengthy reflections. Two senior researchers and group leaders pondered whether male-dominated academic communities excluded them because of their children during the period of declining funding sources. The exclusion took cruel forms, including harassment and discrimination. However, it was not clear to them whether it was the presence of children or some other factor that caused it. Did the myth of the incompatibility of motherhood and academic work prevail in these male-dominated units (Eren, 2022; Nikunen, 2014; Pecis, 2016)?

Children were born ... the support went away somehow, little by little, but of course you can't know if it was because you started a family and had kids or was it because we were approaching ... the end of the [major funding], so in general there was starting to be a kind of battle over positions and funding and who survives.

(Senior researcher, university)

Gendered segregation of women and men across academic fields is one of the cornerstones of gender inequality. Male-dominated work organisations and mixed-gender organisations with male-dominated leadership groups have room for old boys networks (Case & Richley, 2013). These networks and their practices caused disadvantages for interviewees who had small children. As the Finnish RI funding declined significantly from 2009 until 2015, the male networks struggled to keep the posts funded by university core funding and important external funding among themselves (Vehviläinen et al., 2022). The shrinking resources were guarded in male networks and, together with the myth of the unsuitability of women for the highest career stages, produced disadvantages for women's research careers.

Conclusions

The study's context is Finnish society and its gender mainstreaming practices, funding agencies and universities, informed by academic capitalism (Ylijoki, 2003) and membership in the European Union, as well as the Nordic welfare provisions (parental leave, childcare services). We have analysed gender equality in academic research careers in health technology, a field that operates extensively with external funding, through the experiences of motherhood in academic work. Our examples show how gendered practices of funding agencies and academic organisations, and the interplay between these two, either supported women's careers or caused disadvantages.

Although our study is congruent with previous findings that motherhood can cause difficulties for women's careers and underpin gender inequalities in academia (S. Acker & Armenti, 2004; Eren, 2022; Krilic et al., 2019; Thun, 2020), we have argued that funding agencies have the capacity to advance gender equality in academia, especially when funding is directed to individual researchers and research groups (see also Husu & Peterson, this volume). Funding agencies such as the Academy of Finland can influence the success rates of diverse groups of researchers, including mothers, through diversity in expert boards. They can prepare funding contracts that allow for multiple life situations and care commitments for researchers on fixed-term precarious work contracts. In our study, academics at early-career stages in particular benefited from the GEPs of the Academy of Finland, although they are a particularly vulnerable group in non-Nordic countries (Krilic et al., 2019). Funding agencies have unused potential to support gender-equal careers, especially by constructing requirements that influence organisational practices.

Some funding agencies do explicitly make contracts with institutions, and the funding agencies and academic units' organisational practices together shape the gendered careers, including the use of parental leave in each academic unit. These practices can support researchers' careers by ensuring that researchers (mothers, parents) can return from leave and continue their careers even when the funded projects belong to institutions. However, there were examples in our data where academic units sidetracked women researchers when they took parental leave and even gave their projects to other researchers. The interplay of funding and non-supportive practices also implied major disadvantages for women's RI work, especially at the point that women were moving from doctoral studies to postdoctoral research. Good welfare provisions could not alone save women's careers in academia.

Male-dominated academic units stood out because their practices caused disadvantages for women who took parental leave and who had small children (cf. Krilic et al., 2019). Even if the mother researchers were 'supra-performers' (Gatrell, 2011) who fulfilled the norm of long working hours, took only brief leave and produced academic publications and degrees, they could become

2019–2021]. https://www.aka.fi/globalassets/1-tutkimusrahoitus/5-vastuullinen-tiede/suomen-akatemian-tasa-arvo-ja-yhdenvertaisuussuunnitelma.pdf

Acker, J. (1990). Hierarchies, jobs, bodies: a theory of gendered organizations. *Gender & Society*, *4*(2), 139–158. https://doi.org/10.1177/089124390004002002

Acker, S., & Armenti, C. (2004). Sleepless in academia. *Gender and Education*, *16*(1), 3–24. https://doi.org/10.1080/09540250320000170309

Case, S. S., & Richley, B. A. (2013). Gendered institutional research cultures in science: the post-doc transition for women scientists. *Community, Work and Family*, *16*(3), 327–349. https://doi.org/10.1080/13668803.2013.820097

Directorate-General for Research and Innovation. (2021). *She figures 2021: Gender in research and innovation statistics and indicators*. European Commission. https://doi.org/10.2777/06090

Doona, A. (2021). Addressing gender inequality in academia: the role of Irish funding agencies. In E. Drew & S. Canavan (Eds.), *The gender-sensitive university: a contradiction in terms?* (pp. 54–65). Routledge.

Drew, E. (2022). Navigating unChartered waters: anchoring Athena SWAN into Irish HEIs. *Journal of Gender Studies*, *31*(1), 23–35. https://doi.org/10.1080/09589236.2021.1923463

Eren, E. (2022). Never the right time: maternity planning alongside a science career in academia. *Journal of Gender Studies*, *31*(1), 136–147. https://doi.org/10.1080/09589236.2020.1858765

European Institute for Gender Equality. (2016). *What is gender mainstreaming?* https://eige.europa.eu/publications/what-gender-mainstreaming

Evans, M. (2017). *The persistence of gender inequality*. Polity Press.

Gatrell, C. (2011). Policy and the pregnant body at work: strategies of secrecy, silence and supra-performance. *Gender, Work & Organization*, *18*(2), 158–181. https://doi.org/10.1111/j.1468-0432.2009.00485.x

Gaudet, S., Marchand, I., Bujaki, M., & Bourgeault, I. L. (2022). Women and gender equity in academia through the conceptual lens of care. *Journal of Gender Studies*, *31*(1), 74–86. https://doi.org/10.1080/09589236.2021.1944848

Griffin, G., & Vehviläinen, M. (2021). The persistence of gender struggles in Nordic research and innovation. *Feminist Encounters: A Journal of Critical Studies in Culture and Politics*, *5*(2), Article 28. https://doi.org/10.20897/femenc/11165

Huopalainen, A. S., & Satama, S. T. (2019). Mothers and researchers in the making: negotiating 'new' motherhood within the 'new' academia. *Human Relations*, *72*(1), 98–121. https://doi.org/10.1177/0018726718764571

Husu, L. (2001). *Sexism, support and survival in academia: academic women and hidden discrimination in Finland*. Department of Social Psychology, University of Helsinki.

Husu, L., & de Cheveigné, S. (2010). Gender and gatekeeping of excellence in research funding: European perspectives. In B. Riegraf, B. Aulenbacher, E. Kirsch-Auwärter, & U. Müller (Eds.), *Gender change in academia* (pp. 43–59). VS Verlag für Sozialwissenschaften. https://doi.org/10.1007/978-3-531-92501-1_4

Krilic, S. C., Istenic, M. C., & Hocevar, D. K. (2019). Work–life balance among early career researchers in six European countries. In A. Murgia & B. Poggio (Eds.), *Gender and precarious research careers: a comparative analysis* (pp. 145–177). Routledge.

Le Feuvre, N., Bataille, P., Kradolfer, S., del Rio Carral, M., & Sautier, M. (2019). The gendered diversification of academic career paths in comparative perspective. In A. Murgia & B. Poggio (Eds.), *Gender and precarious research careers: a comparative analysis* (pp. 50–80). Routledge. https://doi.org/10.4324/9781315201245-3

excluded when the general funding situation declined. It is, however, difficult to isolate the source of the disadvantage.

Academic work and career paths take place within specific organisational practices and funding sources. When academic units had good resources, (potential) mother researchers were also recruited. When the resources declined, the competition became harsh, and the male networks in male-dominated organisations excluded women with children, in particular those who had reached the career stage of independent researchers. Our study affirms that motherhood is a risk for research careers in male-dominated academic communities (Case & Richley, 2013). Furthermore, the general funding situation of a university unit played a role, not only in terms of individual funding sources, but also in the general decline of resources, and thus cause disadvantages for women's careers in academia.

Our study was conducted in the context of Finnish universities, nation funding agencies and welfare services, and in the interdisciplinary research field of health technology, which has considerable external funding. This foc implied a rather homogeneous group of interviewees (White, European, Ph holders, most of whom had one to three children) and therefore a limit analysis of the intersectionality of gender. Further research should extend t range of interviewees, consider other fields, especially those with few resources, and broaden the focus from national to international fundi agencies. Additionally, the interplay of societal welfare provisions and fund policies requires more attention. Here the welfare services available for int viewed researchers were specific to a Nordic society, and further resea should examine how funding agencies could play a role in supporting gen equal careers in societies with different service structures.

Acknowledgements

This work is supported by NordForsk (grant No. 81520). We would lik thank Tiina Suopajärvi and Minna Leinonen who conducted the interviev

Notes

1 This dataset is also the source for Ylijoki, this volume.
2 The COVID-19 pandemic in 2020–2022 was not part of our data. As childcar vices and schools were closed at some points, and grandparents belonging t groups were less available for childcare, the tensions in having academic wor children presumably grew stronger during the pandemic (see Carruthers Thoma volume).

References

Academy of Finland. (2019). *Suomen Akatemian tasa-arvo- ja yhdenvertaisuussuun 2019–2021* [The Academy of Finland plan for gender equality and non-discrim

Luukkonen-Gronow, T. (1987). University career opportunities for women in Finland in the 1980s. *Acta Sociologica, 30*(2), 193–206. https://doi.org/10.1177/000169938703000205

McGinn, M. K., Acker, S., Vander Kloet, M., & Wagner, A. (2019). Dear SSHRC, what do you want? An epistolary narrative of expertise, identity, and time in grant writing. *Forum Qualitative Sozialforschung/Forum: Qualitative Social Research, 20*(1). https://doi.org/10.17169/fqs-20.1.3128

Ministry of Education and Culture. (n.d.). *Higher education institutions, science agencies, research institutes and other public research organisations.* Retrieved 31 July 2023 from https://okm.fi/en/heis-and-science-agencies

Ministry of Education and Culture. (2016). *Tutkijanuran tilannekuva* [Research career]. https://julkaisut.valtioneuvosto.fi/handle/10024/64967

Nielsen, M. W. (2016). Limits to meritocracy? Gender in academic recruitment and promotion processes. *Science and Public Policy, 43*(3), 386–399. https://doi.org/10.1093/scipol/scv052

Nikunen, M. (2014). The 'entrepreneurial university', family and gender: changes and demands faced by fixed-term workers. *Gender and Education, 26*(2), 119–134. https://doi.org/10.1080/09540253.2014.888402

Nuutinen, A., Mälkki, A., Huutoniemi, K., & Törnroos, J. (Eds.). (2016). *Tieteen tila 2016.* [State of scientific research in 2016]. Academy of Finland. https://www.aka.fi/globalassets/2-suomen-akatemian-toiminta/2-tietoaineistot/aka_tieteen_tila_yksi.pdf

Oksanen, T., Lehvo, A., & Nuutinen, A. (Eds.). (2003). *Suomen tieteen tila ja taso: Katsaus tutkimustoimintaan ja tutkimuksen vaikutuksiin 2000-luvun alussa* [State of scientific research in Finland: An overview of research activities and the effects of research in the early 2000s]. Academy of Finland. https://www.aka.fi/globalassets/a wanhat/documents/tiedostot/julkaisut/9_03-suomen-tieteen-tila-ja-taso.pdf

Ollilainen, M. (2019). Academic mothers as ideal workers in the USA and Finland. *Equality, Diversity and Inclusion, 38*(4), 417–429. https://doi.org/10.1108/EDI-02-2018-0027

Ombudsman for Equality. (n.d.). *What is an equality plan?* https://tasa-arvo.fi/en/equality-planning-at-workplaces

Pecis, L. (2016). Doing and undoing gender in innovation: femininities and masculinities in innovation processes. *Human Relations, 69*(11), 2117–2140. https://doi.org/10.1177/0018726716634445

Pereira, M. do Mar (2017). *Power, knowledge and feminist scholarship: an ethnography of academia.* Routledge. https://doi.org/10.4324/9781315692623

Pietilä, M. (2021). Suomalaisten yliopistojen tutkijanuraa koskevat tasa-arvotoimet [Finnish universities' gender equality measures in academic careers by Nordic comparison]. *Työelämän tutkimus, 19*(4), 520–545. https://doi.org/10.37455/tt.112499

Puhakka, A. (2020). Yliopistojen määräaikaisuuksien epaonnistuneet ratkaisuyritykset [Unsuccessful trials to solve precarious contracts in universities]. *Acatiimi, 2,* 40–42. https://acatiimi.fi/wp-content/uploads/2022/02/acatiimi_2_2020.pdf

Rosa, R., & Clavero, S. (2021). The challenge of neoliberalism and precarity for gender sensitivity in academia. In E. Drew & S. Canavan (Eds.), *The gender-sensitive university: a contradiction in terms?* (pp. 16–27). Routledge.

Rosa, R., Drew, E., & Canavan, S. (2021). An overview of gender inequality in EU universities. In E. Drew & S. Canavan (Eds.), *The gender-sensitive university. a contradiction in terms?* (pp. 1–15). Routledge.

Salmi, M., & Närvi, J. (2017). Pienten lasten vanhempien työmarkkina-asema, tyon epavarmuus ja toimeentulo [Labour market situation, work precarity and income of parents of small children]. In M. Salmi & J. Närvi (Eds.), *Talouskriisi ja sukupuolten tasa-arvo* (Report 4/2017; pp. 36–63). Terveyden ja hyvinvoinnin laitos.

Slaughter, S., & Leslie, L. (1997). *Academic capitalism*. Johns Hopkins Press.

Smith, D. E. (2005). *Institutional ethnography*. Altamira Press.

Stadmark, J., Jesus-Rydin, C., & Conley, D. J. (2020). Success in grant applications for women and men. *Advances in Geosciences, 53*, 107–115. https://doi.org/10.5194/adgeo-53-107-2020

Steinþórsdóttir, F. S., Einarsdóttir, Þ., Pétursdóttir, G. M., & Himmelweit, S. (2020). Gendered inequalities in competitive grant funding: an overlooked dimension of gendered power relations in academia. *Higher Education Research & Development, 39*(2), 362–375. https://doi.org/10.1080/07294360.2019.1666257

Tanhua, I. (2020). *Selvitys korkeakoulujen tasa-arvon ja yhdenvertaisuuden edistämisestä* [Report on the promotion of gender equality and non-discrimination in higher education institutions] (Report 2020:20). Ministry of Education and Culture. http://urn.fi/URN:ISBN:978-952-263-859-5

Thomson, A., Palmén, A. R., Reidl, S., Barnard, S., Beranek, B., Dainty, A. R. J., & Hassan, T. M. (2022). Fostering collaborative approaches to gender equality interventions in higher education and research: the case of transnational and multi-institutional communities of practice. *Journal of Gender Studies, 31*(1), 36–54. https://doi.org/10.1080/09589236.2021.1935804

Thun, C. (2020). Excellent and gender equal? Academic motherhood and 'gender blindness' in Norwegian academia. *Gender, Work & Organization, 27*(2), 166–180. https://doi.org/10.1111/gwao.12368

Toffoletti K., & Starr, K. (2016). Women academics and work–life balance: gendered discourses of work and care. *Gender, Work & Organization, 23*(5), 489–504. https://doi.org/10.1111/gwao.12133

van den Brink, M., & Benschop, Y. (2014). Gender in academic networking: the role of gatekeepers in professorial recruitment. *Journal of Management Studies, 51*(3), 460–492. https://doi.org/10.1111/joms.12060

van der Lee, R., & Ellemers, N. (2015). Gender contributes to personal research funding success in The Netherlands. *PNAS Proceedings of the National Academy of Sciences, 112*(40), 12349–12353. https://doi.org/10.1073/pnas.1510159112

Vehviläinen, M., Ikonen, H.-M., & Korvajärvi, P. (2022). Changes in funding and the intensification of gender inequalities in research and innovation. In G. Griffin (Ed.), *Gender inequalities in tech-driven research and innovation: living the contradiction* (pp. 76–92). Bristol University Press. https://doi.org/10.51952/9781529219494.ch005

Ylijoki, O.-H. (2003). Entangled in academic capitalism? A case-study on changing ideals and practices of university research. *Higher Education, 45*(3), 307–335. https://doi.org/10.1023/A:1022667923715

6

CASTING A LONG SHADOW

COVID-19 and female academics' research productivity in the United Kingdom

Kate Carruthers Thomas

Those of us who follow higher education news will have seen the headlines about the negative impact of the COVID-19 pandemic on female academics' research productivity. But what of the lived experiences beneath the headlines? In this chapter, I address this collection's central concern with gendered repercussions of the research funding imperative, through the consideration of gendered experiences, impacts and implications of the COVID-19 pandemic for female academics' career progression. To do so, I draw on the diaries and interview transcripts of female academics in the United Kingdom (UK) who participated in a small-scale qualitative study in 2021, titled "Dear Diary: Equality Implications for Female Academics of Changes to Working Practices in Lockdown and Beyond" (Carruthers Thomas, 2022a). These data enable me to investigate in some detail how participants navigated the demands of grant applications and related research activity in contexts of workload conflicts, care and service responsibilities, precarity and fatigue.

Before exploring the data, I first summarise the research funding environment of the UK's stratified higher education (HE) sector and the nature of the restrictions imposed within the UK against the COVID-19 pandemic. After describing the Dear Diary research project, I analyse the repercussions of the intersection of gender, research funding and the COVID-19 pandemic through three themes emerging from the data: workload conflicts, research temporalities and new opportunities. Finally, I consider whether and how these themes point to gendered implications for research funding in HE.

DOI: 10.4324/9781003330431-8

Contexts

UK research funding: complex, competitive and uneven

UK research funding is a mixed economy, comprising competitive, performance-based funding from the UK government, grants from a wide range of charitable and commercial bodies, participation in international research programmes, and various small institutional supports. It is a complex arena with which academics, including participants in the Dear Diary study, must engage to further their research careers.

We can identify four main sources of research funding. First, there is UK government funding, itself divided into two routes. The first is 'quality-related' (QR) funding to individual universities determined by their performance in a UK-wide audit, the Research Excellence Framework or REF (see Lucas, this volume). The 2021 REF involved

> expert review, carried out by expert panels for each of the 34 subject-based units of assessment (UOAs). ... For each submission, three distinct elements are assessed: the quality of *outputs* (e.g. publications, performances and exhibitions), their *impact* beyond academia and the *environment* that supports research.
> (Research Excellence Framework, ca. 2017, paras. 3–4)

The precursor of the REF, the Research Assessment Exercise, was established in 1986 and ran until 2008. The introduction of the REF in 2014 saw a new emphasis on research impact beyond academia and assessed institutional performance over the period 2008–2013. A subsequent audit took place in 2021 and the next is anticipated in 2029. The second route to UK government funding is through competitive grants to individuals and research teams from seven disciplinary research councils under the umbrella of UK Research and Innovation (UKRI). These grants include awards aimed at specific academic career stages, for example, early-career and mid-career fellowships.

Charitable and commercial organisations are the second significant source of UK research funding. Awards are made by a broad range of organisations including long-established bodies such as the British Academy and the Wellcome Trust, whose grants are prestigious and much sought-after. The third source is international research funding. However, UK researchers' participation in European schemes was dogged by uncertainty following the 2016 UK referendum decision to leave the European Union, a key example being the Horizon Europe fund. The UK's association in Horizon Europe was not finalised until September 2023 (UKRI, 2023b). At a more modest level, a fourth source is the provision by many UK universities of seed and primer funding to researchers in their institutions.

An understanding of the stratified character of the UK HE sector is key to appreciating that the UK research funding playing field is far from level. Crudely, the sector can be divided into pre- and post-1992 universities, 1992 being the year that UK polytechnics and tertiary institutions were first permitted to become 'new' universities under the Further and Higher Education Act 1992. Many pre-1992 or 'old' universities attach themselves to the label 'research intensive', while many of the post-1992 or 'new' universities embrace their 'teaching-led' identities (Boliver, 2015, p. 613). The 24 research-intensive universities (including Oxford and Cambridge), which have styled themselves as the Russell Group, accounted for 65% of the UK's research judged 4* (the highest rating) in REF 2021 (Russell Group, 2022). It would appear that the mechanism of competitive, performance-based research funding has not dented 'entrenched institutional hierarchies and their dominance' (Papatsiba & Cohen, 2020, p. 189).

Institutional status is not the only form of stratification in research grant application and success in the UK, as elsewhere. Although findings across studies are inconsistent, it is generally thought that women are at a disadvantage in funding competitions compared with men (Sato et al., 2021; Steinþórsdóttir et al., 2020; see also Acker, this volume). There is also a gender disparity in the type of contracts held by academics in the UK that is relevant to research funding. Men are more likely to hold 'teaching-and-research' contracts, for which grant application is part of the job description, while women are more likely than men to hold 'teaching-only' contracts, in which grant application is not expected (Higher Education Statistics Agency, 2022). There are various other contract types with even less job security; for instance, part-time workers on research projects often hold temporary positions.

Gender and ethnic differences are evident in the results of UKRI research council grants. In 2020–2021, across all disciplines, men received 70% and women 28% of principal investigator (PI) awards (UKRI, 2023a, p. 28). The ethnic group differentials in UKRI PI awards over the same period are stark: of UKRI PI grant holders, 81% were White and 8% Asian, while Black, mixed and other ethnic groups constituted 1%, 2% and less than 0.5% of award recipients, respectively (p. 19). Considering gender and 'race' together, White men received 57% and White women 24% of PI awards. Men of Asian background received 6% of PI awards, while the share of other intersectional groups was much smaller (p. 34).[1]

From February 2020 to March 2021, UKRI issued multiple emergency calls for funding of COVID-19-related projects, later reporting a modest increase in applications and awards from women, but that the representation of academics from minority ethnic groups remained very low (Kolarz et al., 2021). Notably, none of the resulting six PI grants totalling £4.3 million awarded by UKRI and the National Institute for Health and Care Research (NIHR) to investigate disproportionate death rates from COVID-19 among people from Black, Asian and minority ethnic backgrounds were awarded to Black academics (Inge, 2020, 2021).

The COVID-19 pandemic: gender and research productivity

On 23 March 2020, the UK government enforced a three-week 'lockdown' against COVID-19. Citizens were only able to leave their homes to shop for necessities; to exercise for one hour a day; to fulfil a medical need including caring for a vulnerable person; or to travel to and from work (but only when absolutely necessary for essential work that could not be done from home) (UK Government, 2020a). Police were given the power to enforce lockdown rules. The initial lockdown period was extended for an additional month before unlimited outdoor exercise was allowed (13 May 2020), with other restrictions lasting into June 2020, after which the country entered a lengthy period of phased opening, local lockdowns and a three-tier system of COVID-19 restrictions (Institute for Government, 2022; UK Government, 2020b). A second national lockdown was imposed from 5 November to 2 December 2020 and a third on 6 January 2021 lasting until 8 March 2021 (Institute for Government, 2022). Schools were closed from 20 March 2020 other than for children of key workers and children deemed vulnerable. Partial opening began on 1 June 2020, with schools reopening to all children in September 2020 but closing again during national lockdowns (Timmins, 2021). Across the UK, from March 2020, access to university campuses was restricted and most course delivery pivoted from face-to-face to online. In the ensuing weeks, some campus facilities were opened to students without access to computer equipment and Wi-Fi at home to enable them to continue their coursework. Thereafter, most universities moved incrementally towards a mixture of online and in-person delivery, which varied according to institution, course type and phase of the pandemic. REF 2021 was put on hold for four months, recommencing in July 2020 with a revised submission deadline of 31 March 2021.

During this period, certain occupations and industries were assigned 'key worker' status, such as health and social care, (school) education, childcare, and provision of food and necessary goods (Office for National Statistics [ONS], 2020). Overall, however, the COVID-19 pandemic resulted in an unprecedented shift of paid labour into the home. Amid growing awareness of the uneven impact of the COVID-19 pandemic on different social groups (Pankhurst, 2020; United Nations, 2020), media reports addressed the issue of women working at home facing simultaneous responsibilities for childcare and home-schooling (e.g. Ascher, 2020; Connolly et al., 2020; Ferguson, 2020). This inequitable situation was reflected in the findings of institutional research I conducted via an online survey in a large post-1992 university at the end of the first UK lockdown in June 2020 (Carruthers Thomas, 2020). Results showed that female academic and professional services staff were more likely than male colleagues to take primary or sole responsibility for home-schooling, household tasks and others' care needs, and less likely to have access to dedicated working space at home.

The survey additionally found that female academic staff within the university, particularly those with care responsibilities for children or elders, were more likely than male colleagues to report that working from home in lockdown had impacted upon their capacity to write grant applications or for publication and to sustain research projects. Boncori (2020) and Pebdani et al. (2023), among others, similarly reported a negative effect on female academics' research productivity while working at home during the pandemic. Media reports noted a decrease in female academics' paper submissions to academic journals (Fazackerly, 2020; Kitchener, 2020).

I pause at this point to observe that the challenges faced by UK female academics should be regarded in the wider context of a global pandemic which disrupted almost every aspect of personal, social and professional lives in the UK and globally, and resulted in nearly seven million deaths worldwide (World Health Organization, 2023). Some disruptions arose from temporary measures with short-term impacts. Others, including the impact of working from home on academic research productivity, are likely to have longer-term implications. This potential outcome arises because the value placed on research income generation and peer-reviewed publications for academic status and career progression means that *any* reduction in research productivity presents a potential risk of longer-term career damage. In the following sections, I set out to question whether, and if so how, such a risk will be disproportionately borne by women in a sector already structured by gender inequality and female under-representation.

The Dear Diary project

In the Dear Diary research project, I investigated UK female academics' experiences of working from home and the resultant changes to working practices between March 2020 and September 2021 (Carruthers Thomas, 2022a). The project also aimed to identify longer-term implications for female academics' careers and gender equality in the sector. Purposive and snowball sampling via social media, sector mailing lists and word of mouth were used to recruit 25 female academic participants employed at 18 UK universities and research institutes. Participants were aged between 28 and 60, drawn from a range of disciplinary backgrounds and occupying roles across the academic career spectrum from PhD student to (full) professor.

A diary, diary-interview method (Kenten, 2010; Latham, 2003; Zimmerman & Wieder, 1977) was used to gather in-depth, qualitative data documenting 'an ever-changing present' (Elliott, 1997, para. 2.4). This method was also a pragmatic choice, given that participants were widely dispersed geographically and the research process was heavily reliant on digital technologies at a time of continuing COVID-19 restrictions. Participants were asked to submit two diary entries, in any format. The first, in May 2021, was retrospective, taking a long view of experiences of living and working since

March 2020, including three national lockdowns, and interim and local restrictions. The second diary entry, in July or August 2021, was contemporaneous. Participants were invited to write in detail about one element or experience, or widely about many, allowing 'leeway to write about what was important to them and to structure as they felt appropriate' (Elliott, 1997, para. 4.2). Following their submission of the diary entries, I interviewed participants via Zoom or Microsoft Teams for 45 to 60 minutes. The semi-structured interview revisited diary entries for clarification and amplification and covered emerging and generic themes relating to career progression and the HE sector. Interviews were recorded and transcribed, and transcripts were returned for verification. At the point of data collection, UK university provision was variably online, in-person or hybrid depending on geographical location, discipline and institution. UK schools had reopened (in March 2021) but children showing COVID-19 symptoms were being sent home to self-isolate.

Each participant dataset (two diary entries and one interview transcript) covered a spectrum of topics including working practices, household arrangements, family relationships, institutional politics, and physical and emotional health. A thematic analysis framed by overarching concepts of gender, space and power produced four core themes – work/home, space/time, new/normal and well/being – each mapping and interlinking public and private, and domestic and professional domains. These core themes shaped the architecture of a key project output, a publicly accessible illustrated digital archive (Carruthers Thomas, 2022b). However, for the purposes of this chapter, I have revisited the data only from participants who wrote or spoke explicitly about research grants. The following section considers these data through three sub-themes: workload conflicts, research temporalities and new opportunities.

Findings: research funding and productivity

Eleven participants (see Table 6.1) wrote or spoke explicitly about research grants in diary entries and/or interviews.[2] References to grant-seeking were equally prevalent for those at pre-1992 (n = 6) and post-1992 (n = 5) institutions. It is useful to note that experiences of applying for research funding were often included in broader discussions of research productivity including conducting research and writing for publication and that engagement with these activities varied given the diversity of participants' career stages and academic roles.

Table 6.1 shows a clear preponderance of social science disciplines, also reflected in the original group of 25 in which only three were from STEM disciplines (science, technology, engineering and medicine). For two of the women in STEM disciplines, applying for research grants was not part of their role.

TABLE 6.1 Participant details

Name*	Pre- or post-1992 university	Age group	Discipline	Care responsibilities at home or locally
Ali	Post	50–59	Education	No
Anita	Pre	30–39	Management	Yes
Ione	Pre	50–59	Education	Yes
Lauren	Post	20–29	Social policy	Yes
Liz	Post	40–49	Art and design	Yes
Maggie	Post	30–39	Psychology	No
Nicole	Pre	30–39	Social policy	No
Nina	Pre	40–49	Education	No
Ola	Pre	40–49	Education	Yes
Sam	Post	30–39	Geography	No
Sarah	Pre	50–59	Social policy	Yes

*Names are pseudonyms.

Workload conflicts

Pre-pandemic, the relationship between 'research' and 'teaching' in the UK HE sector was already troubled. Over the last three decades, student numbers in the UK HE sector have almost doubled (ONS, 2016) and there has been a lionising of the 'student experience' within university missions and metrics (Department for Business, Innovation & Skills, 2010; Sabri, 2011). The combination of the stress on student experience with the increased importance of external research funding to corporate budgets and reputations has created tension within individual academic workloads, only exacerbated by the COVID-19 pandemic.

Academics involved in course delivery needed to rapidly adapt teaching materials and approaches for online delivery, as well as acquire essential technological skills with minimal training. Anita's diary vividly describes the practical demands this 'pivot' placed on teaching staff:

> I used a flipped-classroom technique. This meant videos – lots and lots of videos. By time the 11 weeks of the module were over there were over 70hrs of recorded classes (some live seminar style, some pre-recorded lecture format). The focus on videos meant hours spent learning how to record quality videos; purchasing of specialist equipment, finding the best spot for lighting and sound, learning about captioning and accessibility requirements, not to mention redeveloping lecture material from 2hr classes into 3 short 15 min clips.
>
> *(Anita, diary 1)*

The time required by this rapid learning curve inevitably impacted research activity:

> There has been so much to be done in terms of teaching and support that my research has taken second place, especially in terms of generating output. Research and writing have gone out of the window. Everything seems to be a big pile of admin just now.
>
> *(Nina, diary 1)*

Most UK institutions implement a workload allocation model (WAM), a means of quantifying time spent on teaching, research, administrative or other tasks. Allocations are adjusted for career stage and role focus but 'can vary greatly between institutions, and even amongst departments or schools within the same university' (Boncori et al., 2020, p. 59). WAMs are widely criticised for inadequately reflecting the actual hours worked by academics in the context of an increase in 'teaching and administrative loads ... along with pressure to deliver significant research outputs in an increasingly competitive environment with shrinking funds' (Kenny, 2018, p. 368). During the COVID-19 pandemic, WAMs were used to redirect time towards teaching and student support, with inevitable repercussions for research activity:

> They keep changing our workload balances. It's meant to be 40 research/30 teaching/30 admin but the research time gets really eroded. This year they said, 'Everyone in the department is going to be 50% teaching because of COVID-related things and extra pressures.' It's always the research that goes.
>
> *(Nicole, diary 1)*

The COVID-19 pandemic also exacerbated a particular aspect of existing inequality within the academy, that of female academics' disproportionate responsibility for 'academic housework', a term referring to

> academic service work within the institution ... that receives little recognition within the process of academic career making or within the definition of academic excellence. ... [It includes] tasks that relate to giving back to the community, various teaching and research-related activities, administrative work and gender equality initiatives.
>
> (Heijstra et al., 2017, p. 765)

Within UK universities, personal support provided to students by academic staff, beyond the remit of internal professional departments (Finance, Careers Guidance, etc.), is usually referred to as pastoral care. Participants noted increased demand for pastoral care from their student cohorts during the pandemic and that female academics shouldered this burden to a greater extent than their male colleagues. Ramsay and Letherby (2006) argue that this extra work happens because 'maternal ideologies continue to shape women's experiences at work in higher education organizations' (p. 39).

> I had some students with mental health and family issues that were really struggling to make progress. One of the pieces of advice I was given was to be as motherly as possible and reach out with as much care and compassion as possible.
>
> *(Maggie, interview)*

> A lot of the additional pastoral work with students fell on me, which I think is a gendered issue.
>
> *(Liz, interview)*

Research temporalities

In the previous section, I demonstrated how female academics' research time was pushed to the periphery during the COVID-19 pandemic by multiple competing demands: the pivot to online course delivery, extra administration and increased pastoral care. Yet the imperative for 'research active' staff to generate research 'outputs' (grant applications, publications, completed projects) continued. Such is the hold REF has over all UK universities, financially and reputationally, that this pressure was not confined to participants employed in research-intensive universities. In this section, I explore how diverse temporalities of research activity intensify tensions further.

Most funding calls impose challenging deadlines and involve laborious internal approval procedures prior to grant submission, presenting significant challenges for all academics, especially those with heavy teaching responsibilities. During the pandemic, these challenges were exacerbated not only by home-schooling and care responsibilities but also by a rash of calls for quick turnaround, COVID-specific grants.

> As a full-time academic finding time for my own research and writing is difficult at the best of times. During lockdown with additional pastoral and administrative work due to the pandemic as well as home schooling, it just didn't feel possible to contemplate. My line manager suggested that it was a good time for me to be opportunistic and do additional COVID specific external funding bids. He didn't seem to realise that I was struggling just to get by.
>
> *(Liz, diary 2)*

Ali and Liz, both of whom worked in post-1992 universities, regarded grant-writing as particularly difficult. It may be that the support available was less than that in the pre-1992, more research-intensive institutions. Ali states that 'it took at least three or four months after the start of the first lockdown for me to feel calm enough to write research grant proposals' (diary 1), while Liz, who also had caring responsibilities at home, believed that she lacked 'any mental resources left to generate new ideas or new projects' (diary 2). In contrast, Sarah, in a pre-1992 institution, found the circumstances of the pandemic facilitated her grant-writing productivity:

> Writing for publication, absolutely no chance. You're looking at little blocks of time in between feeding everybody, and I can't write like that. I was much better at task-oriented activity. So even putting a bid together was okay because you could just focus on numbers of interviews or what the sample's going to be. Research-wise, we were successful in two bids.
>
> *(Sarah, interview)*

Sarah prefers to work with 'project time', which is 'a strictly defined time frame with a fixed beginning and end, often with specific milestones between the two' (Ylijoki, 2015, p. 95). Project time contrasts with 'process time', which is non-linear and 'embedded in actual work contexts' (p. 96). Under process time, the research 'takes as much time as is needed to achieve the results and ripening of ideas' (p. 97). The benefits of process time, requiring a deep immersion in work and a sense of timelessness, are impossible for Sarah, Ali or Liz to achieve in pandemic circumstances.

Both the character of the employing institution and the nature of the job contract influence the participants' assessments of their situations. Although employed in a post-1992 'teaching-intensive' institution, Liz is nevertheless keenly aware of the implication of decreased research activity in relation to her academic career and reputation:

> Pausing isn't good for a research career. Two periods of maternity leave made me realise that. I was lucky, I managed to keep going with research last year. But I know that having 'nowt in the pipeline now' will mean that the COVID impact will show in my professional track record for the next couple of years at least.
>
> *(Liz, diary 2)*

For Nina, employed in a research-intensive institution whose reputation is heavily invested in REF outcomes and research income, the future career hurdles are immediately obvious:

> I did manage to put a couple of unsuccessful bids together this year, proposals to very competitive schemes. Our annual review form and promotion criteria do not ask us to list unsuccessful funding proposals – and let me tell you we have a bunch of those! It is just the end product that they are interested in. It is about victories.
>
> *(Nina, diary 2)*

Nina acknowledges that despite these obstacles to promotion, she is fortunate to be on a permanent contract. In contrast, in a post-1992 university, Lauren's account demonstrates the insidious intersection of research funding, caring responsibilities, the pandemic and precarious employment:

> My contract was fixed term and would expire in June 2021. My mission was to try and make myself as employable as possible – write myself a funding bid or get a publication so I get my next job. I volunteered to work on research bids to apply for the COVID funding calls. I'd be waking up at three or four in the morning and start writing stuff. I did a lot of extra work on other grants too. I was like – I am investing in my own future by helping with this research grant. But afterwards I was told there wasn't going to be any money to pay me after all.
>
> *(Lauren, interview)*

New opportunities

So far, this chapter has focused on the challenging and negative impacts of the pandemic on participants' research productivity, including grant applications. However, the forced break with established processes during the pandemic did open up spaces for new ideas and ways of doing things for some participants, if not for all (see also Ylijoki, this volume). The rapid and widespread expansion of digital communication technologies in working practices led to the hypermobility of virtual academic spaces such as online conferences, seminars and network events (Davies et al., 2021). Participating in these activities did not require funding or complex childcare arrangements and brought unanticipated career benefits for some.

> Because of childcare reasons, I had found it really difficult to travel to build the sort of research networks that are needed. This year, I've been able to build up collaborations with others because I don't have to travel for six or eight hours on a train. We can do it quite well on [Microsoft] Teams.
>
> *(Anita, diary 2)*

> Perversely this has been a very good time for me academically. I have really flown, I think, in terms of my reputation. I'm now leading a research network which wouldn't have come together in the old pre-Zoom world. We only got two grand to do it, but it has just opened so many doors and led to various other grant applications.
>
> *(Nicole, diary 2)*

Sam says, 'I've presented at online conferences which I can attend more of, because it's all virtual, there's no or lower costs for attending'. However, Sam points out that universities barely acknowledged that these opportunities were unevenly experienced across the academic workforce:

> I live alone, I don't have kids and I don't have elderly parents who live nearby. It's been good for me, not psychologically, not personally, but academically and promotion-wise because I've worked really long hours. I tried to bring this up in an Equality, Diversity and Inclusion Committee meeting. Will there be some mechanism to take into account those people who have had caring responsibilities or mental health concerns over this time and so haven't been productive? They said they'd minute it. Silence since then.
>
> *(Sam, interview)*

Finally, the pandemic as 'a moment of rupture – that incites action and brings contradictions to light' (Ahmann, 2018, p. 144) provided an opportunity of a different sort for Sarah who strikingly reimagined her academic future:

> I am just exhausted. I have lost a lot of motivation to pursue career-driven goals. It will never be enough, they will always want more and so no, I'm not chasing the money anymore. I'm going to do the research projects that I want to do and I'm not playing the REF game. I will write stuff that I am proud of, that I want to publish. In that sense, it has been quite empowering. I want to share that with my female colleagues.
>
> *(Sarah, interview)*

Conclusion

In the previous sections, I quoted participants' diary entries and interview transcripts to make visible the everyday experiences of female academics' working lives during the pandemic. In drawing on personal, reflective and descriptive data gathered during an unprecedented period of upheaval and change, I have highlighted gendered experiences of competing workloads and research temporalities. These experiences in turn point to gendered repercussions of the research funding imperative in the context of COVID-19 even while the looming REF and the pressures to submit proposals to funding bodies continued to operate. It is important not to overlook the narratives of individuals who found the circumstances of the pandemic conducive to aspects of productivity: Sarah who found writing grant applications more feasible than writing academic papers, Nicole and Anita who discovered new opportunities for research collaboration, and Sam whose productivity increased in social isolation. However, most participants' accounts indicate the burden of care carried by many women during the COVID-19 pandemic, together with physical and psychological challenges across this period, was largely incompatible with institutional pressure to be productive in terms of grant applications and writing for publication. The time and energy required to initiate new research ideas and write complex grant applications were not universally or equally available.

This study contributes to a wider literature on HE and gender and specifically to an emerging body of work addressing experiences and implications of the COVID-19 pandemic for research activity within the sector. I acknowledge that the small number of participants, mostly in social science disciplines, limits the study's explanatory reach. Nor is the sample sufficiently diverse to allow for examination of intersectional experiences and their implications for research funding. The research design comprised three data-collection points within a six-month period, albeit the first being the retrospective diary entry spanning March 2020–May 2021. One avenue for further research would be to approach the same individuals again to ascertain the longer-term impact of reduced (or enhanced) research productivity described during the 2020–2021 period.

However, as a body of evidence, these data point towards the need for a reckoning of the damage done to female academics' research productivity during the COVID-19 pandemic and the identification of longer-term, gendered implications for career progression. The context here is not only that of an unequal research funding environment but also an uneven picture of institutional approaches towards supporting research activity and mitigating the effects of the pandemic. As a starting point, the COVID-19 pandemic should be recognised not as a finite crisis in the past, but as an ongoing phenomenon casting a long shadow. Borrowing from the literature on crisis temporalities, scholars could employ Nixon's (2011) theorising of 'slow violence' as 'a violence that occurs gradually and out of sight, a violence of delayed destruction that is dispersed across time and space' (p. 2) to frame reductions and delays in female academics' research productivity. In the UK, the REF 2029 cycle rolls on, yet unless there is attention to the gendered and raced impacts of the COVID-19 pandemic on research grant applications, awards and research productivity in general, the HE sector risks losing the opportunity of the crisis to 'incite actions and bring contradictions to light' (Ahmann, 2018, p. 144).

Acknowledgements

Funding for the Dear Diary project was provided by the Society for Research into Higher Education. I extend thanks and appreciation to Dr Bally Kaur and Hannah Malpass, research assistants on the Dear Diary project.

Notes

1 Further discussion of these statistics appears in chapters by Tate and by Read and Leathwood in this volume. A full analysis needs to consider those who do not reveal ethnicity (at least 7%) and to disaggregate by research council (because gender-based patterns differ from council to council). Although I have not reported percentages for co-investigators (CIs), they follow similar patterns.
2 Quotations from diaries retain the original spelling, punctuation, abbreviations, etc.

References

Ahmann, C. (2018). 'It's exhausting to create an event out of nothing': slow violence and the manipulation of time. *Cultural Anthropology, 33*(1), 142–171. https://doi.org/10.14506/ca33.1.06

Ascher, D. (2020, May 27). Coronavirus: 'mums do most childcare and chores in lockdown'. *BBC News.* https://www.bbc.co.uk/news/business-52808930

Boliver, V. (2015). Are there distinctive clusters of higher and lower status universities in the UK? *Oxford Review of Education, 41*(5), 608–627. https://doi.org/10.1080/03054985.2015.1082905

Boncori, I. (2020). The never-ending shift: a feminist reflection on living and organizing academic lives during the coronavirus pandemic. *Gender, Work & Organization, 27*(5), 677–682. https://doi.org/10.1111/gwao.12451

Boncori, I., Bizjack, D., & Sicca, L. M. (2020). Workload allocation models in academia: a panopticon of neoliberal control or tools for resistance? *Tamara: Journal for Critical Organisational Inquiry, 18*(1), 51–69. https://tamarajournal.com/index.php/tamara/article/view/462

Carruthers Thomas, K. (2020). *Living and working in lockdown. What's gender got to do with it? Research Report.* Birmingham City University. https://www.thinkthreeways.com/uploads/1/3/2/0/132057820/report_living_and_working_in_lockdown_2020.pdf

Carruthers Thomas, K. (2022a). *Dear Diary: equality implications for female academics of changes to working practices in lockdown and beyond. Final Report.* Society for Research into Higher Education. https://srhe.ac.uk/wp-content/uploads/2022/10/DEAR-DIARY-REVISED-FINAL-REPORT-OCTOBER-2022.pdf

Carruthers Thomas, K. (2022b). *Dear Diary illustrated digital archive.* https://www.deardiaryresearch.co.uk

Connolly, K., Kassam, A., Willsher, K., & Carroll, R. (2020, May 29). 'We are losers in this crisis': research finds lockdowns reinforcing gender inequality. *The Guardian.* https://www.theguardian.com/global-development/2020/may/29/we-are-losers-in-this-crisis-research-finds-lockdowns-reinforcing-gender-inequality

Davies, A., Seaton, A., Tonooka, C., & White, J. (2021). Covid-19, online workshops, and the future of intellectual exchange. *Rethinking History, 25*(2), 224–241. https://doi.org/10.1080/13642529.2021.1934290

Department for Business, Innovation & Skills. (2010). *Securing a sustainable future for higher education: an independent review of higher education funding and student finance* (Reference No. BIS/10/1208). https://www.gov.uk/government/publications/the-browne-report-higher-education-funding-and-student-finance

Elliott, M. H. (1997). The use of diaries in sociological research on health experience. *Sociological Research Online, 2*(2). http://www.socresonline.org.uk/2/2/7.html

Fazackerly, A. (2020, May 12). Women's research plummets during lockdown but articles from men increase. *The Guardian.* https://www.theguardian.com/education/2020/may/12/womens-research-plummets-during-lockdown-but-articles-from-men-increase

Ferguson, D. (2020, May 3). 'I feel like a 1950s housewife': how lockdown has exposed the gender divide. *The Observer.* https://www.theguardian.com/world/2020/may/03/i-feel-like-a-1950s-housewife-how-lockdown-has-exposed-the-gender-divide

Heijstra, T. M., Steinthorsdóttir, F. S., & Einarsdóttir, T. (2017). Academic career making and the double-edged role of academic housework. *Gender and Education, 29*(6), 764–780. https://doi.org/10.1080/09540253.2016.1171825

Higher Education Statistics Agency. (2022, February 1). *Statistical bulletin: higher education staff statistics: UK, 2020/21.* https://www.hesa.ac.uk/news/01-02-2022/sb261-higher-education-staff-statistics

Inge, S. (2020, August 7). UKRI in row over absence of Black PIs in its COVID-19 BAME grant. *Research Professional News.* https://www.researchprofessionalnews.com/rr-news-uk-research-councils-2020-8-ukri-in-row-over-absence-of-black-pis-in-its-covid-19-bame-grant/

Inge, S. (2021, August 20). Black academics hit out at UKRI's lack of public reply to open letter. *Research Professional News.* https://www.researchprofessionalnews.com/rr-news-uk-research-councils-2021-8-black-academics-hit-out-at-ukri-s-lack-of-public-reply-to-open-letter/

Institute for Government. (2022, December 9). *Timeline of UK government coronavirus lockdowns and restrictions.* https://www.instituteforgovernment.org.uk/sites/default/files/2022-12/timeline-coronavirus-lockdown-december-2021.pdf

Kenny, J. (2018). Re-empowering academics in a corporate culture: an exploration of workload and performativity in a university. *Higher Education, 75*(2), 365–380. https://doi.org/10.1007/s10734-017-0143-z

Kenten, C. (2010). Narrating oneself: reflections on the use of solicited diaries with diary interview. *Forum: Qualitative Social Research/ Forum Qualitative Sozialforschung, 11*(2). https://doi.org/10.17169/fqs-11.2.1314

Kitchener, C. (2020, April 24). Women academics seem to be submitting fewer papers during coronavirus. 'Never seen anything like it,' says one editor. *The Lily.* https://www.thelily.com/women-academics-seem-to-be-submitting-fewer-papers-during-coronavirus-never-seen-anything-like-it-says-one-editor/

Kolarz, P., Arnold, E., Bryan, B., D'hont, J., Horvath, A., Simmonds, P., Varnai, P., & Vingre, A. (2021). *Process review of UKRI's research and innovation response to COVID-19: final report.* https://www.ukri.org/wp-content/uploads/2022/01/UKRI-180122-ProcessReviewUKRIResponseCOVID19-FinalReport.pdf

Latham, A. (2003). Research, performance, and doing human geography: some reflections on the diary-photograph, diary-interview method. *Environment and Planning A: Economy and Space, 35*(11), 1993–2017. https://doi.org/10.1068/a3587

Nixon, R. (2011). *Slow violence and the environmentalism of the poor.* Harvard University Press.

Office for National Statistics. (2016, September 20). *How has the student population changed?* https://www.ons.gov.uk/peoplepopulationandcommunity/birthsdeathsandmarriages/livebirths/articles/howhasthestudentpopulationchanged/2016-09-20

Office for National Statistics. (2020, May 15). *Coronavirus and key workers in the UK.* https://www.ons.gov.uk/employmentandlabourmarket/peopleinwork/earningsandworkinghours/articles/coronavirusandkeyworkersintheuk/2020-05-15

Pankhurst, H. (2020, September 30). Forget notions of coronavirus as a great equaliser – women are hardest hit yet again. *The Guardian.* https://www.theguardian.com/global-development/2020/sep/30/forget-notions-of-coronavirus-as-a-great-equaliser-women-are-hardest-hit-yet-again

Papatsiba, V., & Cohen, E. (2020). Institutional hierarchies and research impact: new academic currencies, capital and position-taking in UK higher education. *British Journal of Sociology of Education, 41*(2), 178–196. https://doi.org/10.1080/01425692.2019.1676700

Pebdani, R. N., Zeidan, A., Low, L., & Baillie, A. (2023). Pandemic productivity in academia: using ecological momentary assessment to explore the impact of COVID-19 on research productivity. *Higher Education Research & Development, 42*(4), 937–953. https://doi.org/10.1080/07294360.2022.2128075

Ramsay, K., & Letherby, G. (2006). The experience of academic non-mothers in the gendered university. *Gender, Work & Organization, 13*(1), 25–44. https://doi.org/10.1111/j.1468-0432.2006.00294.x

Research Excellence Framework. (ca. 2017). *What is the REF?* Retrieved on 12 January 2024 from https://archive.ref.ac.uk/about-the-ref/what-is-the-ref/

Russell Group. (2022, May 12). *Russell Group universities produce more world-leading research than ever before.* https://www.russellgroup.ac.uk/news/russell-group-universities-produce-more-world-leading-research-than-ever-before/

Sabri, D. (2011). What's wrong with 'the student experience'? *Discourse: Studies in the Cultural Politics of Education, 32*(5), 657–667. https://doi.org/10.1080/01596306.2011.620750

Sato, S., Gygax, P. M., Randall, J., & Schmid Mast, M. (2021). The leaky pipeline in research grant peer review and funding decisions: challenges and future directions. *Higher Education, 82*(1), 145–162. https://doi.org/10.1007/s10734-020-00626-y

Steinþórsdóttir, F. S., Einarsdóttir, Þ., Pétursdóttir, G. M., & Himmelweit, S. (2020). Gendered inequalities in competitive grant funding: an overlooked dimension of gendered power relations in academia. *Higher Education Research & Development, 39*(2), 362–375. https://doi.org/10.1080/07294360.2019.1666257

Timmins, N. (2021). *Schools and coronavirus. The government's handling of education during the pandemic.* Institute for Government. https://www.instituteforgovernment.org.uk/sites/default/files/publications/schools-and-coronavirus.pdf

UK Government. (2020a). *Prime Minister's statement on coronavirus (COVID-19): 23 March 2020.* https://www.gov.uk/government/speeches/pm-address-to-the-nation-on-coronavirus-23-march-2020

UK Government. (2020b). *Prime Minister's statement on coronavirus (COVID-19): 10 May 2020.* https://www.gov.uk/government/speeches/pm-address-to-the-nation-on-coronavirus-10-may-2020

UK Research and Innovation. (2023a, February 22). *UKRI diversity data for funding applicants and awardees 2020–2021 update.* https://www.ukri.org/publications/diversity-data-for-funding-applicants-and-awardees-2020-21/ukri-diversity-data-for-funding-applicants-and-awardees-2020-to-21-update/

UK Research and Innovation. (2023b, September 7). *Horizon Europe: help for UK applicants.* https://www.ukri.org/apply-for-funding/horizon-europe/

United Nations, Department of Economic and Social Affairs. (2020, April 6). *The social impact of COVID-19.* https://www.un.org/development/desa/dspd/2020/04/social-impact-of-covid-19/

World Health Organization. (2023, July 19). *Coronavirus (COVID-19) dashboard.* https://covid19.who.int/

Ylijoki, O.-H. (2015). Conquered by project time? Conflicting temporalities in university research. In P. Gibbs, O.-H. Ylijoki, C. Guzmán-Valenzuela, & R. Barnett (Eds.), *Universities in the flux of time* (pp. 94–107). Routledge.

Zimmerman, D. H., & Wieder, D. L. (1977). The diary: diary-interview method. *Urban Life, 5*(4), 479–498. https://doi.org/10.1177/089124167700500406

PART 3

Care and conflict

7

FUNDING JOURNEYS IN HEALTH TECHNOLOGY IN FINLAND

The atypical stories of Sara and Heidi

Oili-Helena Ylijoki

In the current neoliberal higher education context, attracting research funding has become a key requirement for universities and academics. In line with academic capitalism (Slaughter & Leslie, 1997), university-based research is dependent on external revenue, compelling academics to compete for grants from various sources. Furthermore, success in securing research funds has turned into an indicator of research excellence as competition per se is believed to ensure that the best get selected, an ideology which Naidoo (2018) calls 'competition fetish'. It follows that funding success has crucial implications for academic career building. Recruitment and promotion decisions favour candidates with impressive records of research grants, preferably from the most prestigious funding bodies with the lowest success rates.

In terms of gender, the imperative of grant-funding success has been seen to work against women academics for several reasons. Women tend to gravitate towards disciplines and research areas, especially social sciences and humanities, which do not belong to the core in the current science policy prioritising the male-dominated STEM fields (science, technology, engineering and mathematics). Thus, there are fewer funding opportunities available, already making the starting points for competition gender biased (Steinþórsdóttir et al., 2020). It has also been suggested that many women feel uncomfortable with the current culture of competitive individualism (Morley & Crossouard, 2016) and may struggle to build or maintain the self-confidence needed to apply for funding and cope with rejections (Leberman et al., 2016). In addition, women tend to be less mobile than men and lack wide collaborative networks that would advance their research productivity and chances of being funded (Uhly et al., 2017). Moreover, compared to men, women focus more on teaching and carry more caring and service duties at home and at work, which take time and energy away

DOI: 10.4324/9781003330431-10

from research (Gaudet et al., 2022). Additionally, subtle but systematic biases in assessing excellence in university recruitments (van den Brink & Benschop, 2012) and funding bodies' decision-making (Sato et al., 2021) may work to women's disadvantage.

In all of these arguments, the relationship between gender and research funding is understood to be unfavourable for women academics, placing barriers into their career trajectories. In this chapter, I want to offer a more nuanced view, pointing to the diversity of women's experiences of research funding. I present two career stories in which acquiring external research funding is not so much a problem but a solution. In these stories, women academics confront severe difficulties in their local male-dominated work environments; however, success in funding competitions enables them to survive financially, socially and emotionally. Although stories like these are rare in academe, I think they deserve to be told in order to show the complexity and multi-layeredness of the relationship among gender, research funding and academic career building.

The stories in this chapter emanate from the Finnish higher education system. Over recent decades, Finnish higher education has witnessed a series of neoliberal changes, turning it into a very competitive and output-oriented system. University budget funding from the Ministry of Education and Culture is performance based, grounded in performance indicators in teaching, research and strategic targets. Apart from this core funding, universities rely on competitive external funding from public and private sources. As a result, the institutional environment of academic work and career building is increasingly competitive and insecure. The majority of academics in Finland, currently 70%, work on temporary contracts (Organisation for Economic Co-operation and Development, 2021), indicating that the competition for permanent university posts is tough. The system follows the usual gendered pattern of vertical and horizontal segregation. In 2022, women held 33% of professor and research director roles, but their representation varied substantially between disciplinary fields, ranging from less than 13% in technology to 50% in the humanities (Vipunen Education Statistics Finland, n.d.).

Data and method

The full dataset consists of 30 career interviews with women researchers working in health technology inside and outside academia in Finland. (This dataset is also the source for the analysis of academic mothers presented by Vehviläinen et al. in this volume.) Health technology is a broad emerging interdisciplinary field. The interviewees' backgrounds were principally either in technology or life sciences, while a few came from the social sciences. The research field had made fast scientific progress, which had also led to the commercialisation of results. As in experimental sciences generally, research was typically carried out in laboratory settings by tightly organised research groups led by group leaders. Nearly all participants had PhDs, but their work history and age varied. Some were early-career researchers in their late 20s; at the other end of the continuum were senior researchers and full professors close to retirement. The interviews lasted one to two hours, and they were recorded and transcribed verbatim. Quotations have been translated into English.

Prior to the interviews, the participants were invited to draw a career line of their work histories and almost all agreed to do so. The drawings typically covered the timeline from finishing high school to the present work situation and entailed such key episodes as university enrolment, degrees obtained, changes in employment, major grants and birth of children. Questions asked in the interview built upon the participants' drawings.

The career stories presented in this chapter are based on two interviews: one with Sara, the other with Heidi. They both are in their 40s and work as research group leaders at research-intensive universities. Neither of them has a permanent position, meaning they must attract external funding not only for their group but also to cover their own salaries. In this sense, they are academic entrepreneurs running their research groups as 'quasi-firms' (Etzkowitz, 1996). This kind of fixed-term employment is common among the interviewees working in Finnish universities, but in other respects, Sara's and Heidi's stories are highly atypical. Prominent in most of the women's accounts are difficulties in grant-seeking and stories of how, for some of the interviewees, failures in getting funding have pushed them away from academic careers. From this angle, these two interviews are success stories, as Sara and Heidi have been particularly successful in securing research funds for years. However, their interviews also include exceptionally gloomy descriptions of harsh working conditions, making them a curious mixture of success and misery worth closer scrutiny.

In presenting the two stories, I follow the sense-making methodological tradition (Weick, 1995), striving to trace the ways the interviewees experience and attach meaning to their career trajectories. Instead of a factual description of what happened, the stories aim to capture how the interviewees understand their career histories and what episodes have been meaningful for them, why and with what implications. As Degn (2018) says, sense-making is 'the ongoing processes wherein individuals and organizations construct a plausible story of "what is going on"' (p. 306) and in the interview situation these stories acted as tools enabling 'certain elements of the past, present and future to emerge and others to wither away' (p. 307).

Next, I present the career stories of Sara and Heidi, and after that reflect on what these stories say about research funding, career building and gender. To protect the confidentiality of Sara and Heidi, the names are pseudonyms and detailed information about the universities, departments, disciplines, family situations and specificities of events are omitted.

Sara's career story

Sara says at the beginning of the interview that she thinks about her career through her academic achievements. This focus is evident also in her career drawing, which, unlike most other participants' drawings, does not include any events from her private life but concentrates wholly on key episodes in her work at universities over 20 years. The drawing presents a steadily rising line until a recent abrupt decline, leaving the future direction open and undefined.

Sara's background is in life sciences. She describes how her doctoral studies aroused 'an enduring love' for her subject and made it clear to her that she wanted to continue in research work. The group where she was based when she wrote her dissertation was ambitious and esteemed, teaching her a routine of working hard and with high standards. The group was led by a woman principal investigator (PI) whom Sara recalls with warmth and who has been her mentor ever since. Nonetheless, after getting a PhD, Sara wanted to move on despite invitations to stay because she was searching for new opportunities to advance her research interests. Sara says that is the sort of person she is: if she has decided something, she sticks to her plan and does not allow others to influence her decision.

Sara had heard about a new research centre in an emerging area of health technology that was about to start in a different city. She became interested, contacted the centre and was quickly recruited there. The centre was established as an independent institution detached from the rest of the university. It was outward-looking and business-oriented, and it came with huge expectations for both scientific and commercial breakthroughs that would boost economic growth and overcome serious diseases. Sara was one of the first people recruited and witnessed the initial hype as the centre got much media visibility and 'everyone wanted to collaborate with us'. For Sara, the centre's hectic start meant that she moved from the position of doctoral student directly to being a PI, without a postdoctoral period.

> We got big funding straight away and then, all at once, I realised that I was establishing my own research group. There was no professor for me, no one whose group I could have entered to. So straight away, I started to hire doctoral students, I was the one who had responsibility of them.

After her PhD, Sara thus jumped directly into the heart of the project world. Applying for external funding, building collaborative networks, managing projects and leading her research group became Sara's core duties. During her doctoral studies, she had not been involved in these activities, which are considered duties of the group leader in her disciplinary tradition. Therefore, she needed to learn new competencies and make an identity transition from a doctoral student to a group leader almost overnight. Although this was a big change, Sara looks back on this period in a matter-of-fact manner. Simply, it was the way the centre operated.

My position was not what I had imagined, so of course it required quite a lot from me. It was hard to know how I should handle this and how I should do things. But on the other hand, all the other research group leaders were in the same position, and we had, and still have, a really strong collegial network. Surely, it didn't go exactly the way it should, but then again, if you have funding and an opportunity, then you learn your lessons while doing them.

In the beginning, the centre was all women, and women remained in the majority over time. The prevalence of women created a strong community spirit, which offered mutual learning and support. Sara says that 'since no one of us had been in a similar situation before, we really worked together and developed, pondered and planned how to start the business'. This sense of togetherness and sharing of experiences was empowering. Sara also had strong self-confidence, which facilitated the adoption of her new role as a research group leader: 'I saw it from the very start that I am capable of doing it.'

Material resources were also of key importance. The overall funding situation for research and innovation in Finland was good at that time, and Sara's field was among the top priorities in science policy. Both the centre and Sara were very successful in attracting research funding from academic and industry-driven funders and from both national and international sources. Accordingly, there was abundant money available at the centre. For instance, Sara mentions that her group was able to conduct extremely expensive laboratory experiments that she could have never imagined. All funding was important, but Sara highlights the big consortium grants from the European Union and the Academy of Finland, which have especially tight assessment systems and low success rates, making them highly valued in the scientific community. This symbolic value of money was very important to Sara since it ensured and strengthened her status and identity as a recognised research group leader in her own and others' eyes:

> This means that the international members of the evaluation panels consider you as an independent research group leader. For me, these have been important, I have been evaluated internationally that I am a qualified group leader and I can get funding. ... It really makes a difference.

Thus, the dependence on external funding was not a problem for Sara but rather a natural element of what academic research is all about. She continued to have funding success, which enabled her to make advances in research and promote young researchers' careers. She highlights how proud she is of all the PhDs she has supervised in her group and who all have secured good positions inside and outside academia. In this way, Sara's career progressed steadily, and she was able to consolidate her position as a successful PI.

Then things changed. In line with the general policy trends to create bigger units to increase efficiency and productivity, the research centre experienced a series of mergers, the last one integrating it with the faculty of medicine. These mergers meant diminishing institutional autonomy and adaptation to traditional university structures and practices which operated by different logics of action compared to the research centre. In Sara's career story, the mergers caused severe tension and finally led to 'a state of war' between her interdisciplinary field and the medical faculty. Sara mentions several intersecting reasons behind this conflict.

To start, the gender aspect was apparent. Sara's centre was predominantly staffed by women and rooted in a communal spirit without strong hierarchies, whereas the faculty of medicine was dominated by men at the top professorial level and strongly attached to traditional hospital hierarchies. This contrast was related to professional status: neither Sara nor any of her colleagues had a professorship but worked as research group leaders with external funding on temporary contracts, a situation that was seen by the medical professors as a mark of lower scientific value. Additionally, the external revenue Sara and her colleagues had gained was underrated because only funding from purely academic sources was seen as valuable, whereas commercial and application-oriented funders, despite their crucial role in Sara's field, were placed into some lower category. Finally, because the centre was focused on research and accountable to its funders, it had few connections to university teaching. Thus medical professors accused the centre's members of not contributing sufficiently to the faculty's teaching duties.

In Sara's career story, this cultural mismatch created a dismissive atmosphere and what Sara called 'girl minimising', which led to open confrontations. Sara describes herself as 'quite strongly feminist' and unwilling to 'tolerate any sort of unequal treatment', and therefore she fought against what she saw as wrong. The conflict culminated when Sara received 'a double jackpot' in the form of simultaneous funding success from two prestigious sources. Again, funding was important not only for money but also for the recognition of her group's work: 'We have been evaluated to belong to the best five per cent in the world.' At this point, she argued that since she had brought in several millions of euros over the years, there must be a way to get funding for her salary from the university. This demand aggravated the already strained working climate and started long and convoluted struggles. Although Sara received support from many directions, both official and unofficial, it was a distressing experience causing 'a total burn-out':

> It really was a tough situation. I even thought I will quit altogether because this doesn't make any sense any more. ... A couple of times I needed to visit a doctor and I also went to a psychologist because I thought I don't want to become bitter about this and stay churning in this. I must get over this.

The outcome of Sara's protest was that her employment conditions were improved but not to the degree to which she would have preferred. Sara says that after these experiences, she has 'zero loyalty' towards her local superiors. She mentions, for instance, that she used to take care of all kinds of common tasks, which in no way were targeted to her, but not anymore. The tough experiences have left an imprint on her, yet she says that she is 'awfully satisfied that I did what I did' and defended her rights.

Her future goal is to get a position as a full professor as soon as possible. She emphasises that she does not 'need this title for getting funding' because she has proved to be successful without it. Rather she sees professorship as a signal of respect and recognition of her work, and conversely, a lack of it as a social stigma. Sara compares herself with her collaborators and colleagues and feels that it is 'ridiculous' that most of them are full professors but she is not, while she has exactly the same job description and she has even brought in more revenue than they have:

> Okay, if I don't now get a professorship, I will not continue with this endlessly. And I also need to have a salary increase. Patting on my head is not enough for me, it tells about respect. ... If I am not valued and if I feel that I am treated like an old rag, I don't need to stay here. In such a case, I can quit and I'm not afraid that I couldn't find something else instead.

Overall, Sara's career future is shadowed by doubts. Yet, she is determined and self-confident: 'I can delegate, I can organise, and I have the guts to do things, I can imagine myself in some more superior position.' The crucial question for her is whether this future will take place in her current university, in another university or outside academe.

Tellingly, Sara's career drawing ends with a big question mark and the words 'to stay or to leave'.

Heidi's career story

Heidi starts the interview by saying that she enjoyed drawing her career line because it made her realise how long her academic path actually is – already 30 years. Heidi's drawing is detailed. It entails two lines presenting the years and verbal descriptions of what happened in each year. In addition to key episodes in her working life, the births of her children are also included.

Originally, Heidi planned to study physics but chose engineering instead. She explains this choice by her family background. She came from a non-academic family from a rural area and could not see herself studying a subject which 'didn't educate to any specific occupation'. Therefore, she chose engineering, which offered good employment prospects, yet had close linkages with physics.

After graduating as an engineer, Heidi spent a few years working in industry and enrolling in various courses in Finland and abroad. During that time, she had 'doubts of career choice', and she also experienced losses in her private life. Heidi says, 'When looking back now, I really see that I wasn't very determined, I couldn't choose what to do, I was partly drifting.' However, Heidi does not regret these years but thinks she needed them to find her own path. Eventually, she ended up starting doctoral studies in Finland. She specialised in health technology, which she found fascinating, and rapidly finished her PhD.

At that point, Heidi decided that she wanted to become an academic. This decision was almost like a surprise to her because she had always thought that a doctoral dissertation would be 'a culmination for her' and 'the maximum I could ever reach'. She enjoyed research work and had sometimes dreamed of continuing in it but found it hard to believe that an academic career path could be available for her. Heidi explains her way of thinking by her family background and gender:

> Surely, I had sometimes thought that I would like to have my own research group, but since I came from rural areas and didn't have any role models in my family, I really couldn't believe that this could be realised, that I could continue as a researcher and have my own research group. It was more like a dream to me. I don't know whether this is typical to women to think this way, albeit I always thought that this is only realistic, but when compared to men, there are studies which show that women underestimate their competences and men exaggerate theirs.

The beginning of her academic career was smooth. The general funding situation in Finland was good, and her technology department was one of the university's core departments with a strong academic reputation. Heidi emphasises that her work environment had a 'dynamic atmosphere' as everybody was expected to write applications fast and keep high standards, but there was also help, training and feedback available. She already had some experience writing applications for small personal grants before her doctoral studies. Under these favourable conditions, Heidi succeeded immediately in getting several important grants. These grants enabled her to recruit people and establish her own research group. For her, as for the whole department, funding was no problem, quite the opposite:

> We had so much money that we hardly knew where to put it. When I look back at that time, I can really say that we had abundantly money, we lived in abundance. We didn't have time to count all the money annually, we had secretaries and coordinators who were managing our money. ... I was able to establish my research group in a good phase with good money and good plans and good support. It was a period of six, seven years, in which we almost started to lose a sense of proportion.

Heidi did not have a permanent position but worked on fixed-term contracts supported by external funding, yet this situation did not bother her. It was a shared working condition among her close colleagues, and she was skilful in attracting money, which made her look at her career future confidently. Besides, at that time, her department offered a supporting, motivating and stimulating working environment with good prospects for career advancement.

However, little by little, the situation changed, and her career turned to 'a dramatically descending curve'. Heidi recalls how she first began to get subtle signals that something was wrong. For instance, she was no longer invited to important meetings, and she heard frequent complaints about her students and her group. At first, she only thought, 'Well, you always get feedback, we need to improve things.' But then, several harsh incidents and bullying took place, and Heidi felt that she had become a target of 'a slander campaign' questioning her competence to lead a research group. Her work was also jeopardised in a more concrete way by hindering her group's access to laboratory space. Faced with these experiences, Heidi searched for professional and legal advice outside the department and finally, after complex negotiations, ended up with an agreement that to some degree calmed things down and protected her.

Heidi calls these incidents gender discrimination and explains them by the drastically deteriorating funding situation both nationally and locally, starting in 2009. When funding became scarce, the competition tightened and 'the game turned out really hard'. According to Heidi, this difficult situation was related to the male domination of the department. She underlines that as an engineer, she has always worked in an environment in which 80% to 90% of her colleagues are men, so male domination was not new nor a problem to her. Yet, she was not prepared to confront the power of the male networks that were activated when the diminishing resources were redistributed. There were a few women professors, but they allied with the men professors and did not challenge the status quo, 'out of fear', Heidi suspects. Furthermore, she also mentions that interdisciplinary research had a much lower value in her department than pure technological research, which also acted against Heidi.

Heidi remembers this time as the darkest phase of her career. She lost self-confidence and faith in the future. It was also a question of livelihood. Due to precarious employment, her situation was financially vulnerable and she needed to take a part-time job as a research administrator to subsidise research work. It was a hard time also for her group members, and she struggled to take care of their well-being too. In this gloomy situation, the support of her long-time colleagues within and outside her department, predominantly women, enabled her to survive and not to give up, although, she says, '99% of researchers would have stopped.'

Then something unexpected happened which turned Heidi's career path into a sharp rise. Through her administrative job, she had good information about EU funding opportunities and almost by accident she decided to make an application to one big programme call. To her great astonishment, she was selected. This success made a drastic transformation in her career path and self-esteem:

> These are European top projects. ... I would have never believed that I could get it, but for some reason I decided to apply for it, that I will not give up yet. And then I got the information that I was selected. My career moved into a totally different sphere. From that moment I belonged to the most distinguished researchers of my field.

In Heidi's story, external funding was thus not a problem but a solution. It provided money, self-confidence and a sense of belonging. While feeling excluded and underrated at her department, the international collaboration and new networks which were opened via EU funding offered her a new welcoming and appreciative 'scientific home'. Heidi says that due to this funding, she made 'an international breakthrough' and got 'an international expert role' with lots of invitations for keynote presentations and reviews.

At the time of the interview, Heidi was still working with external funding on fixed-term contracts. She had pondered the possibility of moving abroad but suspects that she is too old to be recruited to top universities. Not having a professorship is especially problematic in international circles because her international collaborators do not usually know the Finnish system and assume that as an established academic she has a permanent position as a full professor. In this delicate situation, she cannot 'openly tell that in fact I would need a professorship from somewhere'.

In spite of her unsatisfying employment conditions, Heidi is highly motivated and determined to continue in an academic career. She is especially proud of not giving up: 'They thought they can get me out of here, but they didn't get rid of me, I didn't stop my research work.' She underlines that after all her experiences she has learnt to 'take my role', not to be 'somehow submissive' and in the future she will not let anybody 'trample over' her anymore:

> Because of all these experiences I have always somehow questioned myself. Am I really a good researcher, can I really manage this work, am I a competent researcher? But now I won't ask anything from anybody anymore. I will do research as long as I have possibilities to do it. I won't ask anybody what I can do and what I cannot do. I will do whatever I want to, and this has made me awfully happy.

Heidi's career drawing ends with the statement, 'I realise increasingly clearly that I have a right to be a researcher and do research irrespective of whether or not Finland has given me a permanent post! Happy.'

Thinking with the stories

Sara's and Heidi's career stories stand out as atypical among the 30 interviews included in the empirical material of this study. On the one hand, Sara and Heidi have been exceptionally successful in attracting research funding; on the other hand, they have experienced severe hardships in their local work environments. This peculiar combination of success and misery caught my attention in the first place and pushed me to select these interviews for closer scrutiny to better understand the complex and convoluted relations among gender, research funding and academic career building embedded in them.

As regards research funding, Sara's and Heidi's experiences follow the plot of a success story. Under the increasingly competitive funding conditions, only very few succeed, and the majority have to confront rejections and cope with subsequent negative emotional responses, which require resilience and self-belief (McAlpine, 2016, 2020). Sara and Heidi belong to a category of researchers who have for years succeeded particularly well in securing funding for themselves and for their research groups. This achievement could be partly explained by their field. Health technology has been a priority area in science and higher education policies in Finland and beyond, thereby providing substantial resources and funding possibilities (Murgia & Poggio, 2019). There is also an element of good timing as they both happened to enter academic career paths at a time of financial prosperity enabling a favourable start (Vehviläinen et al., 2022). Also, their local work environments were particularly successful and esteemed, which facilitated the creation of a virtuous circle in which money follows money. In this way, the stories attest to the old Matthew effect in science (Merton, 1968): the rich get richer, and the poor get poorer.

Sara's and Heidi's stories also point to the importance of learning the rules of the game in application writing. As McAlpine (2020) highlights, grant success requires not only good writing skills but also 'knowledge of how the funding system operates and how best to navigate it' (p. 12). Sara and Heidi are well aware of these rules. Heidi had learnt to prepare applications during her doctoral studies, whereas Sara had to acquire these skills when starting as a PI, but she did not have to do that alone but in collective learning with her close colleagues who were also early-career researchers. Furthermore, their institutions have provided administrative services and assistance, and collegial feedback and mentoring have been important for them (McGinn & Acker, 2022). Thus, instead of purely individual achievements, Sara's and Heidi's success in research funding has been facilitated by several kinds of formal and informal support structures.

However, funding success did not turn into career success in Sara's and Heidi's stories. This paradox testifies that although funding success may well be a necessary requirement for career progress in academia, it is by no means a sufficient condition. It is noteworthy that for both Sara and Heidi, career success means getting a permanent position as a full professor. This aspiration signals that the traditional linear career model is still deeply embedded in academic culture, regarding a full professorship at the top of the career ladder as a marker of success, respect and authority. Without the status of a professor, Sara and Heidi feel like they have been left on the periphery and lack institutional recognition, which produces a stigma in their social relations. What is more, their career problems are interrelated with experiences of discrimination and bullying in their workplaces, turning their career paths into misery stories at times. This illustrates that it is not enough to have gender equality plans and formal procedures to counter all kinds of discrimination, as is the case in Finnish universities, if actual research practices and cultures do not change accordingly (see also Vehviläinen et al., this volume).

In this way, Sara's and Heidi's stories point to gendered structures and gendering processes in research work, closely connected to subtle disciplinary hierarchies. In line with several other studies (e.g. Müller & Kaltenbrunner, 2019; Turner et al., 2015), the accounts indicate that interdisciplinarity is overshadowed by monodisciplinarity (see also Griffin, this volume). Sara and Heidi work in emergent, female-majority interdisciplinary areas which lack stable institutional positions and rely heavily on external funding, whereas the medical and technological faculties where Sara and Heidi are located are male-majority at the professorial level and have a strong disciplinary status and powerful positions in the institutional structures. Accordingly, the disciplinary elite, comprising men professors, have much power to define what funding sources are most valued, what research excellence means and what counts as core scientific credits in recruitment and promotion decisions (see also Hokka et al., this volume). In the terminology of Becher (1989), it could be said that in both stories, the elite of the academic tribe protected their territory and culture against interdisciplinary newcomers, thereby reproducing prevailing gendered power structures.

Overall, what is prominent in the two stories is that external funding was not so much a problem but a solution for Sara and Heidi in their strained local work environments. First, it was simply a question of money. External funding made it possible to secure their own salaries, run their research group and advance their research interests. Apart from this, funding success was attached with symbolic value (Acker & McGinn, 2021). It was crucial socially because it opened access to new networks and gave visibility and recognition for their work. Funding success was also emotionally empowering and supportive, which was especially important after harsh experiences of being underestimated.

Emotional implications were particularly significant for Heidi, whose story tells about continuous self-doubt and low self-confidence. Sara presents herself as 'a conscious and choosing self' (Acker, 2010, p. 142) who is determined and self-assured, whereas Heidi underlines how she has been uncertain and felt like a stranger in academia. Heidi's perspective points to imposter syndrome linked with intersecting inequalities (Breeze et al., 2022). Correspondingly, Heidi explains her feelings by her gender and non-academic background. In line with

Jones and Maguire (2021), her story shows how the social class experience was 'carried through rather than being left behind' (p. 45) over the many decades of working in academia. This observation stresses the psychological and emotional costs that working-class women academics tend to encounter (Pifer et al., 2023). On the other hand, from a wider intersectional angle, both Heidi and Sara are privileged, White, healthy women who have enjoyed free university education and other benefits of the Finnish welfare state policy. In this sense, their setbacks need to be understood in relative terms, while at the same time acknowledging the lessons to be learnt for building more equal and inclusive universities.

Acknowledgements

This work was part of the Nordic Centre of Excellence Beyond the Gender Paradox funded by NordForsk (grant No. 81520). I am thankful to Tiina Suopajärvi and Minna Leinonen who carried out the interviews.

References

Acker, S. (2010). Gendered games in academic leadership. *International Studies in Sociology of Education*, 20(2), 129–152. https://doi.org/10.1080/09620214.2010.503062

Acker, S., & McGinn, M. K. (2021). Fast professors, research funding, and the figured worlds of mid-career Ontario academics. *Brock Education*, 30(2), 79–98. https://doi.org/10.26522/BrockEd.V30I2.864

Becher, T. (1989). *Academic tribes and territories*. Society for Research into Higher Education and Open University Press.

Breeze, M., Addison, M., & Taylor, Y. (2022). Situating imposter syndrome in higher education. In M. Addison, M. Breeze, & Y. Taylor (Eds.), *Palgrave handbook on imposter syndrome in higher education* (pp. 1–16). Palgrave Macmillan.

Degn, L. (2018). Academic sensemaking and behavioural responses – exploring how academics perceive and respond to identity threats in times of turmoil. *Studies in Higher Education*, 43(2), 305–321. https://doi.org/10.1080/03075079.2016.1168796

Etzkowitz, H. (1996). Conflicts of interest and commitment in academic science in the United States. *Minerva*, 34(3), 259–277. https://doi.org/10.1007/BF00120327

Gaudet, S., Marchand, I., Bujaki, M., & Bourgeault, I. L. (2022). Women and gender equity in academia through the conceptual lens of care. *Journal of Gender Studies*, 31(1), 74–86. https://doi.org/10.1080/09589236.2021.1944848

Jones, L., & Maguire, M. (2021). Investing ourselves: the role of space and place in being a working-class female academic. *Discourse: Studies in the Cultural Politics of Education*, 42(1), 45–59. https://doi.org/10.1080/01596306.2020.1767937

Leberman, S. I., Eames, B., & Barnett, S. (2016). Unless you are collaborating with a big name successful professor, you are unlikely to receive funding. *Gender and Education*, 28(5), 644–661. https://doi.org/10.1080/09540253.2015.1093102

McAlpine, L. (2016). Becoming a PI: from 'doing' to 'managing' research. *Teaching in Higher Education*, 21(1), 49–63. https://doi.org/10.1080/13562517.2015.1110789

112 Oili-Helena Ylijoki

McAlpine, L. (2020). Success? Learning to navigate the grant funding genre system. *The Journal of Research Administration, 51*(1), 10–31

McGinn, M. K., & Acker, S. (2022, December). *Mentorship, sponsorship and the hidden curriculum of research funding* [Conference presentation]. Society for Research into Higher Education conference, Online.

Merton R. K. (1968). *Social theory and social structure.* The Free Press.

Morley, L., & Crossouard, B. (2016). Gender in the neoliberalised global academy: the affective economy of women and leadership in South Asia. *British Journal of Sociology of Education, 37*(1), 149–168. https://doi.org/10.1080/01425692.2015.1100529

Müller, R., & Kaltenbrunner, W. (2019). Re-disciplining academic careers? Interdisciplinary practice and career development in a Swedish environmental sciences research center. *Minerva, 57*(4), 479–499. https://doi.org/10.1007/s11024-019-09373-6

Murgia, A., & Poggio, B. (Eds.). (2019). *Gender and precarious research careers.* Routledge.

Naidoo, R. (2018). The competition fetish in higher education: shamans, mind snares and consequences. *European Educational Research Journal, 17*(5), 605–620. https://doi.org/10.1177/1474904118784839

Organisation for Economic Co-operation and Development. (2021). *Reducing the precarity of academic research careers* (OECD Science, Technology and Industry Policy Papers, no. 113). OECD Publishing. https://www.oecd.org/publications/reducing-the-precarity-of-academic-research-careers-0f8bd468-en.htm

Pifer, M. J., Riffe, K. A., Hartz, J. T., & Ibarra, M. V. (2023). Paradise, nearly forty years later: the liminal experiences of working-class academics. *Innovative Higher Education, 48*(1), 105–125. https://doi.org/10.1007/s10755-022-09601-0

Sato, S., Gygax, P. M., Randall, J., & Schmid Mast, M. (2021). The leaky pipeline in research grant peer review and funding decisions: challenges and future directions. *Higher Education, 82*(1), 145–162. https://doi.org/10.1007/s10734-020-00626-y

Slaughter, S., & Leslie, L. (1997). *Academic capitalism.* Johns Hopkins University Press.

Steinþórsdóttir, F. S., Einarsdóttir, Þ., Pétursdóttir, G. M., & Himmelweit, S. (2020). Gendered inequalities in competitive grant funding: an overlooked dimension of gendered power relations in academia. *Higher Education Research & Development, 39*(2), 362–375. https://doi.org/10.1080/07294360.2019.1666257

Turner, V. K., Benassaiah, K., Warren, S., & Iwaniec, D. (2015). Essential tensions in interdisciplinary scholarship. *Higher Education, 70*(4), 649–665. https://doi.org/10.1007/s10734-015-9859-9

Uhly, K. M, Visser, L. M, & Zippel, K. S. (2017). Gendered patterns in international research collaboration in academia. *Studies in Higher Education, 42*(4), 760–782. https://doi.org/10.1080/03075079.2015.1072151

van den Brink, M., & Benschop, Y. (2012). Gender practices in the construction of academic excellence: sheep with five legs. *Organization, 19*(4), 507–524. https://doi.org/10.1177/1350508411414293

Vehviläinen, M., Ikonen, H.-M., & Korvajärvi, P. (2022). Changes in funding and the intensification of gender inequalities in research and innovation. In G. Griffin (Ed.), *Gender inequalities in tech-driven research and innovation: living the contradictions* (pp. 76–92). Bristol University Press. https://doi.org/10.51952/9781529219494.ch005

Vipunen Education Statistics Finland. (n.d.). *Teaching and research staff at universities.* Retrieved on 12 January 2024 from https://vipunen.fi/en-gb/university/Pages/Henkilöstö.aspx

Weick, K. E. (1995). *Sensemaking in organizations.* Sage.

8

CARING ABOUT RESEARCH

Gender, research funding and labour in the Canadian academy

Marie A. Vander Kloet and Caitlin Campisi

Although scholars investigating research culture generally focus on academic staff, universities are complex organisations containing many different groups of workers. Research undertaken at universities can be organised in several ways and involve different staff groups, for example, principal investigators (academic staff who are grant-holders), other investigators, technicians, project administrators, postdoctoral fellows and so forth. In the project from which we draw our data, two groups of university workers are featured: academic staff and research administrators. Academic staff (our preferred term in this chapter) are generally known as faculty in Canada; research administrators (hereafter RAs) are employees of the university who assist academic staff through the research cycle (pre-award and post-award) and assist the university in managing, documenting and reporting its research operations.

Exploration and examination of work, identity and power relations at academic institutions reveal how academic staff experience working at universities and their frustration with evermore demanding institutions eager for additional research funding (Acker & Wagner, 2019; McGinn et al., 2019). Research administrators are part of this struggle, working with academics but often finding themselves straddling a space between university leadership and academic staff (Vander Kloet & Campisi, 2023; Whitchurch, 2008a, 2008b). In this chapter, we examine the work that is needed to appease the demand for more funding and consider who does this work. Drawing on in-depth, qualitative interviews, we critically consider how work gendered as 'women's work' is included or excluded from what is considered valuable research work. We intend to further scholarship on how academic work is gendered and how feminised labour in seeking research funding has its own hierarchy.

Scholars have documented the extent to which women have been excluded from research due to gender bias in the evaluation of applications for funding

DOI: 10.4324/9781003330431-11

(Side & Robbins, 2007; Witteman et al., 2019), devaluation of methods and publication opportunities used by women (Nakhaie, 2002; Potter et al., 2011), and exclusionary citation practices (Dion et al., 2018; Maliniak et al., 2013). Their time for research is also affected by their heavier burden of teaching, administration and service work (Carruthers Thomas, 2019; O'Meara et al., 2017). Further, compared to White men, women and racialised people are more likely to be contract teaching staff and are more likely to be in the lowest income categories (Foster & Birdsell Bauer, 2018). Even when there is improved representation of women in permanent academic positions, this has not resulted in increased representation of racialised scholars (M. Smith, 2017; Wijesingha & Ramos, 2017), suggesting that gender equity work has largely advantaged White women. In intersectional analyses of gender, it is crucial to attend to how marginalised groups are 'burdened with invisible work' (Social Sciences Feminist Network Research Interest Group [SSFNRIG], 2017, p. 242; see also Dhamoon, 2020).

Women and racialised academics shoulder more care work in the academy; this work is feminised and subsequently devalued (Gill, 2010; Hey, 2001; SSFNRIG, 2017). Lynch (2010) focuses on how a neoliberal model of higher education heightened the demand for 'carelessness' from its workers – what she describes as an ability to be unencumbered by care, that is, completely free to take on more labour when the academy expects it. Lynch offers us the figure of the careless academic who has no care responsibilities (that cannot be delegated) and is thus free to contribute as much as possible to the institution. But women, encumbered with care both within and outside the academy, perennially fail to be what the neoliberal academy desires – careless workers. The care work women contribute to the academy typically does not 'count much for individual career advancement even though [it is] valuable to students and to the reputation of the institution' (Lynch, 2010, p. 56). The figure of the careless academic illustrates how the demand for increased research productivity (and funding) is not genderless (Lynch, 2010, p. 55) and suggests that care has a place in the academy only when it can be professionalised and put to the service of the institution (p. 63).

The COVID-19 pandemic has offered a profound illustration of how inequitably care work is distributed and the consequences of this inequity when it comes to research. Pereira (2021) asks important questions in her comprehensive review of the literature on gender, care and research productivity during the pandemic. Rather than focusing on how to get women to return to their previous, unsustainable work pace, and on what steps institutions should take to make this possible, she demonstrates how inequitable, unsustainable and hierarchical the research landscape has always been and invites others to perform a critical interrogation of the past before they propose recommendations for the future.

Methods

In this chapter, we consider what we can learn from how research work (related to seeking funding and managing funded projects) has been valued and understood by academic and professional staff. This chapter is part of a larger project focusing on the social production of social science research in the province of Ontario, Canada. Following approvals by the research ethics boards in the relevant universities, the research team interviewed 19 RAs and 27 academic staff who focus on social justice issues in their research. The academics, chosen because of their strong research records, worked at seven universities of varied research intensiveness. They were all full-time; 24 were tenured (permanently employed), and three were on the 'tenure track' and close to achieving permanence. As is the norm for tenured or tenure-track academic staff in Canada, most have teaching, research and institutional service commitments. Nearly all academic staff in the study identified as women and over one third identified as racialised (including Indigenous) people. The RAs worked at five universities and were divided between those who worked directly with academic staff (n = 11) and those who also held managerial responsibilities (n = 8).[1] Approximately three quarters of all RA participants were women (n = 14); all but one of the five men held managerial positions. RAs were employed in either local units (n = 8) or central research offices (n = 11). Data were not collected regarding RAs' race or ethnicity.

Interviews were semi-structured and lasted between 60 and 90 minutes. All but two interviews were completed prior to the March 2020 university shutdowns that occurred in Canada because of the COVID-19 pandemic. The remaining two were conducted online shortly thereafter. The interviews were professionally transcribed and subsequently coded individually by the authors of this chapter. To the interviews, we bring two questions:

1. What kinds of work are valued or viewed as meaningful?
2. What kinds of work related to seeking research funding are perceived to be research work?

We are curious about how research work is gendered and pay close attention to how feminised work is valued and claimed as *their* work by RAs and academic staff. This project provides a rare opportunity to look at how two groups of staff involved in seeking research funding at Canadian universities describe and define what counts as research. Reading across these sets of interviews allows us to look at aspects of research culture that would otherwise be difficult to discern from a single perspective.

Findings

The RAs in our study were disproportionately women, and most of the men interviewed held managerial positions; this mirrors what other researchers report about who works in research administration in Canada (and in which kind of roles) (see Kerridge & Scott, 2018). Previous analyses from this project have highlighted how research administration in Canada is a profession in transition and heavily focused on the provision of help to academic staff (Acker et al., 2019). RAs' work with academic staff includes assistance with projects, such as reviewing grant applications, and emotional support, such as engaging in discussion after a rejection. The RAs describe how they skilfully guide academic staff in navigating how to seek funding and manage grants. We note parallels between how RAs from this project discuss their work and how other professional staff in a Canadian university frame their responsibilities (C. Smith et al., 2021). C. Smith and colleagues (2021) explore how professional staff explicitly know that part of what they do is to 'make others' lives easier' (p. 509) and that knowledge and relationships (considered to be a form of social capital) are integral to their ability to do their work.

Our RA participants, half of whom have or are pursuing a PhD, emphasise that the advice they provide is particularly valuable due to their research experience: their support can be logistical (specialised knowledge of application processes, provision of resources) and intellectual (engaging with the substance of applications). RAs also tend to identify with academic staff. For example, Karen Douglas (all names are pseudonyms) states, 'I see my role as attempting to connect people to other researchers or sort of as an information-gathering role that can help enable research to happen.' RAs are aware of how they might be perceived as a part of university management, a connection that they resist. Jason Thorne tries to address this perception:

> I think that there's often an adversarial view between [academic staff] and administration.[2] ... The culture I tried to set for our research office, anyway, was that we were on the researchers' side.

In RAs' descriptions of their contributions to seeking funding and supporting academic staff, we note the connections they draw between themselves and the academics. Our research bears a similarity to studies elsewhere in Canada and in other national contexts about professional staff that highlight how they align themselves with academic staff to differentiate themselves from other non-academic staff (such as clerical staff) and position themselves in the university hierarchy (Allen Collinson, 2007; C. Smith et al., 2021; Szekeres, 2011).

Academic staff, time and research support

Although academic staff and the nuances of their working lives figure prominently in the RA interviews, RAs were mentioned less often in the academic staff interviews. When specifically invited to discuss RAs, some academic staff shared short observations on their experiences with individual RAs and/or with institutional support.

A small number of academic staff in our study, usually those with large grants, hire someone with their research funds to perform administrative tasks.[3] These individuals work under grant-specific contracts and are not university employees. These employees were typically spoken of with high praise and appreciation. Cheryl Evans describes an employee on her grant as 'highly skilled' and as 'the glue that moves everything along, allows me to finish stuff'. She explains that an application would not have been possible without that individual. Sheila Bennett, similarly, states that she 'couldn't do without [name] … because she's a detail person'. Academic staff who hire such employees from their grant funds tend to characterise these people as key in keeping the grants organised, supporting them and being skilful in areas they are not (e.g. organisation, budget). However, few academic staff in the social sciences can hire such employees.

When asked about institutional support, some academic staff could describe their experiences with, and assessment of, working with RAs employed at their universities. Julie Graham discusses how RA supports have been useful to her with managing budgets, which she describes as 'very stressful'. She details working with an RA saying, 'I would sit down with her for two hours and I'd have a great budget that was super solid and I wasn't going to end up being bankrupt.' She also praises RAs as helpful for training student researchers: 'They'd run a series of workshops for our doctoral students and [student] research assistants, so they can learn how to do NVivo and all of these other things.' Contrastingly, Tina Ellis found her research office unhelpful and even interfering in applications:

> I don't really like working with them, but they always have their hands into any research application, because I think, if I see over time, it's all getting funnelled more and more through a centralised process. That wasn't the case before.

This observation was coupled with a concern that institutional supports were being cut. Importantly, this comment also signals what RAs have actively resisted: that they are associated with the bureaucracy of the university and thus perceived as interfering with or in conflict with the interests of academic staff. Academic staff at smaller institutions lamented that research supports were sparse. Nancy Mallory, who moved to a new institution, noted the strengths of a previous research support office and the lack of support at her current university.

Academic staff comments about RA work, both praise and criticism, tend to highlight the types of work that they themselves either do not like or do not know how to do. With most academic staff in our study reporting overwork and limited work–life balance (Acker & McGinn, 2021), it is likely also work they perceive that they do not have time for. Research on academic staff highlights how they experience demands for productivity (and thus more time). It is unsurprising then that some academic staff may welcome supports that are perceived to save them time, while others may also experience a distrust of RAs and be wary of the types of strategies that research offices employ to engage academic staff in grant-seeking (see Beime et al., 2021).

From the academic staff interviews, we can observe how they seek to manage what Gill (2010) describes as the 'punishing intensification of work [that] has become an endemic feature of academic life' (p. 234). Gill's examination of how permanent academic staff experience the demands of the neoliberal university is intricately connected to the growth of precarious academic positions, the unwillingness of academics to discuss financial hardship and the disproportionate burden of precarity borne by women in contract labour (see also Ylijoki, 2013). The connection that Gill makes is important – the time pressure that academic staff experience is only one indicator of myriad troubling changes in the academy that contribute to inequity and precarity.

Categorising research work: 'thinking work' vs. 'admin work'

In the interviews, we hear both what kinds of work RAs and academic staff value and their ability to take up this work. Academic staff and RAs (who are likely to be identified as professional staff) demarcate the work of non-academic staff (particularly administrative support staff) from their own. The administrative support staff referred to in the interviews complete certain administrative work related to research funding such as dealing with online application materials and forms, arranging travel and processing expenses. We might characterise these types of administrative work as feminised with a focus on keeping track of details and distant from conceptual work associated with research.

Sheila Bennett, when discussing sorting out payment of research assistants on a project, insists that this is 'not my job and it's not a student's job. It should be an administrative person's job.' Later in her interview, she describes herself as

> one of those who has been really, really pushing the university to provide us with more infrastructure support. I don't think academic staff should be trying to figure out a budget and phoning up airlines to figure out how much a flight costs.

Similarly, Ruth Cook, in her positive description of institutional research supports, notes the assistance she has had in applying for grants from the Social Sciences and Humanities Research Council (SSHRC):

> There's a woman, for example, who helps me do my SSHRC Common CV.[4] She'll do it for me. She'll help me go on the SSHRC website and you have to accept invitations, you have to verify your CV. I mean all of

that can take you a day or more to do and I have colleagues who are really well-paid sitting there doing their common SSHRC CV, which is just a mind-boggling bureaucratic nightmare, and I say to them 'I have people for this.' I feel a little guilty, but also really glad.

From both Ruth Cook and Sheila Bennett, we observe appreciation for support and also a clear delineation of what they perceive as work worth their time. Academic staff in the study generally see their main or preferred responsibilities as the thinking or creative work of projects. Cheryl Evans argues, 'Our job should be to do the high-level thinking. I still do all my own field work, because epistemologically I think it's really important for me to be in the research setting, because that's where the knowledge gets made.'

It was not uncommon for academic staff to describe analytical and conceptual work as especially worthwhile. But it is not just academic staff who cherish this work. Similarly, RAs relish the creative and analytical work of research. They also seek to distance themselves from being associated with administrative staff responsibilities. Candace Vernon states, 'I don't do people's paperwork for them, but I do help, sort of orient them, to the post-award landscape.' RAs often describe their own training as researchers as connected to their current work. For example, Stephanie Grant notes, 'The best thing I ever got out of my Ph.D. is learning how to learn. ... You learn how to take information from whatever, you learn how to do research writ large, figure out how to process and analyse.' Both academic staff and RAs wished to spend their time with the 'thinking work' – seeing it as integral to who they are. Neither group seemed eager to engage in administrative work, despite recognising it as needing to be done.

Certainly, the participants echo what many academic staff perceive to be essential to their work: to do research, which they associate with creativity, discovery and recognition (Rosewell & Ashwin, 2019). This creative and productive work demands the kind of time that many academic staff feel they lack. Ylijoki (2013) draws on interviews with Finnish academic staff who contrast desirable and undesirable aspects of research: 'real work refers to one's research and to a lesser extent to teaching, whereas wasted time involves all kinds of externally imposed tasks and managerial duties which are perceived as unnecessary or uninteresting' (p. 250). The time for thinking and creative work is highly valued because it is presumed to be the work that matters most. It is thus unsurprising that RAs (many of whom have scholarly training) and academic staff are eager to claim thinking and creative work as their own.

Gendering 'thinking work'

A central thread in how research work is gendered focuses on how thinking and analytical work has tended to be the purview of men, while teaching and administrative work are seen as the responsibility of women (Carruthers

Thomas, 2019; Lynch, 2010; SSFNRIG, 2017). This gendered organisation of academic work also intersects with discourses of race and racism, making access to, and experiences of, the university and research work profoundly difficult for racialised women (Niemann et al., 2020; see also Tate, this volume). Feminist and antiracist scholars have critiqued and interrogated this gendered and racialised organisation of work, which is not to say that it has been dismantled (Henry et al., 2017).

For the academic staff participants, all of whom are involved in research related to social justice and, as noted earlier, are nearly all women and over a third racialised, it is unsurprising that they might strategically prioritise engaging in particular kinds of work. This is a group of academic staff who are likely acutely aware of gender and racial inequity in the academy and that research work is valued more than teaching and service. Some academic staff were mentored on how to address inequity in their working lives; for example, Crystal Seymour describes navigating pay inequity at work:

> A mentor told me that women in the academy would only ever get paid what we should be paid if we move. So, the idea, I reacted negatively to at that time … I try not to tell other people that now, but I think that was a bit true for me, that I felt extremely devalued and disrespected at my prior institution and then came here and feel very much valued, for better or for worse, by this institution.

RAs likewise identified concerns about gender inequity, with several indicating that they did not pursue or stopped pursuing permanent academic positions because of their incompatibility with care work outside the university and the known expectation of being 'careless workers' (Lynch, 2010). RAs also associate their move to research administration as a way out of precarity; for some, the financial security of stable work outweighed their interest in pursuing academic staff positions, increasingly only available in non-permanent forms.[5]

The quest to be productive and funded researchers has meant that most of the academic staff in our study are what Hey (2001) frames as 'time poor' but 'status rich' (p. 77) and what Acker and McGinn (2021) describe as 'fast professors', whose status quo consists of 'working all the time' (p. 90). The academic staff in our study have become successful partly because of their capacity to secure funding, and as noted earlier, many identify with and value highly 'thinking work'. We could consider that undertaking and excelling in particular research activities (e.g. thinking, knowledge production, grant-seeking and research partnerships) is a strategic move that enables access to particular privileges and a more secure position; this is particularly important for women and racialised people who experience exclusion and marginalisation in the academy.

Care work in research

We observe that care work, in contrast to administrative work, which has been similarly devalued in the academy, is often work that academic staff and RAs were willing to engage in. RAs discuss support and care provided to academic staff. For example, Cynthia Quinn has organised an annual retreat for academic staff: 'We are really building a community of writers and supporting academic staff members in focusing on their writing, sharing knowledge, building relationships, learning from each other.' Similarly, Kelly Andrews talks about working with academic staff and how she listens and offers suggestions as they wrestle with career decisions. She describes meeting with a mid-career academic staff member, saying:

> She came, and she said, 'I just want to talk to somebody about this.' She said, 'I started in this and now this is emerging. I haven't given up on this and I'm confused. What should I choose?' And I just said, 'why do you have to choose? Why can't you do both?' And she's 'I'm allowed to do both?' and I'm 'sure, why not?' … and she just seemed so relieved because she really didn't want to abandon what she'd done originally, but this other thing was grabbing her imagination as a researcher.

Here, RAs indicate how they make time and provide emotional support to academic staff as they navigate their work. Their care can be seen as both care for the researchers and for the research itself. By nurturing the researcher, RAs contribute to and sustain research work.

Academic staff frequently describe their experiences of being provided with care and how they, in turn, extend the care they have received to their students and junior colleagues. Debra Carter illustrates this approach:

> It's like 'pay it forward' as they say. There have been people who have done that for me, so of course, I want to do it for other people coming up. … I find that is super helpful if people are willing to help in this way.

Similarly, Judith Lees explains that once she had achieved stability in her career, she was 'ready to collaborate and work with other people and I think it's really quite nice'. Academic staff describe feeling prepared to help others and frame caring for others as a positive experience. Some were concerned that early-career academic staff colleagues might experience a difficult time, given mounting pressure to secure grants and publish frequently. Pamela Underwood states, 'I worry a lot about brand new junior academic staff, particularly women' and that she, reflecting on her own experiences, recommends 'surrounding yourself with people who are supportive and kind'. Descriptions of care that academic staff benefited from, or contributed to, emerged in discussions of career histories, leadership, relationships with project teams, mentoring and supervision.

In the RA and academic staff interviews, acts of caring for people are also a way to care about research. The caring done by RAs and academic staff supports the production of research by enabling those who might be demoralised, uncertain or marginalised to be productive. But it is not just the people who need care, projects are also presumed to need care. Pamela Underwood describes her responsibility for projects saying, 'These projects don't go away; they have a life. They're like babies. They're your children. They're this thing that you are taking care of and stewarding along.' Despite drawing on the intimacy of motherhood and caregiving, the focus of this care is research productivity – not intimacy and love. This care for projects (and staff who work on them) is the kind of caring work that Lynch (2010) posits is professional caring that the academy happily consumes. It serves both a therapeutic and professional function. It makes productivity possible and thus provides something for the hungry institution. Rather than being care work that detracts or interferes with researchers' ability to secure more funding and produce more research output (in the way that women's care work during the pandemic disrupted their ability to produce research; see Carruthers Thomas, this volume; Pereira, 2021), this type of care drives research forward by nurturing academic staff who might otherwise become burnt out or unwilling to work all the time.

Conclusion

Reading across the interviews, we note how deeply RAs and academic staff value research. The conceptual, creative, thinking activity is presumed to be integral to how they understand themselves and their work. Certain kinds of administrative work are eschewed as either not valuable or 'someone else's job'. At first, this sentiment points to how acutely the demand to be what Lynch (2010) frames as careless workers is felt and taken up by participants. But it is never so tidy. Some RAs explicitly discuss stepping off or not applying to the tenure-track path to have time for care work at home, and academic staff described periods of greater or lesser research productivity in relation to when they had greater or fewer care responsibilities (see also Vehviläinen et al., this volume).

Moreover, the kind of care work done for researchers and research itself is more troublesome than perhaps imagined in the careless university Lynch theorises. We observe that many of the women in our study take up and value care work alongside their commitment to thinking work. The desire expressed by the RAs to create an environment for academic staff that is characterised by care and interest, rather than to engage with them as simply tools for securing funding, challenges the kinds of managerial working-upon techniques that might be expected from them (Beime et al., 2021). Further, the academic staff are engaged in social justice scholarship – their care work can be seen as resistance to individualism and competition in research work. Their acts of care might be understood as ways of valuing interdependence and resisting and reframing what it means to do research. This care work speaks to the complexity of gendered labour that can encompass both oppression and resistance.

Through our analysis of care work, a small crack has been exposed in what is valued within research work. Although thinking work is highly valued, participants demonstrate their willingness to trouble what else could count as essential to research. We must then consider administrative support work as another form of feminised labour. In contrast to care work, administrative work remains undesirable. There are many questions to ponder: What makes care work but not administrative work congruent with how academic staff and RAs understand themselves? What could happen if administrative work were valued and seen as an intrinsic part of research? How might hierarchies between staff groups be affected? We pose these questions because we posit that the lack of interest in administrative work continues the distaste for and devaluing of feminised labour. For academic staff, evermore burdened with demands for productivity, eschewing administrative work has not resulted in greater work–life balance. Rather, support from administrative staff is presented as a way to ensure that academic staff can do more. Would it be possible to imagine doing less? Could integrating administrative work into what RAs and academic staff do open up the possibility of running out of time? Perhaps to run out of time is to acknowledge that there is not the possibility of making more work (thinking/creative work or care work) available to the academy. This integration would have significant implications for RAs and academic staff, but even more so for groups we have not yet researched including short-term employees paid by individual grants, other professional and administrative staff, students and community partners. Making space for administrative work as a valued part of research, rather than an interference or distraction, might disrupt the gendered hierarchies of academic labour and the demands for carelessness.

Acknowledgements

The research was supported by the Social Sciences and Humanities Research Council of Canada (435-2017-0104). We thank Sandra Acker, Michelle McGinn, Anne Wagner and Oili-Helena Ylijoki for their feedback on earlier drafts of this chapter.

Notes

1 The RAs working directly with academic staff correspond with Kerridge and Scott's (2018) designation of RAs in operational roles. Likewise, those we describe as having managerial responsibilities correspond with their designation of manager roles with responsibility for a team or area.

124 Marie A. Vander Kloet and Caitlin Campisi

2 In this context, administration refers to university senior leadership; in Canada, this is a combination of academic staff in leadership positions (e.g. dean, provost, president) and high-level professional staff responsible for financial and bureaucratic organisation.
3 Research council grants in the social sciences in Canada are rarely large enough to sustain a full-time staff member (e.g. project manager). Most grants have the expectation or requirement to provide research training for students and most paid employment on grants is given to higher degree students (master's or doctoral). These students may perform some administrative work, but there is strong encouragement to ensure their work on the grant constitutes research training and not clerical work.
4 The SSHRC Common CV is a specifically formatted curriculum vitae required for certain grant applications. The creation of this CV has a reputation as cumbersome.
5 Canadian academic work is characterised by increased precarity. More than half of new academic staff hirings at universities in Canada are for contract teaching appointments, mostly part-time (Pasma & Shaker, 2018, p. 5). Tenured and tenure-track positions are often unavailable. A project at the University of Toronto found that amongst its 10,866 PhD graduates from 2000 to 2015 whose whereabouts could be located, 26% were employed in permanent, tenure-stream positions as of 2016 (Reithmeier et al., 2019). Tenure-stream employment may be even lower for graduates from less research-intensive institutions.

References

Acker, S., & McGinn, M. K. (2021). Fast professors, research funding, and the figured worlds of mid-career Ontario academics. *Brock Education Journal, 30*(2), 79–98. https://doi.org/10.26522/brocked.v30i2.864

Acker, S., McGinn, M. K., & Campisi, C. (2019). The work of university research administrators: praxis and professionalization. *Journal of Praxis in Higher Education, 1*(1), 61–85. https://doi.org/10.47989/kpdc67

Acker, S., & Wagner, A. (2019). Feminist scholars working around the neoliberal university. *Gender and Education, 31*(1), 62–81. https://doi.org/10.1080/09540253.2017.1296117

Allen Collinson, J. (2007). 'Get yourself some nice, neat, matching box files!' Research administrators and occupational identity work. *Studies in Higher Education, 32*(3), 295–309. https://doi.org/10.1080/03075070701346832

Beime, K. S., Englund, H., & Gerdin, J. (2021). Giving the invisible hand a helping hand: how 'Grants Offices' work to nourish neoliberal researchers. *British Educational Research Journal, 47*(1), 1–22. https://doi.org/10.1002/berj.3697

Carruthers Thomas, K. (2019). Genders at work: gender as a geography of power in the academy. In G. Crimmins (Ed.), *Strategies for resisting sexism in the academy* (pp. 187–206). Palgrave Macmillan. https://doi.org/10.1007/978-3-030-04852-5_11

Dhamoon, R. K. (2020). Racism as a workload and bargaining issue. *Socialist Studies, 14*(1), 1–22. https://doi.org/10.18740/ss27273

Dion, M. L., Sumner, J. L., & Mitchell, S. M. (2018). Gendered citation patterns across political science and social science methodology fields. *Political Analysis, 26*(3), 312–327. https://doi.org/10.1017/pan.2018.12

Foster, K., & Birdsell Bauer, L. (2018). *Out of the shadows: experiences of contract academic staff.* Canadian Association of University Teachers Report. https://www.caut.ca/sites/default/files/cas_report.pdf

Gill, R. (2010). Breaking the silence: the hidden injuries of neo-liberal academia. In R. Flood & R. Gill (Eds.), *Secrecy and silence in the research process: feminist reflections* (pp. 228–244). Routledge.

Henry, F., Dua, E., James, C. E., Kobayashi, A., Li, P., Ramos, H., & Smith, M. S. (2017). *The equity myth: racialization and Indigeneity in Canadian universities.* University of British Columbia Press.

Hey, V. (2001). The construction of academic time: sub/contracting academic labour in research. *Journal of Educational Policy, 16*(1), 67–84. https://doi.org/10.1080/02680930010009831

Kerridge, S., & Scott, S. F. (2018). Research administration around the world. *Research Management Review, 23*(1), 1–34.

Lynch, K. (2010). Carelessness: a hidden doxa of higher education. *Arts and Humanities in Higher Education, 9*(1), 54–67. https://doi.org/10.1177/1474022209350104

Maliniak, D., Powers, R., & Walter, B. F. (2013). The gender citation gap in international relations. *International Organization, 67*(4), 889–922. https://doi.org/10.1017/S0020818313000209

McGinn, M. K., Acker, S., Vander Kloet, M., & Wagner, A. (2019). Dear SSHRC, what do you want? An epistolary narrative of expertise, identity, and time in grant writing. *Forum Qualitative Sozialforschung / Forum: Qualitative Social Research, 20*(1). https://doi.org/10.17169/fqs-20.1.3128

Nakhaie, M. R. (2002). Gender differences in publication among university professors in Canada. *Canadian Review of Sociology/Revue canadienne de sociologie, 39*(2), 151–179. https://doi.org/10.1111/j.1755-618X.2002.tb00615.x

Niemann, Y., Gutiérrez y Muhs, G., & Gonzalez, C. (Eds.). (2020). *Presumed incompetent II: race, class, power, and resistance of women in academia.* University Press of Colorado.

O'Meara, K., Kuvaeva, A., Nyunt, G., Waugaman, C., & Jackson, R. (2017). Asked more often: gender differences in faculty workload in research universities and the work interactions that shape them. *American Educational Research Journal, 54*(6), 1154–1186. https://doi.org/10.3102%2F0002831217716767

Pasma, C., & Shaker, E. (2018). *Contract U: contract faculty appointments at Canadian universities.* Canadian Centre for Policy Alternatives. https://policyalterna tives.ca/sites/default/files/uploads/publications/National%20Office/2018/11/Contract%20U.pdf

Pereira, M. do M. (2021). Researching gender inequalities in academic labor during the COVID-19 pandemic: avoiding common problems and asking different questions. *Gender, Work & Organization, 28*(S2), 498–509. https://doi.org/10.1111/gwao.12618

Potter, H., Higgins, G. E., & Gabbidon, S. L. (2011). The influence of gender, race/ethnicity, and faculty perceptions on scholarly productivity in criminology/criminal justice. *Journal of Criminal Justice Education, 22*(1), 84–101. https://doi.org/10.1080/10511253.2010.517653

Reithmeier, R., O'Leary, L., Zhu, X., Dales, C., Abdulkarim, A., Aquil, A., Brouillard, L., Chang, S., Miller, S., Shi, W., Vu, N., & Zou, C. (2019). The 10,000 PhDs project at the University of Toronto: using employment outcome data to inform graduate education. *PLoS ONE, 14*(1), Article e0209898. https://doi.org/10.1371/journal.pone.0209898

Rosewell, K., & Ashwin, P. (2019). Academics' perceptions of what it means to be an academic. *Studies in Higher Education, 44*(12), 2374–2384. https://doi.org/10.1080/03075079.2018.1499717

Side, K., & Robbins, W. (2007). Institutionalizing inequalities in Canadian universities: the Canada Research Chairs program. *NWSA Journal, 19*(3), 163–181. https://muse.jhu.edu/article/224763

Smith, C., Holden, M., Yu, E., & Hanlon, P. (2021). 'So what do you do?': third space professionals navigating a Canadian university context. *Journal of Higher Education Policy and Management*, *43*(5), 505–519. https://doi.org/10.1080/1360080X.2021.1884513

Smith, M. S. (2017). Disciplinary silences: race, Indigeneity, and gender in the social sciences. In F. Henry, E. Dua, C. E. James, A. Kobayashi, P. Li, H. Ramos, & M. S. Smith. *The equity myth: racialization and Indigeneity in Canadian universities* (pp. 239–262). University of British Columbia Press.

Social Sciences Feminist Network Research Interest Group. (2017). The burden of invisible work in academia: social inequalities and time use in five university departments. *Humboldt Journal of Social Relations*, *39*, 228–245. https://digitalcommons.humboldt.edu/hjsr/vol1/iss39/21/

Szekeres, J. (2011). Professional staff carve out a new space. *Journal of Higher Education Policy and Management*, *33*(6), 679–691. https://doi.org/10.1080/1360080X.2011.621193

Vander Kloet, M., & Campisi, C. (2023). Becoming legitimate academic subjects: doing meaningful work in research administration. *Journal of Higher Education Policy and Management*. Advance online publication. https://doi.org/10.1080/1360080X.2023.2222446

Whitchurch, C. (2008a). Beyond administration and management: reconstructing the identities of professional staff in UK higher education. *Journal of Higher Education Policy and Management*, *30*(4), 375–386. https://doi.org/10.1080/13600800802383042

Whitchurch, C. (2008b). Shifting identities and blurring boundaries: the emergence of third space professionals in UK higher education. *Higher Education Quarterly*, *62*(4), 377–396. https://doi.org/10.1111/j.1468-2273.2008.00387.x

Wijesingha, R., & Ramos, H. (2017). Human capital or cultural taxation: what accounts for differences in tenure and promotion of racialized and female faculty? *Canadian Journal of Higher Education*, *47*(3), 54–75. https://doi.org/10.7202/1043238ar

Witteman, H. O., Hendricks, M., Straus, S., & Tannenbaum, C. (2019). Are gender gaps due to evaluations of the applicant or the science? A natural experiment at a national funding agency. *The Lancet*, *393*(10171), 531–540. https://doi.org/10.1016/S0140-6736(18)32611-4

Ylijoki, O. (2013). Boundary-work between work and life in the high-speed university. *Studies in Higher Education*, *38*(2), 242–255. https://doi.org/10.1080/03075079.2011.577524

9

THE GENDERED AFFECTIVE ECONOMY OF FUNDING

Conflicting realities of university leaders and researchers in Finnish academia

Johanna Hokka, Elisa Kurtti, Pia Olsson and Tiina Suopajärvi

Since marketised efforts have entered academia, competition has become a central mechanism by which to govern higher education institutions (HEIs). In both international and national science policy aims, competitive funding mechanisms have been introduced as highly functional governing tools for assuring the quality of research (Wedlin & Hedmo, 2015). At the governmental level, competition has been promoted as a means for modernising HEIs, whereas at the grass-roots level, the all-penetrating competition and performance orientation has involved individual suffering through stress and agony (Gill, 2016) and survival anxiety for managers (Loveday, 2021). These conditions have given rise to a powerful affective economy in which researchers' identities and institutions' prestige are increasingly based on their ability to meet dominant key performance indicators (Morley & Crossouard, 2016). The ever-intensifying competition for funding and resources has led to the polarisation of academia into 'winners' and 'losers', each having different emotional attachments (and detachments) to academia and varying experiences of being part of the academic community (Morley & Crossouard, 2016).

In this study, we apply an affective perspective to analyse gendered practices of research funding in Finland. We are interested in the affective economy constructed by the meaning-making surrounding funding. The concept of the affective economy relies on Sara Ahmed's (2014) theorisations on affect. Rather than psychological dispositions, Ahmed sees emotions as relational, moving in a constant circulation, where emotions signify individuals and collectives morally good or bad or more valuable than others. Emotions may also get 'stuck' with subjects or objects, such as research funding, through repetition of association (pp. 15, 91). Emotions *do* things: they organise social order by aligning individuals into collectives against 'others' and can exclude these others as illegitimate (p. 15). In this chapter, we ask, *what kind of*

DOI: 10.4324/9781003330431-12

gendered affective economy is constructed through university leaders' and researchers' accounts of research funding?

The data in this study consist of individual interviews with university leaders and focus group interviews with researchers in the social sciences and humanities (SSH). It has been argued that in managerially-led universities, managers have been key players in bringing neoliberal values and norms into academia. Consequently, the gap between managers and managed academics has increased. While the managers have internalised goals and working patterns of a corporate management system, the 'managed academics' strive to defend and promote the accounts and values of their professional identities (Winter, 2009). In this study, we relate the leaders' and the researchers' accounts to each other. By this analysis, we can disclose the different realities that come into being through the academic affective economy.

In previous studies, the gendered structure of academia has been illustrated through the dichotomous qualities of feminised care and masculinised, openly individualistic and aggressive competition (e.g. Ivancheva et al., 2019; Lund & Tienari, 2019). It is argued that current academia promotes masculinised competitiveness and bravery for immersion in entrepreneurial and international endeavours, at the expense of feminised ethics of care (Aavik, 2019). By taking affects as a focus of inquiry, we aim to enrich the understanding of these gendered dichotomies. We will show how different affects that are intertwined with these qualities produce and reproduce, but also challenge, the gendered affective economy of academia.

We have chosen to study the accounts of researchers and deans in SSH since these fields are witnessing challenging times under the current technology and innovation-driven science policy context. We have added the accounts of rectors into our analysis, as their notions on funding are crucial in university politics given their top management position. The contemporary science policies that manifest the 'impact' of research, and the methods used to measure that impact, are more favourable for science, technology, engineering and mathematics (STEM) disciplines than for SSH fields (Bastow et al., 2014). This tendency is said to lead to a situation where scholars in SSH must mimic scientists in STEM by focusing more on problem-solving research than on blue-sky thinking in order to survive in the intense competition (Knowles & Burrows, 2014).

Our research context of Finland has one of the most competitive research funding systems in the world, with largely performance-based core state funding and high levels of external, competitive research funding (Kivistö et al., 2019). Although, as elsewhere in Nordic countries, gender equality is strongly promoted at the institutional level, the statistics and previous studies still show the underlying gendered disparities in Finnish academia (e.g. Griffin & Vehviläinen, 2021; Nikunen & Lempiäinen, 2020). Despite the Sámi people and other ethnic minorities living in Finland, race and ethnicity have not historically been part of political consciousness as significant categories of difference (Keskinen et al., 2016); instead, gender has been prioritised as the main line of division and injustice in Nordic societies (Husu, 2000). In this study, the intersectional examination focuses mostly on gender and the implications of masculinised academia but also on the various positions that the interviewees hold from the top of the university hierarchy to grant-funded researchers in precarious situations.

Materials and methods

During the COVID-19 pandemic in 2020 and 2021, we organised three affect cafés over Zoom. These meetings were based on the world café method where participants remain in the same small discussion group throughout the meeting, while the facilitators, each having an assigned theme, move from one group to another (Lorenzetti et al., 2016). The cafés start and end with joint discussions. The open invitation to our cafés attracted 22 participants from SSH disciplines: seven doctoral students, ten postdoctoral researchers and five senior researchers/professors. The participants were affiliated with seven universities. In Finland, the postdoctoral period usually lasts five years, but due to the shortage of funding and positions, it can last up to ten years. All except one of the café participants were women, five held permanent and seven temporary contracts, and nine worked with a scholarship from a research foundation or without funding. All cafés had participants from all career stages. Although some participants were involved in both teaching and research, the focus of the discussions, and consequently our study, is on research. The themes in the cafés dealt with research strategies and their effects on researchers' work, emotions in researchers' work and the daily lives of researchers. The atmosphere in our 1.5- to 2-hour cafés became one of sharing and supporting one another, which created a rather uniform, but still critical, perspective across different career stages. We refer to the cafés with codes AC1–3.

As for the leaders, we held 13 interviews with deans and vice deans (of whom five were from humanities and eight were from social sciences) and seven interviews with rectors and vice rectors (whose backgrounds are in STEM fields, social sciences and humanities) in three universities. Nine of the leaders were women and 11 were men. The participants were contacted by email with details of the project and an invitation to take part in the interviews. All interviews were conducted via Zoom. The interview questions dealt with research strategies, their aims and implementation, emotions concerning the research strategy processes, human resource management, and the interviewees' personal emotions regarding their role in their management positions. Questions about gender and gender-related issues were neither asked in the interviews nor in the cafés. The interviewed leaders were 'manager-academics', as they all had worked in academic roles before becoming managers and did not attain their positions from outside the university (Deem, 2002). We refer to these interviews with codes R (rectors and vice rectors) and D (deans and vice deans) and with identifying consecutive numbers. All participating researchers and leaders are White and most of them have Finnish backgrounds, which reflects the contemporary situation in Finnish academia.

We started our analysis by reading the transcribed materials, listening and watching recordings, and by focusing on the atmosphere and bodily and verbal expressions as signs of emotions that were directed away or towards certain objects and subjects. Quotations from the affect cafés and interviews have been translated into English. During the analysis, we identified three themes related to funding that are affectively dense: (a) research strategies as practices of inclusion or exclusion, (b) disciplinary hierarchies and career opportunities and (c) boasting and distance-taking as competitive practices. Based on these themes, we examined how different objects of emotion, be they academic superstars or SSH researchers opposing competition, are transformed into 'others' within academia (see Ahmed, 2014, pp. 11–12). Through these analyses, we have formulated an affective economy, a web of emotions and their objects, to describe the ambiguous realities in which our study participants live.

Research strategies as practices of inclusion and exclusion

In our analysis, research strategies, a subcategory of university strategies, proved to be emotionally charged since they were tied to particular value judgements. Every university is obliged to formulate strategic goals (commonly referred to as 'strategies') for the Ministry of Education and Culture. Strategies include focus areas (sometimes called key themes or an equivalent), core values, mission statements and so forth. There are specific strategies for areas such as research, teaching, internationalisation and staffing that simultaneously fall under and construct the wider university strategy, which academic units such as faculties are expected to implement. Our interest here is in the research strategies, which contribute to institutional research profiles, i.e. compilations of areas of strength or those that the university wishes to develop. Profiles are meant to differentiate among institutions and concentrate resources and are thus assumed to result in competitive advantages for Finnish universities (Pietilä, 2014). As the broader university strategies and research strategies partially coincide, we have traced their connections in our analysis and, thus, focused not only on specific talk about research strategies but also on how research features in discussions about the broader university strategies.

Research strategies are top-down encouraged priorities for research and research practices, part of the university's strategic management. Strategies provide goals and procedures for publishing, organising research work and applying for funding. At least in theory, each university has a distinguishable strategic profile. In practice, however, these profiles tend to highlight similar aspects when compared to one another. Current strategies incentivise strengthening focus areas for research, applying for international and multi-disciplinary funding, and forming large consortia.

In our research, most of the leaders saw strategies as means by which to 'create a common conversational culture' (D8) and shared goals defined by the community. The leaders present strategies as rational operating principles inclusive of everyone. Nevertheless, the exclusive elements are implicitly part of the strategies as well, as in the argument of a dean that 'strategy is not an order or instruction but a background for people to choose the right things' (D9), suggesting that there are also 'wrong' things to choose. The 'right' choices guide towards excellence, applying for international funding and production of international publications. This idea consequently narrows the scientific heterogeneity and differentiates between valued and less-valued research work. Altogether, for leaders, strategies represent tools by which the university offers facilities and resources for researchers who then are obliged to make the most of them.

In the cafés, most of the researchers, regardless of career stage, had experienced the increasing focus on strategies as alienating or excluding. Strategy 'just puffs from somewhere above' (AC2), forcing oneself to evaluate one's own position in relation to it, in the end even changing oneself and one's research 'so that you would fit into that strategy' (AC1). The problem for them was that the current university strategies implicitly incite researchers to apply for big, multidisciplinary, technology and innovation-oriented project funding. Many of the discussants saw these as distant since they experienced themselves as 'small agents doing small things about small topics' (AC3). They were unwilling to become supporting actors for technological and engineering sciences, which are often associated with economic values and masculinity.

The leaders, by contrast, encouraged SSH researchers to collaborate across multiple disciplines. 'It is clear that if folks do not understand to go beyond the border, to talk with other faculties, then that theme does not have much value in the strategy' (D7). Some rectors even blamed the SSH researchers for passivity and advised them to 'pull themselves together' to create multi-disciplinary collaboration (R6). Especially scholars from the humanities were likely to be rebuked for being the 'ivory tower researchers' who think that 'everything was better before when I was able to do whatever I wanted' (R2). These articulations carry frustration that generates an affective economy, where researchers from the humanities who critique the current situation are the 'others': the passive and moaning killjoys who spoil the university's triumphant goals and who do not have the guts to enter the multidisciplinary and international world of academia. Consequently, they become characterised as non-rational and the emotions become attached to the bodies of humanities scholars, of whom the majority of early-career researchers are women (Academy of Finland, 2021, table 2.11).

Like the leaders, the more senior café discussants, who had participated in strategy making, found strategies mostly inclusive. Some researchers even saw faults in SSH researchers' ways of orienting themselves to the strategy work: 'I somehow wish that [people in the] humanities would be more shameless and braver, that they would make themselves better heard' (AC2). Her criticism is not targeted towards the system but towards those trying to cope within it, as they should change themselves towards a more outspoken, more aggressively competitive character (see Lund & Tienari, 2019; van den Brink & Benschop, 2012). This perspective was supported by some of the discussants who considered that scholars in humanities do not know how to 'sell' their studies strategically in order to thrive and receive large funding. This notion of shamelessness seemingly reflects the neoliberal ideal of the masculinised academic subject (see Lund, 2015).

The value placed on masculinised shamelessness and bravery also become visible in the leaders' interviews, as someone who is ready to 'advance in [their] career and collaborate' (D10) and be vigilant in the face of opportunities is presented as a successful academic. Vigilance is also associated with equality of opportunities, suggesting that women 'can have it all' when it comes to acquiring a family and a successful career. However, rather than seeing equality as a structural factor, it is individualised into personal choices. Accordingly, one must be ready to grasp an opportunity that is beneficial for their career, even if it causes personal sacrifices: 'I get the same answer often: "because I have kids". But I also have [kids] (laughs) … surely, it would be nicer to stay home but if you want to succeed in an academic career, you cannot do that' (R2). This statement is in contradiction with the studies that show how this kind of 'portfolio career' (Blackmore, 2014, p. 93), where people collect skills to enable them to move on career ladders, is constructed around 'mobile men' with fewer care responsibilities both at home and work. Instead of being a question of personal choice, cultural, social and economic structures support men's mobility while preventing women's (Nikunen & Lempiäinen, 2020).

Although gender was not explicitly raised by facilitators in the cafés, it came up in connection with the university hierarchies, challenging the idea of equal opportunities found in the leaders' talk. The related experience in the cafés was that the men, 'the old geezers' club' (AC2), have the power to steer the disciplines (see Monroe et al., 2008). As such, they were considered to have the power to guide money within the university to researchers they considered worth supporting. Those who were criticised were men, but behind this criticism, we read a wider understanding of a specific leadership model that was labelled as masculine. The criticism is targeted towards a non-transparent process, where decisions made in small male-dominated groups exclude not only those whom the decisions affect but also the women who are officially part of the group: 'When you look at our personnel structure, the bosses, there's one woman, and no one listens to her. And the others are like 50-plus old men. It's difficult to become heard, even if you are tenacious' (AC2).

Here, the emotion that is stuck with gender and funding is a combination of frustration and anger. The decision-making processes in academia are still dominated by men, hinting that sufficient progress has not taken place for equality. The use of the word 'club' highlights the fact that the processes are not inclusive but reserved for specific exclusive members of academia. The strategic planning seems to create emotional micropolitics that reproduce hierarchies in academia based on social position and gender (see Bloch, 2012, p. 113). If those who are not participating in the strategic planning are mostly women in SSH disciplines, the risk is that the sense of existing in the academic margin becomes a status quo for them.

Disciplinary hierarchies and career opportunities

Whether or not a researcher should find ways to fit into the strategy was controversial to our café participants. Not fitting in could lead to marginalisation inside the university and make collaboration difficult. In contrast, fitting in and benefiting from it financially and career-wise could mean giving up highly valued academic freedom. Not being able to fit into the strategies generates an affective economy where researchers and their research topics become bypassed or invisible in their organisation (Ahmed, 2014). In the accounts of the discussants, strategies become stuck with fear since they are seen to ignore the relevance of human sciences. Further, their circulation generates anxiety for researchers' career prospects, making them very different from the enthusiastic collaboration and 'hustle' emphasised by the leaders. Some of the deans shared the fear with the researchers by pointing out how, for instance, national thematic funding calls may narrow the freedom of research. A few of the deans also described the university rectors as saturated with naïve 'strategy enthusiasm' since they overestimate the power of strategy over researchers. Hence, while articulating their dissatisfaction with rectors, these deans align themselves with researchers against senior leadership.

In the cafés, academia was described as a ring-shaped structure where the strategy was in the middle and the importance of a research area or discipline was defined by its distance from the strategy. Even when feeling placed in the outer circle, researchers had to strive to find connections with university focus areas in external grant applications (AC2). Connecting one's research application to the university's strategy was seen to be beneficial, or even crucial, to improving one's possibilities for success in large-grant competitions.

Especially deans with a background in humanities called for seeing academic careers as one occupation among others, where being a decent and collegial worker is enough. They also underlined the need to secure the position and freedom of smaller scientific disciplines and saw private funding foundations as important actors in this endeavour. For them, the epistemic premise of SSH fields is to contribute to knowledge formation on the world and humanity, not to mainly support technological innovation, for example.

This aspiration for a better understanding as a core value reflects Lund and Tienari's (2019) depiction of eros: a gender-neutral drive for learning and knowledge-creation for their own sake. The approach is also sensitive to the career-related insecurity that academics face, given that the majority of Finland's researchers do not hold permanent positions (Organisation for Economic Co-operation and Development, 2021).

The hierarchies among disciplines were visible in the highlighted potential of multidisciplinarity, especially in the rectors' interviews. Here, the disciplines in humanities gain legitimacy through multi- and interdisciplinary efforts and funding call successes: 'we are strongly looking for ways how our research in humanities could be connected with other fields of study' (R6). Technology and engineering sciences are presented as higher in the disciplinary hierarchy since the humanities prove their scientific legitimacy by attaching to them. Given the segregation between disciplines, where most academics working in the field of humanities are women while technology and engineering sciences have men in the majority, these legitimation practices make disciplinary hierarchies also gendered hierarchies. These issues were recognised in the cafés, for example, when the discussants wondered how the quantitative arguments made by men in STEM could be considered stronger than the qualitative arguments made by researchers from fields in the humanities with women in the majority. However, in the rectors' strategy talk, worries over the status of SSH disciplines were often brushed off as individuals' needless concerns.

The circulation of affects in the discussions on strategies takes place between those who are and those who are not included in the strategies. The affects stick particularly to individual SSH researchers, whose research themes do not correspond to the strategy due to their small-scale monodisciplinary field. Leaders' interviews (re)construct an ideal academic who is seemingly gender-neutral, agile and supportive of neoliberal science politics yet mostly masculine, since the features of international mobility, pride and confidence in competition are strongly valued (e.g. Blackmore, 2014; Lund, 2015). In researchers' reflections on this 'top scholar', the affective reality they live in is ambiguous: it is shaped by the anxiety of not fitting into the current/future university and by fear of losing academic freedom, and with it, their motivation to do research. In this case, the joyful strategy work that the leaders promote has not (yet) pushed these researchers away from academia but to the margins of it. In the margins, the funding opportunities are different: many researchers in Finland depend on the yearly scholarships of independent foundations since they do not have an employee position at their universities. The bravery of defending disciplinary extensiveness seems to offer academic freedom to study the issues valued by SSH researchers, but simultaneously the economic and career status of these academics remains uncertain. Due to the disciplinary gender segregation in Finnish academia, this status becomes gendered, too.

Boasting and distance-taking as competitive practices

The café discussants brought up the destructive effects of competition for the research community as close colleagues, officemates or even close friends must compete with one another. This was seen to lead to a situation where researchers were willing to share neither disappointments nor successes with their colleagues. Applications are made in secret and the 'wounds are licked alone' (AC1) when the application is rejected. Likewise, received grants are not announced, or they are mentioned in passing, out of awareness of colleagues failing in the same funding call. It also became evident that researchers should show happiness on behalf of a colleague who succeeds, but expressions of bitterness or envy are not allowed.

These aspects of balancing and concealing one's feelings among researchers construct an affective economy that delineates publicly accepted affects. Charlotte Bloch (2012) describes this state of being as an 'academic façade' (p. 43), the upkeep of which is shaped by academics' gender and position. Women and junior academics must be more on their toes than senior men, which includes, for example, not expressing weakness or self-doubt but at the same time not boasting about one's achievements or being angry (pp. 118–127). Ahmed (2021) adds ethnicity, sexuality and disability to this focus on gender by analysing how, for example, Black, Indigenous and transgender academics should adjust to the White, heterosexual histories and structures of Western academia. Meanwhile, White women researchers in precarious positions must make their emotions fit into the marketised, masculinised rules of competition.

In contrast, the leaders openly celebrate the grandeur of getting funding, especially big, international funding such as European Research Council (ERC) money. International funding, the creation of networks and collaboration are mentioned as key factors in the making of research excellence. The university's achievement or the faculty's staff members' funding success is expressed with a contented smile and is attached to thrill and pride, especially when talking about large amounts of funding. ERC funding, for instance, is described as having 'brought in desirable hustle in the faculty' (D2), suggesting that big funding generates a wanted energetic and self-confident atmosphere. The triumphant abstractions, such as 'becoming world-class' or 'world-leading', induce practices of boasting, that on their part, construct an affective economy favourable for global masculinity discourse (Lund, 2015). (Similar boastful language from the United Kingdom government is described by Read and Leathwood in this volume.) According to Lund (2015), global masculinity discourse is connected to regulated international orientation, engagement in market-like behaviour and the adaptation of managerial forms of governance.

In the leaders' interviews, academics who understand the rules of the funding game and are sufficiently agile to find funding are portrayed as reasonable subjects. This agility is associated with bravery in the form of readiness to look for and grasp opportunities. The possibilities for capitalising upon different opportunities can, however, be tied to gendered practices of networking that favour men (see e.g. Monroe et al., 2008). Rationalised neutrality and dismissiveness of structural issues require distance-taking from the object of evaluation. The rationalisation of 'playing the funding game' shapes the power relations by distancing some, often feminised, spheres from power. This affective strategy, via its seeming gender neutrality, can work to normalise patriarchal practices while shrugging off feminist critique as irrational complaints over non-existent problems (Ahmed, 2021).

The researchers brought to light the feeling of always being on the 'losing' side. Social media, especially, tends to construct an image of the 'other' who is always successful and just keeps winning, as was described by a senior researcher: 'the finer points are shared in the social media, and you don't hear all the work behind them [the success]; it is all reduced to the victories' (AC1). The discussion following this argument in the café showed how the academic façade prevents researchers from sharing these feelings, and consequently, the neoliberal mechanism, where the blame is on individuals, continues to work. Altogether, the binary between 'winners' and 'losers', with associated pride and thrill or shame and anxiety (Morley & Crossouard, 2016, p. 151), was reflected in the café participants' descriptions of feelings of bitterness and inferiority arising from other people's success.

The leaders made classifications that expose this polarisation of the affective economy surrounding research funding. Getting funding is seen as proof of academic worth, given the rigorous application evaluation processes. According to a rector, there is no doubt that 'if you get ERC funding, you are a head taller than others' (R3). It becomes clear that minor funding, especially foundation funding, is not as highly acknowledged: 'the three-year Kone Foundation money may be very good for some' (D10). The argument shows that, in the long run, minor funding is not enough, and big funding is invaluable if one wants to continue working in academia. (A similar instance is described by Lucas in this volume.) Despite being aware of the hard competition that researchers must meet, the leaders state how 'this just is the kind of world where you have to bear insecurity' (D5) or 'you have to constantly apply' (D13), suggesting that researchers must be persistent and disciplined to make their way in academia.

The leaders' gloating over big funding is rather distant from the everyday lives of researchers, who bring up how the constant uncertainty of funding influences income and the possibilities of continuing in the academic community. There are, however, deans – both women and men – who show empathy to researchers' constant struggles, ruminating compassionately on researchers' tribulations: 'Constructing one's career is extremely painful. One is rejected many times; does not get funding or positions; the funding period lasts six months or so' (D1). Some deans even note how they have tried to bring in practices to ensure that 'everyone could get a slice of the cake' (D5), so that there would be money to share with a greater number of researchers.

The gendered affective economy of funding **137**

These practices embody empathy towards employees, which is often associated with acts of local and feminised care (Lund & Tienari, 2019). However, these accounts, representing a minority among the leaders, also involved the difficulties in implementing these practices: 'The system works this way, there is nothing to change that. All that can be done is to try to treat the by-products [of the competitive system]' (D12).

The researchers, however, are not powerless in front of the competition. In the cafés, they told how they had started focusing on scientific substance instead of 'wheeling and dealing or power play that would definitely lead to cynicism' (AC2). Focusing on substance works as an affective strategy that enables the grass-roots level mundane interaction and understanding to proceed among disciplines and colleagues while, simultaneously, giving tools for distance-taking from the ongoing competition. According to the researchers, this refusal to follow the competitive rules calls for 'stubborn people' who are ready to 'bang their heads against a brick wall' if needed (AC2). Given this outlook, it may be argued that the refusal to give in to the competition demands even more bravery and obstinacy than obedience to the hegemonic doctrine of competition.

Conclusion

The gendered affective economy generated in the narrated experiences over research funding is constructed by a myriad of circulating emotions, such as fear, frustration, anxiety and thrill. It is also entangled with feelings of bravery and pride, as well as emotional practices of care and persistence. The effects of these emotions are recognised both by researchers and leaders. The researchers live the emotions in relation to their everyday, personal livelihoods. In contrast, the leaders rationalise their organisation's need to survive in the institutional competition, some of them even seem to perceive the neoliberal mechanisms as desirable (cf. Loveday, 2020).

Our study demonstrates the strong affective dissonances between academics and thus reflects the 'othering' in the affective economy described by Ahmed (2014). This othering takes place not only between academic positions but also between different disciplinary interests and epistemic understandings of the role of research. Thus, academic realities can be experienced very differently, depending on the disciplinary background and position one holds in academia. Our analysis also shows that, from the Finnish perspective, the intersectionality within academia is still very much problematised via gender, academic position and disciplinary background, while race and ableism, for instance, did not become topical in the discussions and interviews of this study. This is partly due to the general Whiteness of Finnish academia, but the framing of our research and our recruitment process might not have been completely inclusive either. For example, we advertised the first cafés only in Finnish and we did not ask about discriminatory practices in the interviews.

As our analysis shows, gender is focal in the affective economy of funding. First, it becomes intertwined with research strategies and the way different disciplines are included or excluded. As our focus has been on the SSH fields, areas that often have women in the majority, especially at earlier career stages in Finland, accounts of the researchers and leaders generate a polarised affective economy, where SSH researchers feel excluded from strategies, while the leaders, both women and men, manifest strategies as rational operating tools, open for everyone. Despite the seeming objectivity presented by the leaders, it is the SSH fields that should assimilate to STEM fields, a position that makes the gendered biases visible. However, disciplinary and status hierarchies shape the leaders' sense-making of the funding system and its relation to strategies: the rectors expressed their alignment with neoliberal values more than deans, while deans in humanities were the most critical of such values.

Second, the decision-making processes concerning funding and research strategies are seen as gendered. Our café discussants, nearly all women, argued that the power to make decisions is in the hands of older men. This understanding was combined with leadership that is characterised by secrecy and concentration of power. Meanwhile, most of the leaders described how the processes guiding strategic planning were participatory and communal. Furthermore, the emotional micropolitics (Bloch, 2012) of academia are constructed by balancing between emotions and rationality. On the one hand, this balancing makes the different gendered agencies, the feminist carer and killjoy and the masculine spokesman, visible. On the other hand, the 'equality of possibilities' emphasised by some of the leaders passed over structural factors, such as gender or academic position. The researchers, however, challenged this understanding that individuals were wholly responsible for their fate. Although some deans sympathised with the researchers, it became evident that they found few opportunities to remedy the researchers' conditions. Thus, it may be argued that the neoliberal system sets limitations to implement the practices of local, feminised care at the managerial level.

The entrance of managerialism, the audit culture and competitive logic is said to bring about a neoliberal subject: an ideal academic who is productive, internationally mobile and entrepreneurial (Archer, 2008) and a cultural construction that embraces masculine values and practices (Lund, 2015). The entrepreneurial and internationally mobile orientation calls for carefree travel and networking time and, thus, delegation of care and care work to others, usually to women (Aavik, 2019; Blackmore, 2014; see also Vander Kloet & Campisi, this volume). Besides being carefree, the ideal academic must openly perform competitive spirit, self-sufficient boasting and bravery while immersing themselves in different international and multidisciplinary networks.

The features of a neoliberal university are recognisable from the ways our interviewees and discussants talk about contemporary Finnish academia. However, an affective perspective can reveal varying academic realities. From the leaders' points of view, internationalisation, partaking in big, international funding calls and the creation of multidisciplinary networks often became attached to bravery, in contrast to those SSH researchers who were perceived as comfort-loving, ivory-tower researchers not willing to step into the international and multidisciplinary arena. However, the SSH researchers' acts of distance-taking from the competitive rules and conviction to study a topic regardless of its value as strategically marketable knowledge can be seen as a demonstration of bravery as well. The frustration, anxiety and passion over one's work make these researchers resist the competitive funding rules, while simultaneously, putting their careers and being in academia at stake. In this sense, besides the hegemonic understanding of bravery as vigilance to follow the masculinised competitive rules and practices of academia, bravery may also work as a practice that indicates feminised, and feminist, resistance to the competition.

When focusing on gendered aspects of research funding as an affective economy, multiple lived affective realities come into being. In leaders' interviews and café discussions, a similar ideal academic subject is recognised. Leaders construct it as gender-neutral, though characterised by features that are usually understood as masculine: competitive, opportunistic, mobile and, to some extent, lacking in care commitments. The researchers describe this subject as something opposite to themselves. Not identifying with the ideal employee of one's work community makes these researchers feel unfit for neoliberal academia. Simultaneously, they carve space for a cultural construction of the 'ordinary' employee, giving them some leeway in relation to a hegemonic understanding of an ideal employee. This circulation strengthens the sense of community of the 'non-ideal' academics.

For most leaders in our study, the neoliberal organisation they are managing generates a seemingly rational reality. However, as our analysis shows, both the negative affects the leaders attach to resistant researchers and the frustration and anger aimed at the leadership by the researchers, who oppose and refuse to become the ideal neoliberal subjects, distance the groups from each other. The affective economy constructed in our data also includes worry and care for the future and academic freedom in the SSH fields, a circulation that both the researchers and some of the deans of our study are part of. This circulation stirs the divisive affective movements by pulling researchers and their managers towards each other. Consequently, the constructed affective economy contains realities in universities that are both apart and overlapping.

Acknowledgements

We would like to thank the researchers and leaders who participated in our study. We would also like to thank the Kone Foundation for funding the Academic Affects project and the Finnish Cultural Foundation for funding Elisa Kurtti's doctoral dissertation.

Authors' note

Authors' names are in alphabetical order. The authors have contributed equally to the text.

References

Aavik, K. (2019). Crafting neoliberal futures in the strategic plans of Estonian universities. *Futures: the Journal of Policy, Planning and Futures Studies, 111,* 148–158. https://doi.org/10.1016/j.futures.2018.10.003

Academy of Finland. (2021). *Tieteen tila –tilastot: tutkimuksen honkilöstö* [State of science statistics: research personnel]. https://www.aka.fi/globalassets/2-suomen-a katemian-toiminta/2-tietoaineistot/tieteen-tila–tilastot-tutkimuksen-henkilosto.pdf

Ahmed, S. (2014). *The cultural politics of emotion* (2nd ed.). Edinburgh University Press.

Ahmed, S. (2021). *Complaint!* Duke University Press.

Archer, L. (2008). The new neoliberal subjects? Young/er academics' constructions of professional identity. *Journal of Education Policy, 23*(3), 265–285. https://doi.org/10.1080/02680930701754047

Bastow, B., Dunleavy, P., & Tinkler, J. (2014). *The impact of the social sciences: how academics and their research make a difference.* SAGE. https://doi.org/10.4135/9781473921511

Blackmore, J. (2014). 'Wasting talent'? Gender and the problematics of academic disenchantment and disengagement with leadership. *Higher Education Research & Development, 33*(1), 86–99. https://doi.org/10.1080/07294360.2013.864616

Bloch, C. (2012). *Passion and paranoia: emotions and the culture of emotion in academia.* Ashgate.

Deem, R. (2002). Talking to manager-academics: methodological dilemmas and feminist research strategies. *Sociology, 36*(4), 835–855. https://doi.org/10.1177/00380385020360040

Gill, R. (2016). Breaking the silence: the hidden injuries of neo-liberal academia. *Feministische Studien, 34*(1), 39–55. https://doi.org/10.1515/fs-2016-0105

Griffin, G., & Vehviläinen, M. (2021). The persistence of gender struggles in Nordic research and innovation. *Feminist Encounters: A Journal of Critical Studies in Culture and Politics, 5*(2), 28. https://doi.org/10.20897/femenc/11165

Husu, L. (2000). Gender discrimination in the promised land of gender equality. *Higher Education in Europe, 25*(2), 221–228. https://doi.org/10.1080/713669257

Ivancheva, M., Lynch, K., & Keating, K. (2019). Precarity, gender and care in the neoliberal academy. *Gender, Work & Organization, 26*(4), 448–462. https://doi.org/10.1111/gwao.12350

Keskinen, S., Tuori, S., Irni, S., & Mulinari, D. (2016). *Complying with colonialism: gender, race and ethnicity in the Nordic region.* Routledge.

Kivistö, J., Pekkola, E., Berg, L. N., Hansen, H. F., Geschwind, L., & Lyytinen, A. (2019). Performance in higher education institutions and its variations in Nordic policy. In R. Pinheiro, L. Geschwind, H. Foss Hansen, & K. Pulkkinen (Eds.), *Reforms, organizational change and performance in higher education: a comparative account from the Nordic countries* (pp. 37–68). Palgrave Macmillan. https://doi.org/10.1007/978-3-030-11738-2_2

Knowles, C., & Burrows, R. (2014). The impact of impact. *Etnográfica. Revista do Centro em Rede de Investigação em Antropologia, 18*(2), 237–254. https://doi.org/10.4000/etnografica.3652

Lorenzetti, L. A., Azulai, A., & Walsh, C. A. (2016). Addressing power in conversation: enhancing the transformative learning capacities of the world café. *Journal of Transformative Education, 14*(3), 200–219. https://doi.org/10.1177/1541344616634889

Loveday, V. (2021). 'Under attack': responsibility, crisis and survival anxiety amongst manager-academics in UK universities. *The Sociological Review, 69*(5), 903–919. https://doi.org/10.1177/0038026121999209

Lund, R. W. B. (2015). *Doing the ideal academic – gender, excellence and changing academia* [Unpublished doctoral dissertation]. Aalto University. http://urn.fi/URN:ISBN:978-952-60-6296-9

Lund, R., & Tienari, J. (2019). Passion, care, and eros in the gendered neoliberal university. *Organization, 26*(1), 98–121. https://doi.org/10.1177/1350508418805283

Monroe, K., Ozyurt, S., Wrigley, T., & Alexander, A. (2008). Gender equality in academia: bad news from the trenches, and some possible solutions. *Perspectives on Politics, 6*(2), 215–233. https://doi.org/10.1017/S1537592708080572

Morley, L., & Crossouard, B. (2016). Gender in the neoliberalised global academy: the affective economy of women and leadership in South Asia. *British Journal of Sociology of Education, 37*(1), 149–168. https://doi.org/10.1080/01425692.2015.1100529

Nikunen, M., & Lempiäinen, K. (2020). Gendered strategies of mobility and academic career. *Gender and Education, 32*(4), 554–571. https://doi.org/10.1080/09540253.2018.1533917

Organisation for Economic Co-operation and Development. (2021). *Reducing the precarity of academic research careers* (OECD Science, Technology and Industry Policy Papers, no. 113). OECD Publishing. https://www.oecd.org/publications/reducing-the-precarity-of-academic-research-careers-0f8bd468-en.htm

Pietilä, M. (2014). The many faces of research profiling: academic leaders' conceptions of research steering. *Higher Education, 67*(3), 303–316. https://doi.org/10.1007/s10734-013-9653-5

van den Brink, M., & Benschop, Y. (2012). Slaying the seven-headed dragon: the quest for gender change in academia. *Gender, Work & Organization, 19*(1), 71–92. https://doi.org/10.1111/j.1468-0432.2011.00566.x

Wedlin, L., & Hedmo, T. (2015). Transnational organisations defining quality and excellence. In L. Wedlin & M. Nedeva (Eds.), *Towards European science* (pp. 105–125). Edward Elgar Publishing.

Winter, R. (2009). Academic manager or managed academic? Academic identity schisms in higher education. *Journal of Higher Education Policy and Management, 31*(2), 121–131. https://doi.org/10.1080/13600800902825835

10

BLACK WOMEN ACADEMICS, RESEARCH FUNDING AND INSTITUTIONAL MISOGYNOIR IN THE UNITED KINGDOM

Shirley Anne Tate

In the United Kingdom (UK), the highest academic designation is 'professor',[1] a rank that remains predominantly White and male. In 2021–2022, of 21,760 professors where 'race' was known, 12% were identified as 'ethnic minorities' (Higher Education Statistics Agency [HESA], 2023). This statistic combines Black designations with other 'ethnic minorities',[2] which hides the fact that only 165 – less than 1% – of the UK professoriate was Black. Of the 30% of professors who were women, it is unclear how many were Black. In 2017–2018, there were 35 Black women professors in the UK (Advance HE, 2019, p. 258, Table 5.9).

Black academics are also under-represented in figures for research funding awards from UK research councils (UK Research and Innovation [UKRI], 2023a). Award rates are the percentages of applications that are successful. Statistics are given for principal investigators (PIs), co-investigators (Co-Is) and fellowship recipients. From 2015–2016 to 2019–2020, the award rate for Black PIs was under 15%, less than other 'racial groups' (such as 28% White, 21% Asian).[3] In some of these years, only ten or fewer PI awards were made to Black scholars. For fellowships aimed at early-, mid- or senior-career researchers, Black academics received ten awards across the whole period. UKRI controls some eight billion pounds of government funding (UKRI, 2023c). Access to some of that funding as a PI or fellow is important for Black women's research standing and careers.

For the first time, UKRI (2023a) has published some intersectional data combining gender and ethnicity. PI award rates in 2020–2021 were 16% for Black women and 12% for Black men. The award rate for Asian women was also low at 12%, while for Asian men it was 25%. White men had the highest award rate, at 30%, followed by White women at 28%. The consequence of low award rates is few new PIs: 10 Black women and 12 Black men in 2020–2021.

DOI: 10.4324/9781003330431-13

Black women and Black men each received less than 1% of the PI awards in that year. However, Black women co-investigators had the highest award rate (33%), a finding that calls for explanation (UKRI, 2023a, Figure 20).

This chapter draws on qualitative data from 13 Black women academics at various career stages in the arts, humanities and social sciences in Wales, Scotland and England. From a contact list of 30 academic staff, some of whom were known to me and others who were contacted through snowball sampling, 13 responded to an online questionnaire with closed and open questions asking if they had ever been PIs, Co-Is or research fellows, and for their institutional experiences of applying for research funding, understandings of hindrances to Black women's funding success and suggestions about what would enable better funding outcomes. Data were analysed using discourse analysis (Parker, 1999; Tate, 2005/2020; Van Dijk, 1997).

My analysis focuses on institutional misogynoir – that is, anti-Black woman racism (Bailey & Trudy, 2018) – featuring the respondents' experiences of PI, Co-I and fellowship funding; the 'institutional closed shop' hindrances to accessing funding; and what they believe can help 'beyond less racism'. In the Afterword, I look at the funding future framed by the continuing UK inter-sectionality and critical race studies culture war, meaning that Black women's research will continue to be the target of institutional misogynoir. Let us move to look briefly at the UK funding landscape.

The UK funding landscape

UK research funding is a mixture of government money going directly to institutions and external competitive awards. The Research Excellence Framework (REF) is government performance-based funding rewarding 'excellence', used to shape university management and research outputs (Papatsiba & Cohen, 2020; see also Lucas, this volume). Conducted approximately every seven years, the REF is undertaken by four UK higher education funding bodies: Research England, the Scottish Funding Council, the Higher Education Funding Council for Wales, and the Department for the Economy, Northern Ireland. Its aim is to secure a world-class research base within universities, ensure accountability for public investment in research, produce evidence of impact beyond academia and provide bench-marking for selective funding allocation. Higher-ranked institutions like the 24 Russell Group universities, which include Oxford and Cambridge and some 'redbrick universities' like Bristol and Liverpool, continue to accrue more funding than 'post-1992' universities, former polytechnics and colleges of higher education given university status in 1992, which occupy a lower tier in terms of research capacity, global reputation and financial resources (Papatsiba & Cohen, 2020). The REF assesses three elements in university submissions: 'the quality of *outputs* (e.g. publications, performances, and exhibitions), their *impact* beyond academia, and the *environment* that supports research' (REF, ca. 2017, para. 4). Academics entered for the REF benefit through workload reduction, extra time for research and career progression. A 2023 analysis indicates that Black academics were less likely than White academics, and women less likely than men, to be submitted to the 2021 REF assessment (REF, 2023).

UKRI is a public body launched in April 2018 by the Department for Business, Energy and Industrial Strategy, bringing together seven disciplinary funding councils, including the Arts and Humanities Research Council (AHRC); the Economic and Social Research Council (ESRC); and five others focused on science, technology or medicine.[4] The AHRC and ESRC are most likely to be the funders relevant to the interview participants to be discussed in later sections. Both councils have 'delivery plans' (AHRC, 2022; ESRC, 2022) that set forth their various plans and priorities. Equality, diversity and inclusion (EDI) are included as commitments in both documents but not in great detail, referring to the more general UKRI (2023b) EDI strategy. 'Diversity' is preferred over specific mentions of race or ethnicity in the delivery plans.

The UKRI funds approximately 1,600 fellowships either directly through individual applications to its seven funding councils or through research organisations (including universities) that already have URKI funding and wish to have fellows working with them. Fellowships enable researchers to devote time to research and develop as research leaders through training, mentorship and international placements (UKRI, 2023d). European Union funding has been another source for research grants; however, it has been jeopardised by Brexit from January 2022. The terms for the UK to associate with Horizon Europe and its €95.5 billion (£81.4 billion) funding were formalised in September 2023 (UKRI, 2023e).

Institutional misogynoir and funding

The majority of the 13 respondents had not received PI funding. Of the four who had received PI funding, there was one lecturer, with the others being either associate professors (senior lecturers) or professors. The responses speak to a UK ecosystem of funding from charities, non-governmental organisations, universities and national/local UK governments, but less often the more prestigious UKRI councils and EU funding described in the previous section. The funding sources mean that research is focused on addressing the funders' issues rather than being more desirable autonomous projects (Papatsiba & Cohen, 2020). The researcher with AHRC funding was a Co-I on an AHRC Network Grant specifically targeting research on the African diaspora. The respondent who had PI funding most recently was a lecturer who did not get a research grant but a year-long Impact Grant funded by UKRI–ESRC and her research-intensive university. Impact grants are research fellowships which give the opportunity to develop as a leader in research and innovation by investing in individuals to support individual research, knowledge exchange and professional development. The majority of the respondents had *not* been research fellows and did not know any Black women research fellows. Of the three who had been fellows, one had a week-long fellowship, one had been a fellow at a national centre and another at an international association. However, none of these has the prestige and positive career impact of a UKRI research fellowship.

Irrespective of their career stage, inequity in accessing research funding as PIs and fellows affects promotions and career progression because of the institutional expectation that PI funding is necessary. Two respondents flesh out this point:

> I'm not sure about this but I do get the sense that often at universities Lecturers are expected to have PI experience before being considered for Senior Lecturer roles. In case it's helpful to know, I am a Lecturer.[5]

> It is not explicit but it is certainly implied. PI is favoured over Co-I, but this is not written in documentation, but during annual evaluation meetings, it is clear you should be leading on bids and how that fits within the promotions criteria.

The lack of certainty about the expectations for funding for internal promotion points to a dearth of mentoring. 'Getting the sense' of the requirements means implicit knowledge of the link between PI status and promotion circulating within institutional culture, which is not necessarily a part of the criteria because it is not in institutional documents. It is the unknown and implied that form an institutional culture where institutional misogynoir (Bailey & Trudy, 2018) thrives, repelling anti-racist challenges because of what Deborah Gabriel (2024) calls 'White faculty regimes'.

Gabriel (2024) asserts that racial equity in universities is impossible while discriminatory practices remain that confer White privilege alongside inequalities for Black academic staff (i.e. faculty). UK university equality schemes like Athena Swan and the Race Equality Charter[6] aim to address gender and racial inequality but mask continuing White supremacy and an institutional Whiteness resistant to change (Ahmed, 2021; Bhopal & Pitkin, 2020; Doharty et al., 2021; Tate, 2013). Institutional 'commitment' to equality, diversity and inclusion coexists with intersectional racial disparities, that is, the fact that race, gender, sexuality, gender identity and class, amongst other intersections, impact Black women's academic careers. For example, some respondents say they are routinely spoken to about their research failings and institutional expectations during annual performance appraisals and mentorship meetings. Thus, they are not actively mentored for success in PI or fellowship applications. This is one aspect of an institutional misogynoir in which racial injustice thrives 'without the need for choreographed and pre-meditated racist intentionality' (Meer, 2022, p. 9). This is because White faculty regimes dominate upper and middle management, control who has access to research funding and researcher development funding, determine what counts as research or curriculum and influence who is recruited or who progresses in their career.

White faculty regimes ensure that the majority of the respondents are not encouraged to apply for funding as PIs. If PI funding is an 'implied' and 'unknown' key to promotion and advancement, the Black woman underclass will continue within academia through exclusion. Even for those who responded yes to the question 'Were you encouraged to apply for funding as a PI?', there is a pattern of Black women academics not being mentored by *senior academics*. They access help from institutional research offices which may not have discipline-specific knowledge or from personal professional networks of supportive colleagues elsewhere. There is funnelling of Black women by university research offices towards calls for funding applications that they believe are relevant, such as one from the AHRC in celebration of the UN International Decade for Peoples of African Descent, where for one respondent, 'the research office at my institution flagged up the call, and I applied'. Institutional funnelling restricts the possibilities for applications in a wider range of research areas. The expectation that all Black women academics work on race/racism and want to build their research within that area is a widely held misconception. Significantly too, in terms of systemic inequality is that only two women mentioned discussing research applications with departmental mentors, but only one got feedback on the proposal and institutional research office support:

> I received the staff email about the funding and discussed it with my mentor and one of my colleagues in the department. My colleague … at the time had got a small funding for research, she said that she would send her project for me to see but never did. My mentor gave me feedback when I was shortlisted for the fund. During the process of writing and rewriting the project one of the staff members in the research department was a good support teaching me basic vernacular and administrative procedures in research grant applications.

Despite this one positive example of what mentoring could look like, Black women academics lack institutional mentorship or, indeed, sponsorship, and access to extensive internal academic research networks. Institutional misogynoir hinders women's research prospects because, as one participant says, 'all too often, opportunities are a closed shop'.

Hindrance: 'all too often, opportunities are a closed shop'

Hindrance is the institutional reality. Respondents spoke about institutional misogynoir because of excess workload, the under-representation of Black women academics, inaccessible research networks, rules disallowing shared PI positions, lack of appropriate field-knowledgeable mentors and support staff, absence of good research mentoring, no institutional interest in areas of race intersectional research, knowledge gaps of funders and their assessors about appropriate race-related methods and literature, and funding practices that favour older and elite institutions over post-1992 universities. The (im)possibility of funding is already hardwired into the research ecosystem as an institutional hindrance for Black women.

Sara Ahmed (2021, p. 69) talks about the blockages in institutional complaints in universities from which we can see 'institutional mechanics'. I am reading the respondents' words as windows into the mechanics of institutional misogynoir. For one respondent, institutional misogynoir ensures that she is locked out of opportunities in a context where 'funders do not fund research proposals from Black women' and 'if your research is on race the funding bodies have not funded this area until recently'. For example, government publications tend to use 'ethnicity' as their stand-in for race/racism, which is problematic for shared organisational understandings of strategic institutional approaches to racialised gender spoken about by the respondents. To be a Black woman and to do research applications on race already places you at a disadvantage as PI or fellow material and locates the work outside the normal disciplinary expectations within departments. This othering is part of Black women's experience whatever their career stage.

Black women are located as bodies out of place, both generally (Puwar, 2004; Tate, 2013; Tate & Page, 2018) and in the academy specifically (Gabriel & Tate, 2017; Tate, 2014, 2021). They are made into outsiders through not receiving mentoring, support or research network inclusion. One respondent said what was needed was positive action because of her experience of being left out of White-only cliques, having no research support because of a lack of understanding of race and social justice pedagogy, and *having her proposal changed* by an associate dean, which made it non-feasible and un-fundable. Institutional sabotage is perhaps not uncommon as all applications go through internal review and approval processes before submission. If internal reviewers have no theoretical/methods knowledge while overriding the academics' expertise, then failure is certain. Her words illustrate systematic institutional exclusion of applications for research funding and no positive action measures to address under-representation of Black women academics as PIs:

> I applied for funding on two occasions but the research support team lacked understanding on the subject (race and pedagogy/race and social justice). There were no specific strategies at the university to address that under-representation of Black women as PIs or successfully applying for research funding. But other white colleagues had their own clique and collaborated on funding bids without inviting or including me. In addition, I feel my last funding application to the British Academy would have been successful if the Associate Dean did not change the project timeline from two years to one year, making it unfeasible.

Added to women being funnelled by institutions into race research and the hardwiring of who gets funding into the research ecosystem, we see a bleak research funding landscape. Lack of institutional research support shapes who gets funding, as does where one works. As said earlier and in the next extract, working at a Russell Group university could increase one's chances of being continually funded, but although institutional support could be readily available, institutional misogynoir applies:

> The first issue is that there are very few Black women academics in Arts and Humanities posts in UK universities. The second is that research funding is regularly allocated to high-ranking or 'prestigious' institutions, where there are fewer Black women in post. In the 25 years that I was at my previous institution I was perhaps the third member of staff in the Arts and Literature Faculty to receive funding from an external source. The problem is circular; once an academic receives funding, it becomes easier to be successful with a second application. Success also requires research support and many institutions do not provide this.

Outside research-intensive universities, Black women struggle because their workloads afford them very little time to actively search for grant opportunities. For those on teaching-only contracts, the possibility of time for making such applications is even more constrained. For others who are on teaching-and-research contracts, the expectation is that they will contribute to the REF with 3* or 4*[7] outputs, apply for grants and carry a full workload of teaching and service to the department and university. Time for writing applications is a precious institutional commodity:

> Often it feels as though Black women are facing a cycle of having to 'find' the time to apply for grants to be 'provided' with the time to apply in the first place (particularly when some grant application calls have very tight turn-around expectations). It is difficult for many Black women to even pursue the sort of opportunities that might help them to do the work that they want to do and which may be work that could be beneficial to many people.

Black women are excluded by workload pressures institutionally because they rarely get reductions in teaching, service and pastoral (advising) work to enable them to have the time and resources to apply:

> Also the significant amount of time that is often required in order to complete grant applications means that many people aren't able to submit an application for consideration, particularly Black women, who are among those who are least likely to have reduced workload, e.g. we rarely have reduced teaching, pastoral, academic service expectations, etc., to help provide us with the time and resources to complete such applications.

Lack of grant funding, especially as PIs, means one's career falters. Therefore, respondents often had to make hard career choices and exclude themselves from applying because of health, well-being, and the detrimental impacts of the culture of long hours needed to make applications. The next respondent talks about the decision being bittersweet and frustrating, because of the impacts on career progression internally and externally:

> I recently made the decision *not* to apply for two grants that I was interested in and preparing to apply for. ... Realistically my workload is such that completing these grant applications could potentially come at a cost to my health. ... I would have to do a lot of late night and weekend work/long hour days which I knew could be bad for me (particularly as someone who has been dealing with the ongoing impact of long-COVID for more than a year). It was bittersweet making the decision to pause my potential grant application activities, as it felt good to prioritise my health and wellbeing and boundaries around work, but frustrating to reflect on the reality that without significant forms of workload relief and access to other resources, the work of completing grant applications may be at odds with the health and wellbeing of many Black women, especially those who are chronically ill or disabled.

The next extract highlights the difficulties of grant success working within departments and a funding ecosystem that has a disdain for race research. The extract points to institutional misogynoir's operation in departments, university structures/processes/practices and funder focus on normative disciplinary epistemologies/research methodologies that are inimical to success:

> There is too much of a 'pot-luck' approach to whether a Black woman can 1) get funding and 2) convince funders she is PI material if she hasn't already got an established track record of funding. Money attracts money and this is difficult if she is working in an area like mine (race and education) with a wider disdain for race research (and consequent lack of funding) and a hostile or nonchalant department that does not care whether she obtains funding as PI until it is time to performance manage her out. I have found my department supportive of my work and I have obtained funding as a Co-I, but now writing a bid as a PI, there's a lot of gaps that I am slowly plugging. But it shouldn't take until writing applications to see that.

The question of what needs to be done to ameliorate this situation led to the suggestion that racism was key but what is needed beyond 'less racism' were approaches, knowledge systems and attitudes which would be decolonial and antiracist at individual, university and funder levels.

Help: decolonisation and antiracism

Thinking about what can be done to enable their success, respondents spoke about the REF as needing to be antiracist and decolonised in terms of its judgements of quality and impact; who becomes expert panel members and which research topics, epistemologies and methodologies are valued. The REF is considered to be a type of peer review, as academics are nominated (by organisations with an interest in research) and some of the nominees are then appointed to the panels that assess submitted materials. There is an open application process for chairs of panels. Four overarching subject groupings each contain multiple expert panels.

In recent years, concern has been expressed about the composition of the assessment panels. The report, *Analysis of Full REF 2021 Panel Membership* (REF, 2021), analysed the representation of 'protected characteristics' across REF-appointed panels. (Protected characteristics defined by UK equality legislation include age, disability, race, sex and sexual orientation.) The key points of the report make interesting reading. First, the proportion of the appointed and nominated pool from Black, Asian and minority ethnic backgrounds is 'roughly consistent with the population of permanent professors' (p. 1), although the document stated that 'further work' was necessary to increase Black, Asian and minority ethnic representation (p. 2). As noted earlier, 'professors' are the top tier of academic staff, and it is not surprising that appointments to panels would over-represent this group of scholars. The representation of women overall has improved, and their proportion of appointed members is equivalent to the wider academic population (p. 1); however, the figures on gender are not shown as racially disaggregated. There are no race or gender disaggregated data for disability but there have been increases in the nomination pool and there is alignment with the current academic population with permanent positions (p. 1). Both the nomination process for panel members and the application for chairs are potentially discriminatory. Although uncertain about the process of these appointments, the respondents assert that those within local and national academic cliques, with institutional support to become PIs on funded projects, and a workload giving them time to publish 3* or 4* articles and monographs, will be nominated and appointed.

Within the auspices of the REF, a group named the Equality and Diversity Advisory Panel (EDAP) is charged with advising the funding bodies and the REF teams on issues related to equality and diversity. Based on the shortcomings of earlier REF iterations, the EDAP encouraged increased representation of under-represented groups on REF 2021 panels, as well as introducing a number of other EDI-related measures, such as providing contextual data to nominating bodies on representation of different protected characteristics, introducing a 'Fairness in REF assessment' training unit for panel chairs and later for other assessment panel members (focused on the concept of 'unconscious bias'[8]) and asking panels to complete a monitoring form (REF, 2021, p. 2; REF, 2022).

Analysis of the composition of the REF 2021 panels shows that of the 920 panel members with known ethnicity, only five were Black (REF, 2021, p. 22). The document indicates that there are only 135 Black professors in the academic staff record of the Higher Education Statistics Agency, so the five panel members, like the professors, are 1% of the relevant population. 'Unconscious bias' training, EDI compliance and collecting gap data are the usual REF approaches to EDI, which fail to acknowledge institutional misogynoir and make anti-racist changes. What we see is that under-representation of Black women as professors feeds through into their under-representation in the nomination pool as well as applications to be appointed as expert panel chairs. The EDAP final report (REF, 2022) still urges 'institutions to understand the impact of structural inequalities … and make progress in breaking down long-standing barriers' (p. 28).

If we agree with Encarnación Gutiérrez Rodríguez (2015) that European universities are for White national elites, REF and funders' judgements are impacted by the coloniality of knowledge. The coloniality of knowledge dictates that the disciplinary canon, acceptable research topics, and evaluations of 'quality' and 'impact' are not devoid of institutional misogynoir. Pertinent comments by respondents about the REF and funding bodies were that what is needed is (a) 'to decolonise the REF system so that grant capture and 3*/4* journal publications aren't metrics of excellence but that relevant and socially transformative research is' and (b) 'funding bodies would need to decolonise their selection criteria and selection processes for funding [more Black women PIs and research fellows] to occur'. For one participant, decolonisation of the REF and internal/external funding processes can occur only if the whole research ecosystem shifts to 'incorporate new possibilities to frame research, using different epistemological and empirical frameworks other than the standardised in British universities'. This shift would enable 'new language for creative research committed to Black communities'. As part of decolonisation, 'antiracist practices must be included with specific understanding that Black women are systematically marginalised in the application process'. The need for this shift also extends to prestigious research fellowships.

Only one respondent in a research-intensive university has a UKRI fellowship and no one else had received one or knew anyone who had. As two respondents remind us, 'there may be structural inequalities in the system of awarding funding' and 'greater awareness is needed about discrimination by funders'. Further, 'unless there is recognition of the fundamental white supremacist assumptions in what funding is for and how the system of allocation does not even seem to understand what it is doing, they can't really be helped. It is the decision makers that need their hands held to stop doing what they do'.

Decolonisation and antiracism in research funding councils is a much-needed intervention. For participants, this relates to who reviews funding applications and strategies to engage respectfully with work by Black women focusing on 'the lives of Black people and issues concerning identity and inequality'. In a respondent's view, 'funders seldom approach' the few Black women academics to be reviewers or assessors, so funding applications are 'assessed by colleagues without experience of, knowledge about and methodological approaches, to the study of Black inequality and identities'. Further, funders need to 'involve Black women in doing the call and determining who and what gets researched. Unless there is understanding and mitigation for how the research call is framed and the questions to be explored, we have already lost'. The issues of race, racism, racialisation and racialised gender intersections are not uppermost in funders' imaginings, policies and practices. Funders do not have to demonstrate, 'how they will ensure that the applications of Black women are fairly assessed by people with relevant experience' because EDI continues to be used to obscure institutional misogynoir, as this respondent argues:

> While increasingly funders seem to pay a bit more attention to EDI data related to gender when assessing applications, there is little if any attention paid to race, let alone the intersections of both. I believe that funders need to be strongly compelled to take both matters and their intersections seriously, including by demonstrating how they will ensure that the applications of Black women are fairly assessed by people with relevant experience. Here I am particularly thinking about when the project proposals of Black women focus on matters regarding Black Studies and the lives of Black people, but are reviewed and assessed by people with no understanding or expertise in such areas.

Calls for more transparency in the award process can occur if disaggregated race-based data on reviewers/assessors, the funders and applications for funding are made accessible: 'Sometimes funders claim that they are not receiving applications from particular groups of people, but it can be difficult to determine if this is true without having access to relevant data.'

More radically, to enable transformation in who gets funded, for one respondent there must be 'funding specific for Black women across several disciplines'. As well as this approach to positive action, there needs to be others like:

> Commitment on the part of research councils to ensure where, for example 10 fellowships are available at least 1/3 are protected for Black women. This needs to be matched at institution level by a commitment from the university leadership to establish programmes to advance Black women from the idea stage through to submission of funding applications. Without specific strategies these raced and gendered disparities will continue. This is why Black women are not considered for career advancement as successful funding bids is a criterion for progress to Principal Lecturer/Associate Professor.

For those who are early-career researchers (ECRs), focused mentoring on how to apply for funding and what a successful bid looks like are essential for funding success:

> What is needed is a structure of ECR support that links to skills develop-ment. ... Mentorship is often focused too narrowly on reading a journal article or being a sounding board for issues at work, but not on the lan-guage and phrasing that bidders are looking for. There should be oppor-tunities for Black women to sit on the panels ... reading bids – successful and unsuccessful ones – to get used to seeing what the framings are.

Participants highlight time in the workload, mentoring, 'sufficient resources to apply for grants', being 'included in research clusters/groupings' where making research applications is 'demystified', training on how to make appli-cations 'stand out' and being 'Co-PIs when joint submissions are made' as the missing components in PI funding success. Group solidarity and self-help are also important because 'there are already Black female professors who have a good track record of successfully applying for funding but they do not help junior academics like myself, which is disappointing'. Black women academics have a role in 'mentorship, encouragement, and support through developing an active Black women's network' and 'better comradeship to provide the ladder' based on their 'understanding of the intersectional exclusion of Black women and policy needed to promote our research projects'.

Afterword: UK culture wars and funding futures

Black women academics' lack of PI and fellowship funding has been looked at as institutional misogynoir. Institutional misogynoir is embedded in funders' pre-ference for upper-tier universities, lack of support for Black women as PIs and fellows (Rollock, 2021), time poverty, Black theoretical and methodological fra-meworks not being valued in REF criteria for 3*/4* publications, and not being REF panel members or chairs. Participants posed decolonisation and antiracism as ways forward. However, the UK's ongoing 'culture wars' cast doubt on prospects for decolonisation and antiracism.

Critical race theory and intersectionality were first mooted in parliament in October 2020 as problems by the then Equality Minister, MP Kemi Bade-noch, a Black woman. Members of the Conservative government, headed at the time by Prime Minister Boris Johnson, lambasted Black Lives Matter (#BLM) as 'woke radicals', maintained that slave-holders' statues and prop-erty built with slavery's profits should remain untouched, reparations were unnecessary, colonialism should not be debated, no one should 'take the knee', and critical race studies would be illegal if taught in schools (Trilling, 2020). The widely criticised Commission on Race and Ethnic Disparities (2021) report insisted that as a majority White country the UK was a world leader in race relations, argued there was no evidence of institutional racism in the UK and disparaged critical race theory and intersectionality. The government's influence on the report's conclusions and its denial of institutional racism directly attacked antiracist movements and ideals. The UK as a 'post-race' state is anti-Black as are universities and funders, as illustrated in the use of 20th century EDI approaches while institutional misogynoir continues. If not challenged, institutional misogynoir will stymy the decolonisation and antiracism that respondents view as necessary for equity in funding.

Notes

1 Approximately equivalent to North America's full professor, the designation 'professor' applies to 10% of UK academic staff compared to over a third in Canada and slightly fewer in the United States. Ten per cent may be an underestimate, as managerial positions such as heads of department are not included but can be held by professors (Higher Education Statistics Agency, 2023). Note, also, that 'race' is unknown for 1,755 professors in these annual statistics. Other positions for academic staff, depending upon the institution, include senior lecturers, readers (often now called associate professors), principal lecturers and lecturers (the entry grade). These positions normally involve both teaching and research. Different terms are used for research pathways and for teaching-only streams. Some universities have altered their preferred terms in recent years.

2 Official and other documents have until recently used both BME and BAME to refer to racialised populations described as 'Black and minority ethnic' or 'Black, Asian and minority ethnic'. Although still in common parlance, it is increasingly understood that there are problems with these designations, as they specify certain groups and not others and obscure differences among subgroups. UK Government (2021) now recommends against their use, and Higher Education Statistics Agency (2023) uses the term 'ethnic minority'.

3 UK Government (2021) indicates that 'Asian' includes people of Indian, Pakistani, Bangladeshi, Chinese and other Asian descent; Black as African, Caribbean and other Black descent; White as British, Irish and other White. There are also 'mixed', unknown and not disclosed groups.

4 UKRI also coordinates two other funding bodies that are less explicitly disciplinary: Research England and Innovate UK.

5 Quotations retain original wording, punctuation and capitalisation found in respondents' emailed responses.

6 Athena Swan was established by the UK Equality Challenge Unit in 2005 as a national charter mark to recognise good practice in gender equality in universities. The Race Equality Charter (REC) was introduced by the Equality Challenge Unit to address racial inequalities for academic staff and students in UK universities. Policy enacted through the REC benefits universities by reinforcing and perpetuating White privilege without addressing racial disadvantage (Bhopal & Pitkin, 2020).

7 In the REF, 4* is research quality that is world-leading in terms of originality, significance and rigour; 3* is research quality that is internationally excellent in terms of originality, significance and rigour; 2* is research quality that is recognised internationally in terms of originality, significance and rigour; 1* is research quality that is recognised nationally in terms of originality, significance and rigour.

8 Tate and Page (2018) have critiqued unconscious bias as an 'alibi for white supremacy' (p. 146).

References

Advance HE. (2019). *Equality in higher education: staff statistical report 2019.* https://www.advance-he.ac.uk/knowledge-hub/equality-higher-education-statistical-report-2019

Ahmed, S. (2021). *Complaint!* Duke University Press.

Arts and Humanities Research Council. (2022, September 30). *AHRC strategic delivery plan 2022 to 2025.* UK Research and Innovation. https://www.ukri.org/publications/ahrc-strategic-delivery-plan/ahrc-strategic-delivery-plan-2022-to-2025

Bailey, M., & Trudy. (2018). On misogynoir: citation, erasure and plagiarism. *Feminist Media Studies, 18*(4), 762–768. https://doi.org/10.1080/14680777.2018.1447395

Bhopal, K., & Pitkin, C. (2020). 'Same old story, just a different policy': race and policy making in higher education in the UK. *Race, Ethnicity and Education, 23*(4), 530–547. https://doi.org/10.1080/13613324.2020.1718082

Commission on Race and Ethnic Disparities. (2021). *Commission on race and ethnic disparities: The report.* https://www.gov.uk/government/publications/the-report-of-the-commission-on-race-and-ethnic-disparities

Doharty, N., Madriaga, M., & Joseph-Salisbury, R. (2021). The university went to 'decolonise' and all they brought back was lousy diversity double-speak! Critical race counter-stories from faculty of colour in 'decolonial times'. *Educational Philosophy and Theory, 53*(3), 233–244. https://doi.org/10.1080/00131857.2020.1769601

Economic and Social Research Council. (2022). *ESRC strategic delivery plan 2022–2025.* UK Research and Innovation. https://www.ukri.org/wp-content/uploads/2022/09/ESRC-010922-StrategicDeliveryPlan2022.pdf

Gabriel, D. (2024). Do Black lives really matter? Social closure, white privilege and the making of a Black underclass in higher education. In R. Andreasson, C. Lundström, S. Keskinen, & S. A. Tate (Eds.), *Routledge international handbook of new critical race and Whiteness studies* (pp. 170–181). Routledge.

Gabriel, D., & Tate, S. A. (Eds.). (2017). *Inside the ivory tower: narratives of women of colour surviving and thriving in British academia.* Trentham.

Gutiérrez Rodríguez, E. (2015). Sensing dispossession: women and gender studies between institutional racism and migration control policies in neo-liberal universities. *Women's Studies International Forum, 54,* 167–177. https://doi.org/10.1016/j.wsif.2015.06.013

Higher Education Statistics Agency. (2023). *Higher education staff statistics: UK, 2021/22* (Statistical Bulletin SB264). https://www.hesa.ac.uk/news/17-01-2023/sb264-higher-education-staff-statistics

Meer, N. (2022). *The cruel optimism of racial justice.* Policy Press.

Papatsiba, V., & Cohen, E. (2020). Institutional hierarchies and research impact: new academic currencies, capital and position taking in UK higher education. *British Journal of Sociology of Education, 41*(2), 178–196. https://doi.org/10.1080/01425692.2019.1676700

Parker, I. (1999). Introduction: varieties of discourse and analysis. In I. Parker & the Bolton Discourse Network (Eds.), *Critical textwork: an introduction to varieties of discourse and analysis* (pp. 1–12). Open University Press.

Puwar, N. (2004). *Space invaders: race, gender and bodies out of place.* Bloomsbury.

Research Excellence Framework. (ca. 2017). *What is the REF?* Retrieved on 12 January 2024 from https://archive.ref.ac.uk/about-the-ref/what-is-the-ref/

Research Excellence Framework. (2021). *Analysis of full REF 2021 panel membership.* https://archive.ref.ac.uk/publications-and-reports/analysis-of-full-ref-2021-panel-membership-ref-202101/

Research Excellence Framework. (2022). *Equality and Diversity Advisory Panel final report.* https://archive.ref.ac.uk/media/1863/ref-edap-final-report-2022-final11.pdf

Research Excellence Framework. (2023). *Analysis of inclusion for submission, representation in outputs attribution and scoring.* https://archive.ref.ac.uk/media/1919/ref-2021-analysis-of-inclusion-for-submission-representation-in-outputs-attribution-and-scoring.pdf

Rollock, N. (2021). "I would have become wallpaper had racism had its way": Black female professors, battle fatigue and strategies for surviving higher education. *Peabody Journal of Education, 96*(2), 206–217. https://doi.org/10.1080/0161956X.2021.1905361

Tate, S. A. (2013). Racial affective economies, disalienation and 'race made ordinary'. *Ethnic and Racial Studies, 37*(13), 2475–2490. https://doi.org/10.1080/01419870.2013.821146

Tate, S. A. (2014). 'I can't quite put my finger on it': racism's touch. *Ethnicities, 16*(1), 68–85. https://doi.org/10.1177/1468796814564626

Tate, S. A. (2020). *Black skins, Black masks: hybridity, dialogism, performativity.* Routledge. (Original work published 2005)

Tate, S. A. (2021). On brick walls and other Black feminist dilemmas: anger and racial diversity in universities. In M. Crul, L. Dick, H. Ghorashi, & A. Valenzuela, Jr. (Eds.), *Scholarly engagement and decolonisation: views from South Africa, the Netherlands and the United States* (pp. 83–102). Sun Media. https://doi.org/10.18820/9781928314578/03

Tate, S. A., & Page, D. (2018). Whiteliness and institutional racism: hiding behind (un)conscious bias. *Ethics and Education, 13*(1), 141–155. https://doi.org/10.1080/17449642.2018.1428718

Trilling, D. (2020, October 23). Why is the UK government suddenly targeting 'critical race theory'? *The Guardian.* https://www.theguardian.com/commentisfree/2020/oct/23/uk-critical-race-theory-trump-conservatives-structural-inequality

UK Government. (2021). *Writing about ethnicity.* https://www.ethnicity-facts-figures.service.gov.uk/style-guide/writing-about-ethnicity

UK Research and Innovation. (2023a). *UKRI diversity data for funding applicants and awardees 2020 to 21 update.* https://www.ukri.org/publications/diversity-data-for-funding-applicants-and-awardees-2020-21/ukri-diversity-data-for-funding-applicants-and-awardees-2020-to-21-update/

UK Research and Innovation. (2023b). *UKRI's equality, diversity and inclusion strategy: research and innovation by everyone, for everyone.* https://www.ukri.org/publications/ukris-equality-diversity-and-inclusion-strategy/ukris-equality-diversity-and-inclusion-strategy-research-and-innovation-by-everyone-for-everyone/

UK Research and Innovation. (2023c, July 19). *Research England publishes university research and KE budget.* https://www.ukri.org/news/research-england-publishes-university-research-and-ke-budget/

UK Research and Innovation. (2023d, July 28). *Our fellowship opportunities.* https://www.ukri.org/what-we-do/developing-people-and-skills/develop-your-research-career/find-fellowships-and-other-funding-for-researchers/

UK Research and Innovation. (2023e, September 7). *Horizon Europe: help for UK applicants.* https://www.ukri.org/apply-for-funding/horizon-europe/

Van Dijk, T. (Ed.) (1997). *Discourse as structure and process.* Sage.

PART 4

Funding and defunding

11

STATUS HIERARCHIES, GENDER BIAS AND DISRESPECT

Ethnographic observations of Swedish Research Council review panels

Lambros Roumbanis

Fairness and impartiality are crucial to maintaining the legitimacy of grant peer review as a mechanism for distributing funds in science. In most European countries today, public funding agencies are regularly trying to improve their evaluation methods to ensure that money is spent on the most qualified applicants with the strongest research ideas. Yet there are several issues that continue to haunt this evaluation process – issues that go to the very heart of the contemporary academic ethos and meritocracy. Gender equality is one of those issues, and policymakers in Sweden have worked hard to improve the conditions for women in research across all disciplines during the last couple of decades. To be sure, the assessment of research proposals often leads to very different interpretations and scorings from one reviewer to another, without entailing any unfair treatment or gender bias. Based on many previous studies, the common understanding is that peer-review decisions are notoriously influenced by arbitrariness, chance and disagreements (Lamont, 2009; Mutz et al., 2016; Roumbanis, 2022). More insidiously, however, gender biases can creep into negotiations, partly as a result of reviewers becoming immersed in the talk and carried away by it, making them oblivious to other things, including their own behaviour (Goffman, 1957). They may assume that they are free of bias while failing to recognise ways in which deep-rooted beliefs, past socialisation or unexamined positions of privilege contribute to the evaluation of others. Thus, a male reviewer can identify himself as a supporter of women in science and be an outspoken advocate of meritocratic values in academia but still respond quite differently when debating with his male and female colleagues. This social phenomenon can also be related to what has been identified as gender-based status inequalities, 'with its connotations of greater or lesser worthiness and esteem' (Ridgeway, 2019, p. 5). As a consequence, even highly qualified female scientists will sometimes

DOI: 10.4324/9781003330431-15

struggle to make their voices heard in the peer-review process. I believe this topic has been somewhat neglected, because the largest bulk of research on gender bias in grant peer review has mainly focused on how it affects the applicants, not the reviewers assigned to evaluate the proposals.

In the present chapter, I explore the issue of gender bias in research funding by using the sociological theory of status hierarchies and status inequalities in group interactions. The empirical data consist of a unique sample of ethnographic observations from Swedish Research Council (SRC) panel groups within the natural and engineering sciences. I will describe several concrete situations in which disrespectful treatment was shown in the way some male reviewers responded to the arguments presented by their female colleagues. The analysis is intended to shed new light on the social dramaturgy of gender-based status inequalities in the peer-review process. In addition, I hope to improve our understanding of how gender can play a role during panel group deliberations, which raises questions regarding the legitimacy and adequacy of peer review as the dominant mechanism in contemporary research funding.

The social dramaturgy of status hierarchies

Status is one of the classical concepts in the history of social science, a Latin word with its etymological root in the proto-Indo-European word *stā-*, meaning 'position, state or condition' (in Ancient Greek *stasis*, 'standing'). In the early days of sociology, Weber (1922/1978) introduced the notion of status to complement his analysis of power and class by using the equivalent German word *stand* to point out what is crucial: 'social esteem in terms of positive and negative privilege' (p. 305). The concept of status was later incorporated into new theoretical frameworks and even given new names. For example, Bourdieu (1984/1988) emphasised the impact of status by using his concept of 'symbolic capital' to analyse the hierarchies and habitus formations within the French academic world.

Here, I aim to pinpoint the concept of *status hierarchies*, using it as a theoretical framework for my empirical analysis. Status hierarchies exist everywhere in social life, affecting individuals and groups alike; it is, as Cecilia Ridgeway (2019) wrote, 'an ancient form of inequality that nevertheless interpenetrates modern meritocratic institutions' (p. 2). This is a central idea that I will elaborate on through the analysis that follows. Despite political and normative changes that promote equal treatment of men and women, deep-rooted gender stereotypes and implicit biases[1] still exist as integral parts of the creation of status hierarchies at the interpersonal level. As a motive for actions, status can be just as significant as money and power (Ridgeway, 2019). In fact, status, money and power often come together, such as in the case of research funding and academic careers (Blau, 1994; Edlund & Lammi, 2022). But how can we move from these rather basic premises regarding the importance of status hierarchies to a more concrete sociological understanding? I believe we have to start from Goffman's 'front stage' (1959), that is, the place where people interact face to face. Most people have probably experienced the occurrence of status hierarchies when joining a group that is engaged in some form of shared activity. This is what I would like to call the social dramaturgy of status hierarchies. For example, it often becomes apparent after a while that some individuals are talking more than others, and that 'others are reacting by paying more attention to and offering more approval for the comments of some than others' (Ridgeway, 2019, p. 6).

Most people are relatively familiar with the experience of status hierarchies, but how such hierarchies actually emerge is still a bit of a mystery (Ridgeway, 2019). This obliqueness is probably because status comes into existence through the communication flows and all the small, seemingly unimportant actions that individuals rarely notice. Hence, status is not always easy to capture, because it can be hidden in many different types of behaviour. During conversations, the individual can, as Goffman (1957) explained, 'become unthinkingly and impulsively immersed in the talk and carried away by it' (p. 47). Status inequalities can be expressed through subtle gestures, jokes or silence, but they can also be manifested by harsh comments, arrogance or dismissiveness. And these expressions must always be viewed in the light of how other individuals are treated when they talk in the group. Disrespectful behaviour with a gender dimension is always context-dependent and relational. In addition, the social dramaturgy of a status hierarchy is typically influenced by 'a substantial element of contingent uncertainty', that is, how it evolves depends on the contingent reactions of the different members in the group (Ridgeway, 2019, p. 29). In the present chapter, I will focus on gender-based status inequalities by analysing concrete situations where disrespectful treatment could be discerned during panel group discussions.

Ethnography of meetings

The empirical data I used were collected during the late summer of 2013 when I conducted ethnographic observations of ten panel groups of the SRC, representing sub-disciplines of natural or engineering sciences, and charged with assessing and ranking research proposals. I was given permission by the funding agency to join these meetings as an external researcher; in other words, I was not an official observer of the SRC. This was a unique opportunity to examine the peer-review process from a close distance. Studying formal meetings has been shown to be a fruitful method that can provide detailed insights into how discussions and decision-making play out in practice (Sandler & Thedvall, 2017; Schwartzman, 1989). What happens during a meeting often presents a rather good picture of the exchange of views and the emotions people may express spontaneously when they interact. By taking extensive handwritten field notes during the panel meetings, both disrespectful treatment and people's emotions could be documented in a fairly objective manner.

Although several years have passed since I conducted my research project, very little has changed in the way this review process is organised today.[2] Basically, all the reviewers are assigned a subset of proposals that correspond with their scientific expertise. In order to assess the value of a proposal, all panellists have to translate their qualitative judgement into numerical scores, and they are also expected to rank each proposal against all other proposals they have reviewed. All the individual scores are then later calculated into average scores, which form a preliminary group ranking. The main goal of the meetings is for the panellists to reach a consensus regarding which proposals should be prioritised for funding. The results finally agreed upon provide the basis for the subsequent funding decisions, which are formally made by the SRC Board. However, the board usually follows the recommendations made by the collective body of expertise in each panel group, so the time-consuming construction of consensus per se is indeed very crucial (Roumbanis, 2017).

To be sure, gender equality is taken very seriously by the SRC. As a result, most panel groups are composed of a relatively equal share of men and women, and the statistics for the 2013 funding call also show a proportionate share (19%) of men and women receiving grants (SRC, 2014; see also Cruz-Castro & Sanz-Menéndes, 2019).[3] The SRC informed all of their panel groups before every meeting of the importance of gender equality and the rules to use to avoid potential conflicts of interest. The examples presented in the following analysis are not representative of all of the ten panel groups; I will illustrate situations from the two panel groups where I found the most significant instances given the particular scope of this study.

The reason why ethnicity/race is not in focus in my analysis is because of the total absence of reviewers with a non-Western background in the material. Not a single reviewer was African, Asian or from the Middle East, as far as I could judge from looking at their surnames and physical appearance. An overview of all the panels for 2021–2022 within the natural and engineering sciences indicates that this is no coincidence. Of the 233 reviewers, only ten had names that I identify as originating from non-Western countries. There are certainly methodological limitations in trying to identify ethnicity/race in this way, yet it gives a rather good picture of the general situation. The results from this analysis are also indirectly confirmed by Behtoui and Leivestad's (2019) study on how researchers in Sweden with immigrant backgrounds from non-Western countries are marginalised and excluded from the most powerful decision-making units in academia.

There are several status-related differences in panel groups other than gender, including, for example, differences in academic experience. Scientific achievements and academic reputation are also naturally of paramount importance in this context. A methodological technique I used to reconstruct an approximate picture of the status relations was to look up the panel members in Google Scholar to compare their publications and citation indexes up to 2013. To add more colour to these 'status pictures', I also looked at each reviewer's particular research fields (basic/applied), organisational affiliations, funding success, age and academic career positions. Thus, the brief background information I gathered functioned as basic proxies for the status hierarchies, making it possible to discern some of the gender/age-based aspects of status inequalities.

Results and analysis

A status hierarchy in the light of 'eccentric' men

In the first panel group I will present, there were 12 reviewers, five women and seven men.[4] The chairperson was a professor in her early 50s, well-established and with a good publication record. I will call her 'Anna'. The other four female reviewers all had strong career positions, but three of them were slightly younger than Anna. One of these reviewers, 'Ingrid', came to play a significant role in the situations I will describe later. The fourth reviewer was around 60 years of age and very well-qualified. I will call her 'Karin'. Her main expertise was in an applied science field, and she had long experience in developing new methods, while the other women (including Anna) were mainly experimentalists and theoreticians doing basic research. The male panellist I will focus on, 'Kristoffer', was in his 50s and worked at one of Sweden's largest universities. He was well-established in his research field and had many strong publications. In this panel group, Kristoffer stood out to me as being rather eccentric and quite dominant, but not just in relation to his female colleagues. Still, the way he treated the male and female group members could differ. For example, he diminished the importance of the female panellists' arguments and sometimes completely ignored them. When he responded to his male colleagues, even when criticising their judgements, it always seemed to be in a spirit of 'friendly rivalry',[5] as if they were more worthy opponents (e.g. 'I think you are wrong about x, ... but okay, you are completely right about y'). To be sure, Kristoffer was not like this all the time, yet his behaviour exposed some gender/age aspects of the status hierarchy in this particular panel group. The other male reviewers in this group were 55 to 65 years old, except for one younger man who was in his early 40s and kept a rather low profile. One of the male professors had recently been awarded a prestigious prize and was well-known internationally. I will call him 'Lars' and, as I will show, he also demonstrated some of the gender aspects of the status hierarchy in the way he acted in the meeting room.

Situation 1

Ingrid had just presented one of her favourite proposals. She seemed to make her best effort to convince all her colleagues that this proposal was great. In her view, the proposed work was state-of-the-art, the project was very promising, and she concluded: 'The proposal was a pleasure to read and she [the PI] has really strong merits.'[6] The two other reviewers with the responsibility of assessing this proposal, the young male reviewer and Karin, looked at the ranking list. Both liked the proposal, but they had not been as generous with their scores as Ingrid had been. Karin mumbled something, and the young male reviewer looked rather puzzled. Suddenly, Kristoffer broke the silence. Even though he had not read the proposal, he exclaimed in a rather arrogant tone of voice, 'Please, can you explain what you mean when you say strong merits? To be honest, I am not at all impressed by the publications you mentioned.' And he then went on to dismiss other things Ingrid had just told the group. Some of the other male panellists seemed to agree with his critique, looking at each other and nodding. Yet Ingrid did not seem intimidated by Kristoffer's confrontational approach; she responded to his argument and again urged her fellow assessors to raise their scores. The discussion went on for a few minutes, and they finally decided to wait with this proposal so they could compare it with three other proposals. Without saying anything more, Kristoffer's response revealed his low esteem for Ingrid's expertise, as if he did not expect her judgement to be sufficiently valid, even though she was actually one of the assigned experts on this proposal. The contrast became evident when comparing his responses in other similar situations; Kristoffer never used the same kind of patronising rhetoric when he disagreed with some of his male colleagues, even in situations when he disputed the plausibility of their judgements.

Situation 2

In the next situation I present, Kristoffer explained to the group the great importance of funding a proposal he praised to the skies. One of the female reviewers asked him a question about the feasibility of the project, a question that Kristoffer completely ignored and failed to answer. Instead, he turned towards the chairperson, Anna, and asked her if they could begin calibrating the scores. However, Anna dismissed his request and asked the group if anyone wanted to add something to the discussion. Now, Ingrid, who had also read this proposal, asked if he (Kristoffer) might have overestimated this PI's publications a bit, reminding him of the proposal she had previously supported. Kristoffer immediately answered, 'X's project is unique. You cannot compare these two proposals.' And he went on: 'Your PI hadn't read the literature. There are many important methods, such as A and B. ... Have you heard about them?' This seemed to be a rather humiliating comment for Ingrid, as if she was not knowledgeable enough regarding these methods and did not understand the different qualities of these two proposals. She replied that she knew about the methods Kristoffer had mentioned, but he did not seem to bother about this. Then after a few minutes and some minor discussions, Anna finally told them to adjust their scores. The panel group managed to reach an agreement in what seemed to be a good collegial spirit. Still, what some of the group members may have perceived as just an expression of hard negotiations and Kristoffer's idiosyncratic rhetorical style could also be interpreted as a gender-based status inequality in his disrespectful and patronising approach to his two female colleagues.

Interlude

During a coffee break, three of the female reviewers and one female administrator talked separately. They discussed the issue of gender and how often it affects the funding results; they agreed that men and women are often judged by slightly different standards regarding their merits, originality or independence. Still, one of the reviewers added, 'But this group is pretty okay.' What stood out in this conversation, in my view, was their focus on the rights of the female applicants, ignoring the role of gender during the meetings in which they themselves were involved. This kind of consideration might hide a taboo. Nevertheless, it adds an important piece to the picture of status hierarchies and the peculiar kind of normality that it establishes in the group. One of the reviewers acknowledged that she had to calm herself down in one situation, to avoid 'causing a fight'. Her disclosure may also explain certain aspects of how status inequality functions in practice, that is, how it prevents some people from truly expressing what they think and feel in front of the group ('emotional labour' in Hochschild, 1983). Status was also palpable in how Kristoffer later responded to the statements of a male colleague, admitting that he was not an expert: 'I didn't understand the importance of this project. This topic seems to be well-studied. In this respect, not being in the field, I wasn't that impressed.' As far as I could discern, this type of humble attitude was seldom expressed in his comments to his female colleagues, the only exception being his deference to the older female professor, Karin, which probably signals the importance of age as an intersecting factor in this case. However, as Søndergaard (2005) illustrates, in other situations, older female researchers might be disregarded, while younger female colleagues are appreciated for their enthusiasm and vivacity.

Situation 3

With the last observation from this group, I will highlight the issue of status in relation to the chairperson's ambivalent authority. The group had reached a critical moment, and Anna asked her reviewers how they should handle three proposals placed just below the funding threshold. All three proposals had female PIs, and Anna therefore proposed: 'Maybe we should consider raising one of them?' But nobody in the group answered, not even the female reviewers, possibly because some of their older male colleagues had expressed strong feelings for some of the proposals just above the funding line. While it is impossible to know how they really felt, it nevertheless seems plausible to assume that the status hierarchy in the group played a crucial role in this sensitive situation, even for a highly esteemed person like Karin. Then, a peculiar thing happened. Instead of responding to Anna's request, Lars proposed that they should consider raising one of the male PIs who was also below the threshold. As Lars was one of the high-status professors in the meeting room, his comment immediately opened up a new conversation, especially among two other male reviewers. Even if discussions about the ranking in principle are important as regards proposals in the 'evaluative grey area', Lars's action illustrates how status hierarchies manifest themselves during the deliberations. In the end, none of the four proposals were awarded a grant, yet Anna's request was ignored by her group, because they deferred to Lars and not to her (the chairperson). This was actually the only panel group in which the chairperson was not listened to in such a highly sensitive decision-making situation. My interpretation is that Anna's relatively young age in relation to several of her male colleagues, in combination with her gender, partly explain her position in this status hierarchy. Anna's more general situation as a female academic could also be described in the words of Ridgeway (2019): 'We all feel the power of status inequality in the subtle (and sometimes unsubtle) ways in which we are treated with attention and respect in one context or overlooked and dismissed in the next' (p. 150).

The unbearable lightness of a gender argument

Scientific quality is the most important criterion according to the SRC rules, and gender can only be used as a special boundary condition (*randvillkor*) in situations where some proposals are judged to be of the same scientific quality and therefore hard to differentiate. However, among experts on peer review, it is commonly understood that quality judgements can differ considerably, both within and between panel groups. Research quality can mean many different things to different reviewers at different moments in time, as it basically concerns the future promise of a project that has yet to be performed (Roumbanis, 2021). Against this background, we might ask, what is a gender argument worth in relation to scientific quality, despite the uncertainty and arbitrariness of the criterion?

The group I will present next included ten members: six men and four women. The chairperson, 'Nicklas', was a relatively young professor in his late 40s. He was what one would call 'a rising star' and had received a number of prestigious prizes and grants. In other words, this was a man with high academic status. One of the other panellists, 'Axel', was a senior professor in his 60s with a solid career in basic research and many high-impact papers co-written with international colleagues. Another reviewer, 'Yvonne', was a very well-qualified professor in her late 40s working with applied research and with a strong reputation. She had many high-impact papers, and she was also involved as an expert in a couple of industry-related research projects.

Situation 1

The reviewers had been discussing several proposals during the first hour after lunch on the first meeting day. The negotiations went rather smoothly with only a few minor disagreements. In fact, the overall impression of this panel group was that the members collaborated relatively well. However, Yvonne looked anxious. Until this moment, she had kept a rather low profile, even in situations when her opinion was not given appropriate attention and approval by some of her colleagues. Two male reviewers had taken a lot of space in the group, one of them being Axel. He often went through the PIs' publication oeuvres and frequently used standard arguments to raise the proposals he liked or lower those he disliked. But at this moment, Yvonne raised her hand, and Nicklas gave her the floor. She said:

> I think some of the PIs have been really unfairly treated. As a group we have been inconsistent in how we judge some of the proposals that have almost identical qualifications. In her [name of PI] case you said the publications were okay, but then later when you discussed X's merits you said he had excellent publications. I can't really see any substantial differences, yet you gave him higher scores.

After Yvonne had finished, Axel looked at her and said, 'Scientific quality is always the most important', going on to defend his judgement in the case mentioned by Yvonne. He then underscored that the female PI had gaps in her publication list, gaps that the male PI did not have. And then he added, 'I am also a bit concerned about her independence as a researcher. Her role in paper A and B was not that clear.' At this moment, the group members were silent for a few seconds. But Yvonne replied, and this time she seemed rather upset, judging from the tone of her voice:

> There is nothing wrong with her independence. The proposal is very good and deserves to be funded. But you and MB [another male reviewer] lowered it, and now it hasn't a chance. But this doesn't feel right because there are few women above the funding line. And the reason is that we don't have a broader perspective in this group. I mean, we are not really considering the gender issue at all. You know, it's really difficult being a mother of young children and at the same time having a career as a woman in this research field. We cannot compare quality in such a mechanical way between these two PIs, they are competing on different terms.[7]

Axel looked remarkably unaffected by Yvonne's line of reasoning, and instead, he whispered something to the male reviewer sitting next to him. Another male reviewer took the opportunity to share his view. He emphasised that there were fewer female PIs in their pool of candidates, which naturally resulted in fewer women ending up above the funding line. He then added that most of the proposals with female PIs were also of much lower quality, and he presented this conclusion as if it were an indisputable fact, despite not having read all of them. To my surprise, none of the other reviewers expressed any support for Yvonne's argument, nor did they challenge the claim that most proposals with female PIs were of lower quality. However, one reason for this lack of challenge might have been the time pressure, which constantly forces reviewers to employ a 'pragmatic attitude' (Brenneis, 1994; Lamont 2009) despite the fact that some reviewers are just being disrespectful.

Situation 2

Near the end of the second meeting day, the panellists had worked hard to complete the new ranking list. Most of the group members looked tired. The chairperson, Nicklas, asked the group, 'The SRC would be happy to have feedback from you. Do you have anything you would like to say?' One of the male group members was irritated because of the low budget and said he thought it was a total waste of time having them read all these proposals if so few could receive money. 'What's the point?' he said. Then Yvonne raised her hand, and again she gave voice to her frustration with the gender issue, which she thought had been completely neglected by the group. 'Why is it that men are overrepresented among the grant recipients in this group?' she asked. Nicklas immediately responded in a rather loud voice: 'I don't think gender is such a big problem. Scholars with non-Swedish backgrounds are, in my experience, much more discriminated against than women.' As pointed out earlier (see Behtoui & Leivestad, 2019), Nicklas may be right in that ethnic diversity is a pressing issue in Swedish academia (but what about the disadvantage of non-Western women, that is, the intersection of gender and ethnicity?). However, it was the way in which he disagreed with Yvonne that made the greatest impression in this situation, how he avoided recognising her view by shifting the focus away from the gender issue. In the next second, the group had moved forward and was discussing other issues. It might be worth emphasising again that SRC takes gender equality very seriously (Husu & Peterson, this volume). Still, the negotiations are, first and foremost, focused on judging research quality and selecting the most promising applications. In such a context, support or dismissal can be discreet indicators of gender-based status in the group.

Concluding remarks

Promoting fairness and reliability in the peer-review process is considered a main priority for funding agencies all around the world. What is often forgotten in this context, however, is the working climate within these groups. Status-related biases can be quite difficult to separate from legitimate disagreements, partly because everything is embedded in conversations that are full of epistemic prestige, personal idiosyncrasies, and intellectual jargon. A harsh response may just be a harsh response. The entire situation is also deeply influenced by the fierce competition over scarce resources that is dominating research today. Still, the way these meetings are organised entails, among other things, that each reviewer should show colleagues respect and have a solution-oriented mindset, as the goal is to reach a consensus under time constraints. Moreover, the peer-review process is dominated by the systematic use of scores and average values to decide which applications should be awarded funding (Roumbanis, 2017). During my ethnographic fieldwork, the discussion climate was generally good and respectful. But that was not always the case, as I have illustrated.

The theory of status hierarchies and gender-based status inequalities provides an important key for understanding a force that permeates everyday social interaction across organisational contexts. Gender, age and esteem based on academic accomplishments intersect in complex and sometimes unpredictable ways. An older woman with superior achievements might be shown greater respect, while a middle-aged or younger woman trying to perform as a leader might be disregarded. By zooming in on the reactions of some of the reviewers involved in the panel group meetings, my aim has been to uncover some sensitive ethical issues in the peer-review process. To be clear, some reviewers will always be listened to more than others because of their academic status as scientific experts, as that is simply how peer review works (Lamont, 2009; Roumbanis, 2022). Still, legitimate academic status and gender-based status inequalities can sometimes be intertwined. Old gender stereotypes that associate male scientists with brilliant ideas and great discoveries (due to the historical exclusion of women from science) are probably one of the reasons for the occurrence of unequal treatment and double standards in review panel groups, even in Sweden, which is generally ranked as one of the most gender-egalitarian countries in the world (European Institute for Gender Equality, 2021).

In her celebrated magnum opus, *The Second Sex*, Simone de Beauvoir (1949/1972) declared, 'One is not born a genius, one becomes a genius; and the feminine situation has up to the present rendered this becoming practically impossible' (p. 133). No matter how we choose to interpret the word 'genius' today, it still seems to represent an individual disposition that is very much framed by gender, thereby influencing the social distribution of intellectual status in academic life. There are findings showing that even top-performing women are significantly less likely than men to be described as 'geniuses' or 'superstars' due to gender bias (see Rivera & Tilcsik, 2019; see also the discussion of equity issues associated with assessing research excellence by Tamtik and Sutherland in this volume). Fortunately, things are slowly changing, and the situation has certainly improved in recent years. For example, if we look at the statistical results from the SRC funding calls of 2013 and 2021 (see note 3), the organisation seems to have achieved at least some form of distributive justice between male and female applicants. The SRC has also conducted its own gender observations, which have resulted in new recommendations to improve gender fairness. Nowadays the reviewers are in general more careful in how they discuss the applicants. And yet, there is great reason to believe that gender-based status inequalities will not just disappear in academia. Moreover, gender is but one of several social categories that intersect each other. If the impact of status inequalities and unfair treatment on future decision-making is to be avoided, the entire funding system will probably have to be changed. I think we must ask ourselves the following question: why should the merits and the realisation of the research ideas of a relatively large number of applicants depend on the judgements of a small group of individuals? I will close the chapter by recalling what Arendt (1954/1977) wrote, 'Meritocracy contradicts the principle of equality, of an equalitarian democracy, no less than any other oligarchy' (pp. 176–177).

Acknowledgements

I would like to thank the editors for the opportunity to write this chapter and for their many valuable comments.

Notes

1 See Bursell and Olsson (2021) for a sociological account of 'implicit bias'.
2 Since 2016, the SRC has reworked its rules on gender equality. However, these rules do not say anything about how the reviewers are expected to treat each other during the meetings, only how to monitor gender issues with regard to, for example, the gender composition of panel groups and the goal of producing an equal distribution of grants between men and women (SRC, 2022). Another change, put into effect during the COVID-19 pandemic, was for panels to meet online (Peterson & Husu, 2023), with impacts such as stricter chairing, fewer interruptions and loss of opportunities for socialising, changes that might conceivably alter some of the patterns reported in this chapter.
3 The statistics on the funding distribution between men and women principal investigators (PIs) within the natural and engineering sciences for the 2013 call show the following: 38 of 204 female PI applicants received a grant (19%) as did 190 of 1,014 male PI applicants (also 19%) (SRC, 2014). The corresponding figures for the 2021 call show 55 of 246 female (22%) and 215 of 954 male PIs (23%) received funding (SRC, 2022).
4 I decided not to reveal the reviewers' nationality/country of origin, and the reason for this is mainly because it was difficult from the existing observational data to say anything significant regarding this social factor and the manifestation of status inequalities.
5 The term 'friendly rivalry' originates from the Ancient Greek ευγενής άμιλλα (*evgenís ámilla*).
6 One of the four main assessment criteria used by the SRC is 'the merits of the applicant'. The word 'merits' refers to the *qualifications* of the applicant in terms of productivity and achievements.
7 For similar views, see Sato et al. (2021).

References

Arendt, H. (1977). The crisis in education (D. Lindley, Trans.). *Between past and future* (pp. 170–193). Penguin Classics. (Original work published 1954)

Behtoui, A., & Leivestad, H. H. (2019). The 'stranger' among Swedish 'homo academicus'. *Higher Education*, *77*(2), 213–228. https://doi.org/10.1007/s10734-018-0266-x

Blau, P. M. (1994). *The organization of academic work* (2nd edition). Transaction Publisher.

Bourdieu, P. (1988). *Homo academicus* (P. Collier, Trans.). Stanford University Press. (Original work published 1984)

Brenneis, D. (1994). Discourse and discipline at the National Research Council: a bureaucratic Bildungsroman. *Cultural Anthropology*, *9*(1), 23–36. https://doi.org/10.1525/can.1994.9.1.02a00020

Bursell, M., & Olsson, F. (2021). Do we need dual-process theory to understand implicit bias? A study of the nature of implicit bias against Muslims. *Poetics*, *87*, Article 101549. https://doi.org/10.1016/j.poetic.2021.101549

Cruz-Castro, L., & Sanz-Menéndez, L. (2019). *Grant allocation disparities from a gender perspective: literature review* (GRANteD Project D1.1). https://doi.org/10.20350/digitalCSIC/10548

de Beauvoir, S. (1972). *The second sex* (H. M. Parshley, Trans.). Penguin. (Original work published 1949)

Edlund, P., & Lammi, I. (2022). Stress-inducing and anxiety-ridden: a practice-based approach to the construction of status-bestowing evaluations in research funding. *Minerva*, *60*(3), 397–418. https://doi.org/10.1007/s11024-022-09466-9

European Institute for Gender Equality. (2021). *Upward convergence in gender equality: how close is the Union of equality?* Publications Office of the European Union. https://eige.europa.eu/publications/upward-convergence-gender-equality-how-close-union-equality

Goffman, E. (1957). Alienation from interaction. *Human Relations*, *10*(1), 47–60. https://doi.org/10.1177/001872675701000103

Goffman, E. (1959). *The presentation of self in everyday life*. Doubleday.

Hochschild, A. R. (1983). *The managed heart: commercialization of human feeling*. University of California Press.

Lamont, M. (2009). *How professors think: inside the curious world of academic judgment*. Harvard University Press.

Mutz, R., Bornmann, L., & Daniel, H.-D. (2016). Funding decision-making systems: an empirical comparison of continuous and dichotomous approaches based on psychometric theory. *Research Evaluation*, *25*(4), 416–426. https://doi.org/10.1093/reseval/rvw002

Peterson, H., & Husu, L. (2023). Online panel work through a gender lens: implications of digital peer review meetings. *Science and Public Policy*, *50*(3), 371–381. https://doi.org/10.1093/scipol/scac075

Ridgeway, C. (2019). *Status*. Russell Sage Foundation.

Rivera, L. A., & Tilcsik, A. (2019). Scaling down inequality: rating scales, gender bias, and the architecture of evaluation. *American Sociological Review*, *84*(2), 248–274. https://doi.org/10.1177/0003122419833601

Roumbanis, L. (2017). Academic judgments under uncertainty: a study of collective anchoring effects in Swedish Research Council panel groups. *Social Studies of Science*, *47*(1), 95–116. https://doi.org/10.1177/0306312716659789

Roumbanis, L. (2021). The oracles of science: on grant peer review and competitive funding. *Social Science Information*, *60*(3), 356–362. https://doi.org/10.1177/05390184211019241

Roumbanis, L. (2022). Disagreement and agonistic chance in peer review. *Science, Technology, & Human Values*, *47*(6), 1302–1333. https://doi.org/10.1177/01622439211026016

Sandler, J., & Thedvall, R. (2017). *Meeting ethnography: meetings as key technologies of contemporary governance, development, and resistance*. Routledge.

Sato, S., Gygax, P. M., Randall, J., & Schmid Mast, M. (2021). The leaky pipeline in research grant peer review and funding decisions: challenges and future directions. *Higher Education*, *82*(1), 145–162. https://doi.org/10.1007/s10734-020-00626-y

Schwartzman, H. (1989). *The meeting: gatherings in organizations and communities*. Springer Science.

Søndergaard, D. M. (2005). Making sense of gender, age, power and disciplinary position: intersecting discourses in the academy. *Feminism & Psychology*, *15*(2), 189–208. https://doi.org/10.1177/0959353505051728

Swedish Research Council. (2014). *Årsredovisning 2013* [Annual report 2013]. Vetenskapsrådet. https://www.vr.se/analys/rapporter/vara-rapporter/2014-01-06-arsredovisning-2013.html

Swedish Research Council. (2022). *Årsredovisning 2021* [Annual report 2021]. Vetenskapsrådet. https://www.vr.se/analys/rapporter/vara-rapporter/2022-02-24-arsredovisning-2021.html

Weber, M. (1978). *Economy and society: an outline of interpretative sociology* (H. Gerth & C. Wright Mills, Trans.). University of California Press. (Original work published 1922)

12

TRACING EXCELLENCE AND EQUITY IN RESEARCH FUNDING

Policy change in the Canada Research Chairs Program

Merli Tamtik and Dawn Sutherland

Research funding agencies are key stakeholders in distributing public money. Given their worries over accountability, these agencies tend to institutionalise the discourse of excellence through peer review, which is often grounded in claims of 'scientific', 'objective' and 'neutral' knowledge. Critics have expressed concerns about the reliability and fairness of peer review, pointing to bias and systemic inequities in funding decisions (Hicks & Katz, 2011; Tamblyn et al., 2018). The mounting criticism over the lack of equity in research funding outcomes has led to specific policy responses from these agencies, but more needs to be done. Moreover, scholars regularly note that the activities of funding bodies regarding equity have been underexplored in the academic literature (Jong et al., 2021).

The Canada Research Chairs Program (CRCP) serves as an important illustrative case for unpacking the complexity and resistance in policy change that aims for enhanced equity in funding decisions. The CRCP was announced in 1999 and launched in 2000 with the intent to better position Canada as a world leader of excellence by providing federal funding to degree-granting institutions across the country to create over 2,000 chair positions for 'world-class' researchers. The process of defining and determining excellence within the CRCP has played a key role in who is appointed as a chair.

The objective of this chapter is to examine equity-related policy change in the CRCP within the context of research excellence, tracing policy shifts and examining their underlying factors, while illustrating the tensions and complexities involved in the move towards equitable approaches for awarding chair positions. The following question guides this chapter: *In what ways has the Canada Research Chairs Program responded to calls for equity?* We conduct a critical policy analysis from an equity standpoint of CRCP documentation from the programme's inception in 1999 until 2022. We argue that an equity agenda

DOI: 10.4324/9781003330431-16

174 Merli Tamtik and Dawn Sutherland

is difficult to achieve and may rely upon changes in understandings of excellence, institutional will and continuous advocacy work by equity-seeking groups,[1] such as women researchers and racialised scholars.

The Canadian research funding landscape

Federal research funding is the most significant source of research support in Canada. This research funding is primarily administered by three federally affiliated agencies: the Canadian Institutes of Health Research (CIHR), the National Sciences and Engineering Research Council of Canada (NSERC) and the Social Sciences and Humanities Research Council of Canada (SSHRC). These agencies offer funding for individual scholars, teams of collaborators or institutions. Each agency was created independently through an Act of Parliament and has a governance structure that is responsible for developing its strategic directions and goals and evaluating overall performance. The three agencies (often referred to as the tri-agencies) create common policies, regulations and guidelines for the administration and use of federal research funds. Canada's provincial governments have the responsibility for regulating and providing direct operating support to post-secondary institutions (i.e. universities, colleges and institutes) and provide some research project funding. Funding for research projects is also available from other sources, including institutions themselves as well as industry.

Canada Research Chairs Program overview

The announcement of the CRCP in 1999 initiated a shift towards more direct involvement and financial support from the federal government in Canada's research funding landscape (Jones, 2000), combined with heightened concern over attaining world-class excellence (Fallis, 2013). Canada Research Chairs can be appointed to one of two streams: tier 1 and tier 2. Tier 1 chairs are outstanding researchers, typically full professors, 'acknowledged by their peers as world leaders in their fields', while tier 2 chairs are 'exceptional emerging researchers, acknowledged by their peers as having the potential to lead in their field' (CRCP, 2019a).[2]

For each tier 1 chair, the institution receives 200,000 CAD (£118,000)[3] annually for seven years; for each tier 2 chair, the institution receives 100,000 CAD (£59,000) annually for five years plus an additional 20,000 CAD (£12,000) annual research stipend for the chairholder in their first term. Other than the tier 2 stipend, institutions have flexibility in how they use the funding. The institution may allocate some of the funding to the chair and will negotiate what teaching and administration are expected. In general, chairs must establish research programmes, secure relevant research funding and contribute to the strategic priorities of an institution. They are expected to provide mentoring and training opportunities for students by exposing them to cutting-edge research. Institutions may also support chairs to apply for infrastructure funding (for example, for laboratories) from another fund, the Canada Foundation for Innovation (CFI). Chair positions can be renewed at the same institution for one additional term. Renewals require a progress report and other demonstrations of excellence.

The CRCP is jointly administered by the three granting agencies through the Tri-agency Institutional Programs Secretariat (TIPS) (CRCP, 2019b). TIPS is responsible for the day-to-day administration of the programme. Governance of the programme is maintained by a management committee (looking after peer reviews, policy development) and a steering committee (responsible for strategic advice on the programme's overall direction). The steering committee oversees the work of the management committee and reports to the Minister of Innovation, Science and Industry. The deputy ministers of Industry Canada and Health Canada have seats on the CRCP steering committee.

The identification of prospective Canada Research Chairs occurs at the level of the institutions, which determine their own selection processes, normally involving some level of peer review. Chairs may be recruited externally or nominated internally. Only recently have institutions been required to advertise these positions. The institutional nomination must make a case that establishes the 'excellence' of the nominee and their proposed research programme. Each nomination is then subjected to external peer review through the CRCP College of Reviewers.

Every five years, the CRCP determines the allocation of a number of chairs to each eligible institution (CRCP, 2021b). The allocations are based on the research performance (amount of tri-agency funding, with certain exclusions) of each institution in the previous three years, which means that most chair positions are allocated to research-intensive universities. As of 2021, there were 2,285 chair positions, of which 2,148 were 'regular' chairs allocated by agency: 39% to NSERC (837 chairs), 39% to CIHR (837 chairs) and 22% to SSHRC (474 chairs). A small number (137) of 'special' chairs that can be filled across any agency are reserved to assist less research-intensive institutions (CRCP, 2021b).

Research excellence, peer review and the CRCP

Excellence, determined by bibliometric indicators and/or peer review, has been used as the gold standard to establish promise and make research funding decisions (Jong et al., 2021). Critical scholars argue that to assume excellence is readily measured overlooks the systemic barriers to research funding that disadvantage individuals from equity-seeking groups (Ahmed, 2012; Hicks & Katz, 2011; Mohamed & Beagan, 2019). Viewing knowledge in neutral terms creates power hierarchies where a dominant group asserts its inherent cultural values, assumptions and societal norms over others, leading to bias in peer review and highly unequal distributions of research funding (Tamblyn et al., 2018). Furthermore, ignoring equity aspects in the assessment of excellence misses the unique research potential that emerges from individuals who do not fit the standard measurement criteria. Gender bias in the awarding of research grants, whether individual or systemic, has been identified by scholars (e.g. Steinþórsdóttir et al., 2020; Witteman et al., 2019). Although the CRCP (2023c) defines equity in systemic terms, requiring 'the removal of systemic barriers and biases enabling all individuals to have equal access to and to benefit from the program', it retains conventional ideas about research excellence.

The instructions to reviewers encapsulate 'research excellence' within the programme (CRCP, 2021a). For tier 1 chairs, the nominee is to be an outstanding researcher whose accomplishments have made a major impact on their fields; be recognised internationally; have a superior record of supervising higher degree students and postdoctoral fellows; and be proposing an original, innovative, high-quality research programme. Tier 2 chair nominees are to be excellent emerging world-class researchers who have demonstrated research creativity; have the potential to achieve international recognition; have the potential to attract trainees; and, like tier 1 nominees, be proposing an original, innovative, high-quality research programme.

Unlike similar chairs elsewhere, scholars do not apply directly but are nominated by the institution. At that institutional stage, some type of peer review may take place, but its structure is not mandated. Once a nomination is put forward, there is a formal external peer-review process. At least three members from the CRCP College of Reviewers assess each nomination in relation to research excellence and make a recommendation to TIPS about funding the position. These peer reviewers are commended for their 'proven ability to recognize excellence' (Picard-Aitken et al., 2010) and are seen to make an outstanding contribution 'to the current landscape of Canadian research excellence' (CRCP, 2018). Available data from 2012–2017 show that the list of the most active peer reviewers is heavily male-dominated (CRCP, 2018). Most reviewers are from research-intensive Canadian institutions, with only a few reviewers from the United States and other countries. This peer review tends to be largely a formality, as the acceptance rate of institutional chair nominations is 98% (CRCP, 2023d).

Conceptual framework

This chapter is grounded in critical policy analysis (CPA) literature examining the discourses of policy change towards equity, diversity and inclusion in the CRCP. CPA attends to the 'difference between policy rhetoric and practiced reality' (Diem & Young, 2015, p. 843). CPA examines the circulation of power, the ways policy creates 'winners' and 'losers', and the strategies of resistance some individuals exert (Diem et al., 2014, p. 1072).

We understand policy as an interpretive process enacted in specific historical, geographical, social, economic, cultural and political contexts (Ball, 1994; Bowe et al., 1992; Ozga, 2000; Rizvi & Lingard, 2010). Policies are not value-free; they serve the interests of particular stakeholders in power and do not follow a standard implementation path. We are guided by Bacchi (2012), who argued that policy is something to be critiqued and troubled rather than accepted at face value.

With CPA as a conceptual framework, we examine where and how policy is made and re-made in the context of the CRCP, who benefits from the policy, who loses and what has been the role of equity-seeking groups in policy change. As such, CPA helps to reveal tensions and highlight policy struggles in the decision-making and equity efforts of the CRCP with regard to research excellence.

Method and data sources

We adopted a qualitative case study approach. The first step involved gathering relevant policy documents related to the CRCP issued between 1999 and 2022. As well as examining current publicly available data on the CRCP website, we reviewed and analysed 15 CRCP governance publications (programme description, programme evaluation reports, CRCP formal responses to reviews); 15 CRCP equity, diversity and inclusion (EDI) action plans from research-intensive universities; six EDI policy documents (released to the institutions as best practices); and four documents associated with human rights complaints involving the CRCP. The purpose of the document analysis was to collect information and examine the narratives of policy shifts towards increased equity in the CRCP. We performed textual analysis of the documents, tracing inequities in peer review, discourse changes around research excellence and indications of power in the distribution of resources and knowledge. Open coding, categorising and selective coding led to a final set of themes.

Findings: phases in the CRCP vis-à-vis EDI

Our findings indicate the following distinct phases in CRCP policy change with regard to EDI approaches: the early years and equity concerns (1999–2002); moving the equity process beyond monitoring (2003–2006); establishing institutional targets (2007–2018) and targets are not enough, time to get tough (2019–onwards). The phases are closely tied to the responses of TIPS to external programme reviews, which were conducted every five years, and to the work of equity-seeking individuals who launched complaints to the Canadian Human Rights Commission. Those formal complaints have been followed in some cases by modifications to the CRCP. Each phase is described in detail in the following sections.

The early years and equity concerns (1999–2002)

The 2000 CRCP budget announced an initial allocation of 900 million CAD (£530 million) to the programme. The original distribution of awards according to granting agency was CIHR 35%, NSERC 45% and SSHRC 20% (Fallis, 2013). As described earlier, institutions were allocated chair positions according to their share of tri-agency grants. In order to receive a regular chair, an institution had to have an annual external grant income of at least 100,000 CAD (£59,000) (Fallis, 2013). As a result, the larger, more research-intensive universities, whose academic staff members had been securing tri-agency grants, received most of the chair allocations.

In the first few years of the CRCP, several equity concerns surfaced concerning the distribution of chairs. First, this funding approach not only discriminated against the less research-intensive institutions but also against the humanities and social sciences, spaces where women academics were relatively well-represented. The unequal distribution across subject areas was based on the relative value of the agencies' budgets, thus compounding existing inequities. Furthermore, when the programme was launched, institutions had to submit strategic research plans to show their research strengths and strategic direction and recommend candidates who showed high potential to contribute to the institution's strategic vision. Again, as men and those in male-dominated fields often had stronger records using conventional indicators, the system rewarded the established 'winners'. One feature of 'excellence' was a record of securing research grants (Hickling Arthurs Low, 2002), which in some cases worked against potential women candidates or others who may have had interrupted careers.

In addition, the governance mechanism of the CRCP was seen to be potentially discriminatory to equity-seeking groups. The five-person CRCP steering committee from 2000 to 2004 was composed exclusively of men, and a majority (83%) of the College of Reviewers' 2,000 appointed experts were men (Side & Robbins, 2007). No equity data other than sex was available for these reviewers. The combinations and interactions of all these factors meant that there was systemic bias built into the chair allocation process from the start.

TIPS's third-year external review of the nomination and approval process was published in 2002 (Hickling Arthurs Low, 2002). Research excellence was defined as success in obtaining funding from the tri-agencies (p. 9) and the language of equity was missing from the report. The report also noted that 26% of tier 2 women chairholders expressed concerns with the nomination process (compared to 15% of men), pointing to the limited transparency in promoting the opportunity among all eligible scholars (p. 11). The report recommended that TIPS should work with institutions to achieve gender balance and that there should be greater recognition of circumstances, such as time away from research to have children, that may affect the career research productivity of women.

An additional gender-based analysis of CRCP was requested by TIPS to analyse women's representation in institutional nominations. The evaluation found fewer tier 1 and 2 nominations of women, including far fewer women nominated for tier 2 chairs in the social sciences and humanities than what would be expected given the pool of eligible nominees (Nicole Bégin-Heick & Associates, 2002). After these reports, the CRCP policy was adjusted so that tier 2 nominees could have no more than ten years of postdoctoral experience (not including leaves) in an effort to counterbalance a tendency of institutions to nominate more senior researchers, which could result in disproportionately higher numbers of men.

Moving the equity process beyond monitoring (the Human Rights Settlement) (2003–2006)

In 2003, a human rights complaint was launched by eight women academics (Marjorie Griffin Cohen, Louise Forsyth, Glenis Joyce, Audrey Kobayashi, Shree Mulay, Michele Ollivier, Susan Prentice and Wendy Robbins), asserting that the CRCP, and thus the federal government, discriminated based upon sex, age, race, sexual orientation, colour, disability, nationality, ethnic origin and family status (Morgan, 2003). The complainants alleged that the programme failed to collect statistics on the appointment of chairs from equity-seeking groups (except women). They also argued that the programme failed to introduce standardised policies that required institutions to comply with employment equity legislation intended to ensure that workplaces are representative of the working-age populations and individuals from disadvantaged groups (Morgan, 2003). The complaint, initiated and executed by equity-seeking individuals, was a formal step to hold the federal government accountable for structural discrimination in the CRCP.

Gender bias was also noted in the fifth-year external review report of the CRCP, which suggested that in order to attain gender balance, women's representation in chair allocations across both tiers must significantly increase (Malatest & Associates, 2004). The recommendation of this report was to continue monitoring the gender distribution of chairholders. Best practices for institutions to achieve gender parity included prioritising fields where women were populous and engaging equity officers on the institutional CRCP advisory committee (Malatest & Associates, 2004). The approach to research excellence (programmatic and individual) remained unchanged. The response of the CRCP Steering Committee (2005) to the fifth-year review noted that 'the Chairs program will continue to apply existing peer-review mechanisms for evaluating Chairs nominations' (p. 2).

In 2006, TIPS and the eight human rights complainants successfully negotiated a settlement whereby TIPS agreed to collect information on the status of nominees; establish targets for members of the under-represented groups; incorporate gender and diversity-based analyses; secure a transparent, open and equitable nomination process; and conduct a review of systemic barriers that hinder the nomination process for equity-seeking individuals (Canadian Human Rights Tribunal [CHRT], 2019, Appendix A). Despite the CRCP's defence of its policies of excellence and peer review, the 2003 human rights complaint set in motion a long-term battle against inequity in the programme.

Establishing institutional targets (2007–2018)

Gradually, TIPS amended policy and processes in line with the 2006 settlement. Institutions were asked to start tracking CRCP nominations by tier and discipline in order to address the issue of under-representation of women (and other equity-seeking groups) in their planning documents and annual reports. Targets for the under-represented groups were established in 2007 with a deadline for compliance by December 2019: approximately 31% for women,[4] 15% for members of visible minorities, 4% for persons with disabilities and 1% for Indigenous peoples. TIPS committed to monitoring participation rates against these targets. The tenth-year review report (Picard-Aitken et al., 2010) further explored the impact of the initial and continued barriers to access within the programme. This evaluation report was authored by six individuals, four of whom were women. The report identified four under-represented groups in the CRCP (based on protected groups listed in the Canadian Human Rights Act): women, members of visible minorities, persons with disabilities and Aboriginal people (Picard-Aitken et al., 2010).

The consequences of zooming in on equity issues were apparent in the Picard-Aitken et al. (2010) review. Examination of systemic barriers was introduced as part of the evaluation design across programmes, institutions and chairholders, and the language used in the report was critical compared to previous evaluation reports. Peer reviewers and institutional nominating committees were warned against assessing members of the under-represented groups based on productivity, as they are more likely to have career gaps in their academic paths. Systemic barriers in the CRCP were reported by 15% of the chairholders belonging to the four under-represented groups, and the CRCP design was said to further perpetuate the already existing barriers with key problems associated with selection and nomination to the programme (p. viii). The observations in the document directly challenged institutions to improve their limited efforts in attending to equity concerns (pp. 112–113). Following the tenth-year review, in 2012, the CRCP established an advisory committee on EDI policy with a mandate to provide guidance on advancing equity across the programme and the research ecosystem in higher education.

Human rights claims continued. In 2016, a University of Ottawa law professor, Amir Attaran, filed a case primarily based on race. He described how several White men in his department had been promoted from tier 2 to tier 1 chair positions, while as a racialised individual, he was denied the same opportunity (Greenfield, 2021). The 2003 human rights case also took a turn in 2017, when the complainants argued that too little progress had been made on the terms of the settlement (Munroe, 2021), which subsequently led to a federal court order and an amendment to the earlier settlement (CHRT, 2019).

In May 2017, the tri-agencies initiated the EDI action plan to clearly lay out the implementation of EDI requirements for institutions to be eligible for tri-agency funding (Canada Research Coordinating Committee, 2018). TIPS provided new targets for the under-represented groups (CRCP, 2023b) and introduced a guidebook of best practices as a tool to support the recruitment, hiring and retention of academics to meet equity objectives (CRCP, 2021c). In 2017, the allocations of chair positions shifted across agencies, resulting in decreases for NSERC, the agency with the lowest overall participation rates for women (from 45% to 39%), and increases for CIHR (from 35% to 39%) and SSHRC (from 20% to 22%).

Since the launch of the EDI action plan and best practices guidebook, institutions have further introduced changes to their CRCP recruitment processes. In their institutional action plans, there are mentions of conducting institutional employment equity reviews, engaging in targeted recruitment for chairholders from the under-represented groups, inserting equity statements in employment postings, providing search committees with specific guidelines for broadening candidate pools and introducing unconscious bias training for academic and other staff. As a result, there seemed to be some gradual increases in representation of the four under-represented groups. For example, between 2016 and 2019, the percentage of chair positions held by women increased from 28.9% to 37.6%, by racialised scholars from 13.1% to 21.0%, by Indigenous peoples from 1.0% to 3.2% and by persons with disabilities from 0.6% to 5.4% (CRCP, 2023d).

Targets are not enough, time to get tough (2019–onwards)

Further development occurred in the human rights cases in this period: an amendment to the settlement agreement from the 2003 complaint was released in 2019 (CHRT, 2019) and the Attaran case was settled in 2021 (CHRT, 2021). Enforcement of targets was characterised as more stringent, potentially leading to the loss of chair positions, and institutions were required to finalise their equity-focused action plans (Munroe, 2021). From about 2019, we see changes in language, targets, scope and urgency in the documents concerning the CRCP. Updated targets to be met by December 2029 for each of the four under-represented groups were much higher than in the past: women and gender equity-seeking groups[5] 50.9%, racialised individuals 22%, persons with disabilities 7.5% and Indigenous peoples 4.9% (CRCP, 2023b). In addition to increasing targets, the language in the documents also changed. The 2019 addendum to the original 2006 human rights settlement moved away from using the word 'Aboriginal' and used 'Indigenous' instead.

The document also mentioned for the first time the need to attend to gender identity and sexual orientation (CHRT, 2019), which were subsequently added to the self-identification data collected from nominees and chairholders. The programme also asks institutions to consider intersectional identities that may create additional equity barriers for researchers (CRCP, 2021c). A small segment of the guidelines issued by TIPS broadens the concept of excellence for job postings: 'Use encompassing, clear, flexible criteria for assessing excellence that fully document, recognize and reward the scholarship of teaching, professional service, community service, outreach, mentoring and research training, and account for non-traditional areas of research and/or research outputs' (CRCP, 2021c). Nevertheless, it remains unclear how to reconcile this advice with the standard criteria for identifying excellence that has been part of the CRCP all along (world-class recognition, etc.).

In March 2023, chairholders included 45.8% women and gender equity-seeking groups, 26.1% racialised scholars, 6.3% persons with disabilities and 3.9% Indigenous peoples (CRCP, 2023d). Failure to meet the identified targets (which gradually increase from 2022 to 2029) now results in some consequences for the institution. So far, it seems that these consequences are primarily in the scope of naming and shaming. In July 2023, two (out of 78) institutions had not met the December 2019 targets. For those two institutions, new nominations (excluding renewals) were limited to candidates who self-identify as belonging to one or more of the four under-represented groups; this restriction was lifted in August 2023 by which time all institutions had met the targets (CRCP, 2023a). At that time, two institutions were facing sanctions, one for an unsubmitted progress report and the other for a partially satisfactory institutional EDI action plan. Peer-review decisions and associated funding were being withheld for these two institutions.

In addition to holding institutions accountable through targets and applying consequences, TIPS has introduced financial incentives for institutional compliance. For example, in April 2020, the CRCP introduced a new EDI stipend of 50,000 CAD (£29,000) to encourage higher education institutions to tackle systemic barriers in their institutions that prevent individuals from the under-represented groups from participating in the CRCP.

Discussion

Our analysis has examined the long and winding road towards achieving equity in the CRCP. We demonstrate the importance of 'bottom-up' pressures from equity-seeking individuals, the positive role of programme evaluations and the slowness of change in the face of deeply entrenched notions around research excellence.

In terms of pressures, a small group of women researchers and later a racialised man were key initiators of policy change. The claims were made within the larger context of Canada's legal position on human rights issues.

Another important influence on CRCP policy change stems from the series of evaluation reports conducted on the CRCP. These reports provided quantitative data on representation and regularly emphasised systemic barriers, pointing out how achieving excellence and equity are intertwined and should not be considered disjointedly. We anticipate that agency staff may have contributed behind the scenes to policy change (see Husu & Peterson, this volume).

Based on these concerted efforts, TIPS altered a number of its procedures, for example, creating a 'mid-point attestation' where institutions must demonstrate they are following EDI-compliant recruitment and nomination processes before the nomination can be filed. Targets for representation of under-represented groups were introduced and increased over time. By 2021, the CRCP process looked much more equitable than it did originally, its language was more inclusive, and targets had been met in most institutions. The diversity categories have been broadened over time, demonstrating gradually increased awareness of who might be marginalised within the CRCP and research funding practices more generally. In 2002, the specific focus was on gender balance, with three other under-represented groups added in 2010, gender minorities and intersectionality formally recognised in 2021, and a shift in 2023 from the term 'gender minorities' to 'gender equity-seeking groups' (CRCP, 2023b).

However, issues remain. Our analysis demonstrates that EDI considerations in the CRCP still tend to have a checkbox nature in policy documents – measured primarily by tracking targets across equity groups, without stronger institutional accountability over systemic issues persistent in higher education. The existence of targets or quotas does not address issues individuals may face after starting their research programmes (e.g. persistent institutional racism, predominantly White knowledge spaces) nor the impact on colleagues who do not receive chair positions. More work needs to be done at the institutional level to really challenge systemic barriers in the nomination process and to go beyond targets.

The process is still closely tied to limited ideas about how excellence should be framed and measured in a federally funded research programme. Our findings demonstrate that for many years, excellence and equity were seldom considered together. The 2003 human rights complaint brought equity issues to centre stage. What followed was a reactive scrambling to mitigate the voices of equity-seeking individuals by gradually developing better informed perspectives and proactive action such as comprehensive definitions of equity, EDI action plans, institutional repercussions, considerations around intersectionality and awareness of tokenism.

At the heart of this policy puzzle is the concept of excellence, intertwined with the peer review charged with identifying it (see Acker, this volume). Our analysis shows the definition of excellence in the CRCP remained unchanged for decades. While recently TIPS has provided recommendations for being somewhat flexible in approaching excellence, it is likely that peer review still focuses heavily on assessing research production based on quantifiable indicators (e.g., peer-reviewed publications, international conference presentations, grant acquisition), favouring the dominant knowledge pool and its producers. Although excellence is defined in three different ways in the CRCP – as programmatic excellence (overall capacity), individual excellence (productivity) and excellence in peer review (ability to identify excellence) – the meaning in practice is determined and measured by the dominant groups (e.g. university administrators, government policymakers). As a result, the CRCP produces an elite academic class based on rankings in peer reviews, validating and rewarding dominant knowledges and overlooking others.

To fully integrate equity concerns into the process, there is a need to deliberately consider alternative perspectives on the concept of excellence in higher education. Tamtik (2023) describes how Indigenous perspectives have taught higher education administrators to view excellence and innovation from a decolonising lens, resisting endless competition but considering ways in which learning from a colonial past and healing can teach institutions new ways to pursue excellence. However, to date, efforts to reframe the narrative of research excellence using different standards that would be more inclusive of alternative knowledge frameworks or provide incentives to think about excellence and innovation in decolonial terms are absent.

Within the context of practice, it becomes clear that there has been a change in the rhetoric of TIPS from one of omniscient to responsible funder. As an omniscient funder in the initial implementation of the programme, the TIPS narrative established a programme that was absolved of responsibility for the nomination process. Indeed, the TIPS policy reflected a reluctance to hold institutions accountable for their identified EDI targets until very recently. The autonomy of institutions in the nomination process and the application of a discriminatory definition of excellence seem to be the two assumptions that inhibited a quicker or more proactive approach to equitable policy in the CRCP.

Conclusion

As is evident from this analysis, organisational attempts to address equity through policy change take significant time, effort and often strong bottom-up advocacy work from equity-seeking groups. Following the tenets of CPA, and taking as its subject a particularly important innovation, the Canada Research Chairs Program, our study points to the contextual and situated nature of research funding policy in Canadian higher education. Although policy change in the direction of equity has been achieved over several decades, it tends to have a checkbox nature (e.g. a focus on numeric targets) and does not sufficiently address systemic change in a comprehensive, all-encompassing manner nor does it substantially challenge normative practices in assessing excellence.

Much responsibility is left up to the higher education institutions. Unusually, compared to some other countries, nominations in the CRCP are made by institutions and centred on the practices of 'star searches', which invariably miss many qualified researchers (Picard-Aitken, 2010, p. 112). Peer review takes place in unstandardised ways in the institutions (despite 'guidelines') and in prescribed ways once the nomination is made, yet it is still located in the context of conventional ideas about excellence that prioritise international reputations and cutting-edge research. Although non-compliance with equity requirements of the programme has direct financial and potentially reputational consequences for higher education institutions, there is still significant diversity in how those criteria are enacted within individual institutions. Furthermore, even with declared strict consequences for non-compliance, there is still flexibility for institutions to quickly 'correct their mistakes' to continue receiving funding.

The most vulnerable aspect of the CRCP design with regard to equity issues is that individual institutions decide who to nominate and how to allocate the funding received. Despite improvements over time, the continuing limitations in transparency hide barriers faced by particular scholars. We might also conclude with the observation that making selections equitable within the CRCP does not detract from the inherent elitism of the programme itself, which naturalises a division between the 'chosen few' (Angervall et al., 2015) and the rest.

Notes

1 We are intentionally using the term 'equity-seeking' (rather than 'equity-deserving') to denote the active participation, purposeful advocacy and political power of marginalised individuals in disrupting the structural and systemic barriers in society and organisations. This language also aligns with the terminology used on the CRCP website as of January 2024.
2 The term 'researcher' does not mean an academic engaged exclusively or near-exclusively in research, as it might in some of the other countries represented in this volume. In most cases the nominees are academics with responsibilities in teaching, research and service (administration). Once they become a Canada Research Chair, the distribution of their activities is negotiated with the institution.
3 Currency conversions as of January 5, 2024.
4 The target for women was based upon the overall participation rates for women in CIHR, NSERC and SSHRC grant competitions (35%, 21% and 45%, respectively). Institutional targets, therefore, varied depending upon the number of chair positions allocated to each agency.
5 'Gender equity-seeking groups' comprise individuals who self-identify as transgender, gender-fluid, nonbinary or Two-Spirit (CRCP, 2023b). As of 2021, gender equity-seeking groups were included in the equity target for women; however, gender equity-seeking groups and women are reported separately in the programme statistics (CRCP, 2023d).

References

Ahmed, S. (2012). *On being included: racism and diversity in institutional life.* Duke University Press.

Angervall, P., Beach, D., & Gustafsson, J. (2015). The unacknowledged value of female academic labour power for male research careers. *Higher Education Research & Development, 34*(5), 815–827. https://doi.org/10.1080/07294360.2015.1011092

Bacchi, C. (2012). Why study problematizations? Making politics visible. *Open Journal of Political Science, 2*(1), 1–8. https://doi.org/10.4236/ojps.2012.21001

Ball, S. J. (1994). *Education reform: a critical and post-structural approach.* Open University Press.

Bowe, R., Ball, S. J., & Gold, A. (1992). *Reforming education and changing schools: case studies in policy sociology.* Routledge.

Canada Research Chairs Program. (2018, August 17). *College of reviewers.* https://www.chairs-chaires.gc.ca/peer_reviewers-evaluateurs/college_members-membres_college-eng.aspx

Canada Research Chairs Program. (2019a, June 25). *Program details.* https://www.chairs-chaires.gc.ca/program-programme/index-eng.aspx

Canada Research Chairs Program. (2019b, November 28). *Governance.* https://www.chairs-chaires.gc.ca/about_us-a_notre_sujet/governance-gouvernance-eng.aspx

Canada Research Chairs Program. (2021a, March 16). *Instructions to College of Reviewers members.* https://www.chairs-chaires.gc.ca/peer_reviewers-evaluateurs/instructions-instructions-eng.aspx

Canada Research Chairs Program. (2021b, July 29). *Method of allocating chairs.* https://www.chairs-chaires.gc.ca/program-programme/allocation-attribution-eng.aspx

Canada Research Chairs Program. (2021c, November 17). *Creating an equitable, diverse and inclusive research environment: a best practices guide for recruitment, hiring and retention.* https://www.chairs-chaires.gc.ca/program-programme/equity-equite/best_practices-pratiques_examplaires-eng.aspx

Canada Research Chairs Program. (2023a, August 2). *Consequences of not meeting the program's equity, diversity and inclusion requirements.* https://www.chairs-chaires.gc.ca/program-programme/equity-equite/consequences-eng.aspx

Canada Research Chairs Program. (2023b, August 9). *Establishing equity targets for 2021 to 2029.* https://www.chairs-chaires.gc.ca/program-programme/equity-equite/targets-cibles-eng.aspx

Canada Research Chairs Program. (2023c, August 9). *Frequently asked questions.* https://www.chairs-chaires.gc.ca/program-programme/equity-equite/faqs-questions_frequentes-eng.aspx

Canada Research Chairs Program. (2023d, August 9). *Program representation statistics.* https://www.chairs-chaires.gc.ca/about_us-a_notre_sujet/statistics-statistiques-eng.aspx

Canada Research Chairs Program Steering Committee. (2005). *Response to the fifth-year evaluation of the Canada Research Chairs Program.* https://www.chairs-chaires.gc.ca/about_us-a_notre_sujet/publications/fifth_year_response_e.pdf

Canada Research Coordinating Committee. (2018). *Tri-agency equity, diversity and inclusion action plan (2018–2025).* https://www.nserc-crsng.gc.ca/InterAgency-Interorganismes/EDI-EDI/Action-Plan_Plan-dAction_eng.asp

Canadian Human Rights Tribunal. (2019). *Settlement agreement* (addendum to October 24, 2006, settlement agreement) (CHRT T11118/9905). https://www.chairs-chaires.gc.ca/program-programme/equity-equite/pdf/addendum_to_2006_agreement-eng.pdf

Canadian Human Rights Tribunal. (2021). *Minutes of settlement* (CHRT T2241/6317). https://www.chairs-chaires.gc.ca/program-programme/equity-equite/2021_settlement-reglement-eng.aspx

Diem, S., & Young, M. D. (2015). Considering critical turns in research on educational leadership and policy. *International Journal of Educational Management, 29* (7), 838–850. https://doi.org/10.1108/IJEM-05-2015-0060

Diem, S., Young, M. D., Welton, A. D., Mansfield, K. C., & Lee, P.-L. (2014). The intellectual landscape of critical policy analysis. *International Journal of Qualitative Studies in Education, 27*(9), 1068–1090. https://doi.org/10.1080/09518398. 2014.916007

Fallis, G. (2013). *Rethinking higher education: participation, research, and differentiation.* McGill–Queen's University Press.

Greenfield, N. M. (2021, April 8). University research chairs ruling enforces equity targets. *University World News.* https://www.universityworldnews.com/post.php?story=20210408151948785

Hickling Arthurs Low. (2002). *Third-year review of the Canada Research Chairs Program.* https://www.chairs-chaires.gc.ca/about_us-a_notre_sujet/publications/third_year_review_e.pdf

Hicks, D., & Katz, J. S. (2011). Equity and excellence in research funding. *Minerva, 49*(2), 137–151. https://doi.org/10.1007/s11024-011-9170-6

Jones, G. (2000). The Canada Research Chairs program. *International Higher Education, 21,* 22–23. https://doi.org/10.6017/ihe.2000.21.6896

Jong, L., Franssen, T., & Pinfield, S. (2021). *'Excellence' in the research ecosystem: a literature review* (Research on Research Institute Working Paper No. 5). https://doi.org/10.6084/m9.figshare.16669834.v1

Malatest & Associates. (2004). *Fifth-year evaluation of the Canada Research Chairs Program.* http://www.chairs-chaires.gc.ca/about_us-a_notre_sujet/publications/fifth_year_review_e.pdf

Mohamed, T., & Beagan, B. L. (2019). 'Strange faces' in the academy: experiences of racialized and Indigenous faculty in Canadian universities. *Race Ethnicity and Education, 22*(3), 338–354. https://doi.org/10.1080/13613324.2018.1511532

Morgan, R. C. (2003). *Human rights complaint concerning the Canada Research Chairs Program.* https://www.academicwomenforjustice.org/downloads/Cdn-research-chairs-prg-complaint.pdf

Munroe, I. (2021, June 29). Latest settlement in CRC equity issue sets hard deadline for targets. *University Affairs.* https://www.universityaffairs.ca/news/news-article/latest-settlement-in-crc-equity-issue-sets-hard-deadline-for-targets/

Nicole Bégin-Heick & Associates Inc. (2002). *Gender-based analysis of the Canada Research Chairs Program.* https://www.chairs-chaires.gc.ca/about_us-a_notre_sujet/publications/gender_e.pdf

Ozga, J. (2000). *Policy research in educational settings: contested terrain.* Open University Press.

Picard-Aitken, M., Foster, T., Labrosse, I., Caruso, J., Campbell, D., & Archambault, E. (2010). *Tenth-year review of the Canada Research Chairs program: final evaluation report.* https://www.chairs-chaires.gc.ca/about_us-a_notre_sujet/publications/ten_year_evaluation_e.pdf

Rizvi, F., & Lingard, B. (2010). *Globalizing education policy.* Routledge.

Side, K., & Robbins, W. (2007). Institutionalizing inequalities in Canadian universities: the Canada Research Chairs Program. *NWSA Journal, 19*(3), 163–181. https://www.muse.jhu.edu/article/224763

Steinþórsdóttir, F. S., Einarsdóttir, Þ., Pétursdóttir, G. M., & Himmelweit, S. (2020). Gendered inequalities in competitive grant funding: an overlooked dimension of gendered power relations in academia. *Higher Education Research & Development*, *39*(2), 362–375. https://doi.org/10.1080/07294360.2019.1666257

Tamblyn, R., Girard, N., Qian, C. J., & Hanley, J. (2018). Assessment of potential bias in research grant peer review in Canada. *Canadian Medical Association Journal*, *190*(16), E489–E499. https://www.doi.org/10.1503/cmaj.170901

Tamtik, M. (2023). Indigenous innovation and organizational change towards equitable higher education systems: the Canadian experience. *AlterNative: An International Journal of Indigenous Peoples*, *19*(2), 345–355. https://doi.org/10.1177/11771801231170277

Witteman, H. O., Hendricks, M., Straus, S., & Tannenbaum, C. (2019). Are gender gaps due to evaluations of the applicant or the science? A natural experiment at a national funding agency. *The Lancet*, *393*(10171), 531–540. https://doi.org/10.1016/S0140-6736(18)32611-4

13

WOMEN ACADEMICS UNDER RAE AND REF

The changing research funding policy landscape in the United Kingdom

Lisa Lucas

Since publishing *The Research Game in Academic Life* (Lucas, 2006), I have been writing and reflecting on the United Kingdom (UK) system of research funding and evaluation with an interest in the ways it affects universities and the work and careers of academics. In this chapter, I continue that focus by reviewing changes over time in the UK evaluation and funding framework known initially as the Research Assessment Exercise (RAE) and then as the Research Excellence Framework (REF) (subsequently RAE/REF in this chapter). These exercises were established with the stated intention to improve the quality of research in UK universities and use the results to allocate selective funding to universities for research.

The UK was one of the first countries to initiate this form of national assessment, since copied by other countries with slightly different formats (Hicks, 2009). Its initiation can be traced to political shifts in the 1980s when the Conservative government of Prime Minister Margaret Thatcher aimed to intensify central government control over universities by making them more accountable. As part of the 1988 Education Reform Act, there were important changes for the higher education sector such as ending the entitlement of academic staff to permanent positions. Through the RAE/REF, research performance was elevated to a major concern for universities, not only because funding depended on it but also because of its reputational value in an era in which global and national rankings have increased competition over the positioning and prestige of universities (Naidoo, 2018).

The question of gender equity in the RAE/REF is an important consideration that I have not focused on specifically in previous writings. In this chapter, therefore, the issue of gender equity is brought to the fore to consider whether

DOI: 10.4324/9781003330431-17

equity has improved over the many years of the RAE/REF or whether women academics continue to be disadvantaged by the process as Yarrow (2018) found.

I begin with an overview of the RAE and REF exercises and some of the equity policies developed in recent years. I then consider the scholarly literature on the RAE/REF and relevant work on women academics. I draw upon two research studies, paying particular attention to the interviews with women in each study as a means of highlighting the gender equity implications of these exercises and to attend to changes and continuities in what the participants saw as being required of them. In a conclusion, I bring the discussion up to date and look towards possible future developments.

Overview of the UK RAE/REF

Since the establishment of the UK Research Assessment Exercise (RAE) in 1986, it has gone through many changes, with successive exercises conducted in 1992, 1996, 2001 and 2008 and then as the renamed Research Excellence Framework (REF) in 2014 and 2021. Its purpose is to assess the quality of research across disciplines (called units of assessment or UOAs) in UK universities and then to use a funding formula based in part on these evaluations to determine an annual allocation of quality-related (QR) research funding. The funding is allocated to institutions to support research across the university, normally involving some devolving of funds to faculties. Until 2018, the Higher Education Funding Council for England (HEFCE) was responsible for the RAE/REF, but it is now undertaken by Research England, part of UK Research and Innovation (UKRI).[1]

The RAE/REF is conducted through a process of peer review with specialist panels evaluating the research work of academic staff at all universities in the UK. For example, for REF 2021 (REF, ca. 2022), there were 34 sub-panels overseen by four broad-subject main panels; assessors included 900 academic evaluators (including 38 'international members') and 220 'research users' drawn from various sectors (e.g. health, media). The grading scale utilised by the RAE/REF panels involves star ratings: 0 (unclassified), 1* (nationally recognised), 2* (internationally recognised), 3* (internationally excellent) and 4* (world-leading). Previously, there was a 1* to 5* scale but still corresponding to levels of national and international excellence.

The RAE/REF panels assess outputs, environment and, in later years, impact for each UOA. I have extracted the main points from the detailed submission guidelines for REF 2021 (REF, 2019). Prior to REF 2021, institutions could select which academic staff members to consider in each UOA rating, whereas, for REF 2021, there was a requirement to include all eligible 'category A' academic staff, defined as academic staff with a contract of employment of 0.2 full-time equivalent (FTE) or greater, whose primary role is to undertake either 'research only' or 'teaching and research'.

The *outputs*, which made up 60% of the total calculation in REF 2021 (previously 65% in REF 2014), were assessed based on the proportion of research publications that met the 3* or 4* rating thresholds. From RAE 2001 to REF 2014, the ratings were based on the best four research publications for each academic in the UOA. In REF 2021, instead of requiring four research publications for each member of academic staff, a minimum of one output per person was required and a total number of outputs equal to 2.5 times the summed FTE of the submitted staff for the UOA.

For REF 2014, the evaluation of *impact* was added with a 20% weighting; this weighting increased to 25% in REF 2021, demonstrating the greater significance given to this aspect. Impact case studies (ICSs) were required to be submitted to demonstrate the influence of research in wider society. The number of ICSs to be included was calculated based on the number of FTE academic staff submitted, with a minimum of two ICSs per UOA.

Finally, the *research environment* formed 15% of the total calculation, and for this measure, the judgement was made on the vitality and sustainability of the university and departmental environment. Narratives were submitted that documented details of research income, number of completed doctorates, and research culture and leadership.

Concerns about equity in the assessment process led to the establishment of a REF Equality and Diversity Advisory Panel (EDAP). EDAP's final report (REF, 2022) described measures put in place to increase equity, diversity and inclusion (EDI) in the operation of REF 2021. EDAP also analysed the environment submissions within the REF and reviewed statements from universities about their REF-related policies and procedures. In addition, EDAP provided advice about 'circumstances requests', a feature of REF 2021 that allowed some individuals and groups to claim special considerations impacting upon their productivity (such as illness or parental leave). A separate blog entry by three members of the EDAP panel emphasised the importance of continuing to increase the numbers of researchers of Black, Asian and minority ethnic backgrounds on panels and in research-active roles more generally (Khan et al., 2022; see also Tate, this volume).

In considering gender equity in UK higher education, it is important to mention the Athena Swan (Scientific Women's Academic Network) Charter, which was launched in 2005 and was initially premised on improving women academics' careers in science disciplines but was expanded to include all disciplines in 2015. Universities that apply are awarded levels of attainment of either bronze, silver or gold based on achieving accreditation, and must accept and promote the Athena Swan principles, undertake an audit of their procedures for ensuring gender equity, and develop a gender equality action plan. In recent years, Athena Swan has moved towards a more intersectional approach and become less prescriptive (Advance HE, 2021). A connection between Athena Swan and research funding emerged in 2011 when the National Institute of Health and Care Research (NIHR) began requiring a silver award for funding eligibility (although this requirement was dropped in 2020) (Müller & Tzanakou, 2022; NIHR, 2020).

Research on the RAE/REF and gender equity

The research on the experiences of women in academia is extensive, and there is also substantial literature on the impact of the RAE/REF and similar arrangements in other countries; surprisingly, however, there is limited research specifically connecting the RAE/REF and gender equity. Here I review some key studies but note that a full account of the literature on women academics and gender inequities is beyond the scope of this chapter (for relevant work, see Kandiko Howson et al., 2018; Leathwood & Read, 2009; Morley, 2016).

In *The Research Game in Academic Life* (Lucas, 2006), there was evidence of an intensification of the management and organisation of research activities within universities in response to successive RAEs. This 'new managerialism' involved manipulating staff workloads and auditing staff outputs and achievements to determine whether they were eligible for submission to the RAE and hence considered 'research active' or 'research inactive'. Being ineligible for submission to the RAE – and hence potentially being labelled as 'research inactive' – could have extremely negative consequences for academic staff and their careers in terms of a threat of redundancy (Lucas, 2006). With the shift to inclusion of all research-involved staff for REF 2021, there was potentially more risk to career and status as anyone deemed ineligible for submission to the REF might be even more likely to be encouraged or required to move to a 'teaching-only' contract. Academics in the UK are normally employed on one of three 'pathways', namely 'teaching and research', 'teaching only' and 'research only', with increasing numbers of teaching-only positions. Wolf and Jenkins (2021) found an 80% increase in teaching-only positions from 2005–2006 to 2018–2019 compared to a 16% increase for teaching-and-research positions. From 2018–2019 to 2021–2022, teaching-only contract positions increased by a further 22%, while teaching-and-research numbers remained stable with an increase of less than 2% (Higher Education Statistics Agency [HESA], 2023, Figure 2). In the same time period, women have consistently held about 43% of teaching-and-research contracts, but 54% of women's contracts are for teaching only (HESA, 2023, Figure 2).

Much of the research evidence produced has been critical of the impact on academic work in the audit cultures of RAE/REF with the intensification of academic working environments emphasised (Loftus, 2006; Sikes, 2006). Only a few studies have linked gender inequities with the RAE/REF. Some of the research on women academics provides clues as to potential connections. For example, in a case study of a British university, Fagan and Teasdale (2021) report that 'deeply embedded gendered expectations pervade organisational structures and cultures, with gender performances created and re-created in the workplace' (p. 779). Fagan and Teasdale also note that achieving excellence in research by securing funding and publishing is crucial for promotion and success in academic life. However, women's research success can often be hampered by heavy involvement in teaching and what is sometimes referred to as 'academic housework' that enables institutions to function and students and staff to be supported (Heijstra et al., 2017; Macfarlane & Burg, 2019).

Although Fagan and Teasdale do not specifically discuss the RAE/REF, their consideration of structures and cultures and the importance of research success is relevant to my analysis. In a study that did reference the RAE/REF, Leathwood and Read (2013) interviewed 71 academics in Britain over email and found that women participants reported less time for research due to increased workloads in relation to teaching and administration. However, some women (and men) noted that they could now have their research efforts valued within their departments and that the RAE/REF allowed them to have a more successful research career. Nevertheless, it was clear that substantial inequity remained in the system. Moreover, an analysis of inclusion in REF 2021 showed that women and Black academics, even when eligible, were less likely to be submitted to REF 2021 (REF, 2023).

In a case study of a research-intensive British university, Yarrow (2018) argues that 'unconscious bias', together with the operation of informal networks that favour men, can affect the advancement of women academics, including their lesser likelihood of being submitted to REF 2014. Chubb and Derrick (2020) take another approach, as they interview researchers and evaluators on the meaning of the REF impact criteria and tease out some of the subtle gendered associations connected to 'hard' (masculine) and 'soft' (feminine) images of impact. Finally, it is important to emphasise that inequalities are exacerbated in relation to intersectional factors, particularly for women of colour. Bhopal and Henderson (2021) show how and why 'race' has received less attention than gender in university diversity efforts, while Rollock (2021) argues that Black women remain 'under-represented and invisible' (p. 206) in these institutional initiatives. (See also Tate, this volume.)

Findings from my research studies relating to academic work and the RAE/REF

In this section, I outline two research studies on the life and work of academics in the UK and what influences their experiences of the RAE/REF and their success or struggles in achieving research recognition through funding and publishing.

The first study relates to the research reported in my book *The Research Game in Academic Life* (Lucas, 2006), in which I investigated the experiences of university managers and academic staff in three disciplinary departments (biology, sociology and English) in each of two universities in the UK. A total of 70 interviews, including 12 with women, were conducted across the two universities. The study explored the changing research environments and their influence on academic work and identity.

A second study, conducted with colleagues, involved mid-career academics in research-intensive environments in six Australian and six English universities (Brew, Boud, Lucas, & Crawford, 2018; Brew, Boud, Namgung, et al., 2016). This study explored how academics make sense of the competing pressures of teaching, research and administration in academic work. Using purposive sampling, semi-structured interviews were conducted with 27 academics five to ten years beyond their doctorates in a variety of fields. There were 13 interviews, including six with women, across five UK universities.

Both studies involved convenience samples that are not considered representative of all academics in terms of experience and positioning; notably, none of the UK participants identified as scholars of colour. The data for the Research Game in Academic Life project (henceforth RGAL) were collected around 1997–1998 just after RAE 1996 and in preparation for RAE 2001. The data for the Mid-Career Academics project (henceforth MCA) were collected in 2013 in preparation for REF 2014.

The interviews from both datasets were reviewed to explore the experiences of the 18 UK women academics during these different time periods. Three key themes captured their experiences of the relevant RAE/REF and attempts to build or sustain a research profile: (a) being RAE/REFable – the challenges of building and maintaining a research profile, (b) the imperative of research funding and publishing and (c) research support and mentoring. Each of these themes is discussed next.

Being RAE/REFable: the challenges of building and maintaining a research profile

The idea of being labelled as 'research active' and being considered 'worthy' of inclusion in the RAE/REF was central to the experiences of the academics in RGAL. During the period in which the research was conducted (1997–1998), it was possible for academics not to have a doctorate and perhaps to be registered in a doctoral programme while working at a UK university. Today this scenario would be highly unlikely, as a doctorate and a track record of publications is typically the minimum requirement for an entry-level lecturer position. At the time, the introduction of these changes and the rising expectations could be disorienting and provoke anxiety about one's career (Lucas, 2006). As Kate[2] stated:

> The university are really driving research, so you cannot get a job here, or be internally promoted, if you don't have a PhD, and that has created huge problems because we have members of internal staff who, because it just wasn't the done thing ... don't have a PhD and now cannot get promoted.
>
> *(Kate, senior lecturer, MCA)*

Kate referred to the university's rising expectations and the uncertainty that resulted:

> We've obviously got the REF coming up. We don't know yet who is in, who is not in. We've got a good idea, but the university has basically said that there is an expectation that we will be producing at least one 3* [internationally excellent] piece per year.

She indicated that consequences for not meeting expectations were unclear but could be dire: 'and there is a long, long process that you will go down if you do not produce that [and] the bottom line is transfer to a teaching-only contract. Whether that will happen, I have no idea.'

Building a research profile has become essential to gaining entry to and sustaining an academic career. Moreover, being able to maintain a research profile means having the capacity to do research, within circumstances that can enable publishing and applying for funding while juggling all the other commitments of academic life, as well as life outside academe. This juggling can be challenging in the early stages of an academic career and throughout. The women academics across both projects were keen to build their research profiles and to be included within the RAE/REF but talked of the challenges of achieving these objectives due to the pressures of high teaching loads and the expectation that they, more so than men, would take on significant administrative positions, often in relation to programme leadership (a common form of 'academic housework').

One example from RGAL is Ms Chandler, a lecturer on a part-time contract. She was not submitted to RAE 1996. Ms Chandler led two modules, one with 200 students. For her, 'research is something that goes on in my unpaid time'. She was working towards a PhD and aimed to have four publications and be included in the next RAE in 2001.

A similar situation was found with Emily, an early-career researcher and senior lecturer from the MCA project, who from the outset had a 'full-on teaching load', although she felt that there was at least recognition of her efforts:

> And I remember one day the head of school popping in on my door, and he was lovely, he was so good, and I think he realised that they'd sort of given me a baptism of fire with all this teaching in the first year. ... He was saying, oh, you know, I appreciate this. Thank you very much.

Emily's initial workload involved not only extensive teaching but also administrative leadership roles. She wondered if she had made the right choices:

> When I first arrived here, I took over [student] admissions ... and then I was director of undergraduate studies. So, I've had quite meaty admin roles, and given the size of the department they are quite heavy, you

know, sort of quite large roles. So, I think I spent a lot of time on admin-related [work] rather than my research earlier on in my career.

Emily talked of 'ending up' doing a lot of teaching and saw it as a personal decision to take on more programme leadership and administrative roles, as opposed to seeing this workload as acquiescing to the structural and cultural expectations of the department about women academics. The thank you from the head of school suggests that a powerful man giving praise for feminised behaviour may act as an incentive for exploitation. Another participant, Jane, a senior lecturer in the MCA study, began to wonder whether such flattery is not what it seems:

> I've been at the stage where, you know, if people ask me to do something, you know, I'm so flattered that I have to say yes. ... I think maybe that's a gender thing as well. I think I've learned in the last few years ... I need to try to resist, or I need to try to bargain a little bit better.

Building and maintaining a research profile is clearly a challenge for these women academics. The changing standards of research engagement and excellence, particularly influenced by the RAE/REF, coupled with high teaching loads and expectations to take on administrative or leadership positions, are difficult to navigate.

The imperatives of research funding and publishing

The women academics in both projects talked about their experiences of applying for research funding and publishing, which are important for building their research profiles and being selected for submission to the RAE/REF, as well as for getting promoted. What type of research funding was obtained might also be relevant. Jane, in the MCA study, commented that 'it had taken me quite a while to get promoted. I got turned down a couple of times.' Neither her administrative/leadership roles, nor her teaching, nor several small research projects were sufficient for promotion to senior lecturer: 'The thing that tipped the balance was getting the ESRC [Economic and Social Research Council] project. ... I had British Academy projects, small ones, but I suppose they didn't see that as financially [important] as a research council grant.'

As highlighted earlier, increased expectations for publishing and being successful in securing research funding could be challenging for those women academics already struggling to manage a workload filled with teaching and administrative responsibilities. The anxiety was evident as academics who had formerly focused on teaching pondered how to obtain grants and do research:

> Senior management has gone from [a focus on teaching excellence] to, right now, we want you to get money. ... To me, research has always

been at the bottom of the heap, and you need space and time to think. ... What scares me is that I'm expected to do what I'm doing and still produce three or four research applications a year. And I don't know [how], I work 16 hours a day already.

(*Natalie, senior lecturer, MCA*)

Although Natalie may have overstated the expectations around research grant applications, she sees what senior management is asking for as unattainable when she is already working '16 hours a day'. Natalie's discussion suggests she lacks the prior research experience from which to build and sustain the research profile necessary for successful funding applications.

In contrast to the experience described by Natalie, one strategy that worked for Emily was first securing small grants, including internal institutional funding, to build a foundation in a particular research area and work up to applications for larger amounts of research funding:

And I've really found a niche in the research side ... and that was only with a small-scale project ... where I got a small grant, and that gave me the real desire to do empirically funded research. And since then, of all the grants I've applied for, I've got them all, which is very lucky. And touch wood, that sort of success rate will continue. So, I feel that I've found an area that (a) I like, (b) ... I'm quite strong at and (c) is in my area of expertise ... but it took me a while to find that niche.

Securing those initial pots of research funding, let alone building them into larger funding streams, was not inevitable and required creativity and planning. Dr Kirby, a senior lecturer in the RGAL study, described such a strategy:

The first way I got industrial money is I actually wrote a letter, a begging letter if you like, saying here I am, I have this amount of ... experience, would you like to fund some work with us, these are the kinds of areas which we work on. And it was very tongue in cheek in some respects ... and then people just came, they came for meetings to see what we'd got and who I was because I wasn't known. And [company name] were brilliant because they were the first people who gave me money and supported a PhD studentship.

In addition to finding a niche or specialist area of research and gaining small pots of research funding, participants' experiences showed that it is also crucial to build networks and find collaborators, particularly when aiming to apply for larger competitive grants (Brew, Boud, Namgung, et al., 2016):

When I first came here, almost the only thing I knew was that we had to publish ... and you had to bring in income. But, often, the income was done as a group. ... [In my previous institution] there was so much going on in terms of proposals being written [that] you would always be involved.

(Rosemary, principal lecturer, MCA)

Being able to work in larger collaborations both internally and externally appeared crucial for securing larger research funding bids if that is a goal, and it often is, as evidenced earlier by Jane, who needed to secure more extensive funding to be considered for promotion. Emily described how she and others looked for 'data gaps' in their field. Acquiring funding and conducting research, however, did not guarantee being submitted to the RAE/REF, where time frames may not be in alignment and judgements are made by others about whether publications are of sufficient quality to merit inclusion. As Jane explained:

> So, I suppose I feel a little bit frustrated by the REF because for me, personally, my ESRC project, having finished in January, there's just no way my publications are going to be out in time for that. So, it's great for the next REF round, but it's not great now. And whilst I have enough publications for [this] REF, I just have to, you know, wait for the final scoring or whatever in terms of whether I'm going to be submitted or not.

Jane's statement points to the significant amount of instrumentalism and strategising found in the accounts of these women academics in their efforts to be considered 'worthy' of inclusion in the RAE/REF. However, the desire to do research that is meaningful and worthwhile in terms of intellectual value is also emphasised. Emily has the final word here:

> And I think you can only be true to yourself and do the work that you think is appropriate for you. ... I think ultimately I want to make a difference, and I want to feel that the work I'm doing is assisting in some way.

Research support and mentoring

What became apparent by talking to institutional and departmental leaders in the RGAL study was that major changes in research infrastructure within the university and departments were happening from the early 1990s. Research committees, research administration and internal research funding were all enhanced and extended. The level of research infrastructure and support that might now be taken for granted in universities was still in formation, but it became pivotal along with research mentoring in enabling some academics to build their research profile and to successfully be entered into the REF. Ms Chandler, for example, mentioned receiving some institutional funds (known as QR funding that would have been drawn from institutional income from RAE 1996) to help support her writing.

We have already seen that Emily from the MCA project developed strategies for building a research career. She faced challenges like those experienced by other women academics with a heavy teaching and administrative load, but she also talked about the support available that enabled her to do this:

> There's a previous research director who was incredibly encouraging and has been encouraging in terms of the grant applications that I've done [and] ... a colleague ... who has gone above and beyond the call of duty in looking at grant applications, suggesting amendments, making suggestions as to improvements, suggesting cutting that particular bit and focusing on something else, when he wasn't required to do that ... and [he] was a real factor in helping me get that first grant, and that spurred me on to the next few.

The significance of getting support and help from more senior academics was also emphasised by others in the MCA project, such as Jane:

> My co-investigator on the ESRC project was very supportive and we wrote the bid for me to be the PI [principal investigator] and that he would support me in doing that ... and another colleague, who is a former colleague here ... she's always been pretty supportive. We've put in bids together for research council grants, that kind of thing, and I suppose – and now ... they're my friends. They're not just my colleagues.

Kate pointed out that collaboration, support and mentoring were crucial in developing large funding bids, which, as previously discussed, can often be pivotal in being considered for promotion:

> To get big, funded bids, you need to go on the tailcoats of somebody who has [done so] and luckily the two people in [other university] have. So, I'm hoping that that will tip the scales. They know what they're doing.

Institutional research funding and support can be crucial in enabling women academics to build a research profile but mentoring and collaboration are also important and so these practices need to be embedded in the culture of universities to ensure the nurturing of potential and greater equity of outcomes.

Conclusions and looking forward

To give a perspective on staffing trends over time, the list of academic staff members for all six departments in the RGAL study was compared to the staff complement for the same departments in 2022. This analysis is not exact as university web pages on staff members are not always accurate. In biology, women's representation had increased at both universities from 15% and 22%

in 1998 to 38% and 40%, respectively, in 2022. In the two sociology departments, there were increases from 10% and 62% to 49% and 71%. In the English departments, women's share moved from 31% and 30% to 61% in both institutions. We see the increase in biology, the high participation in sociology (despite the low start in one department) and the lower initial but higher later representation in English. There are also changing academic titles from 1998 to 2022 with the more frequent appointments in 2022 of associate lecturers and teaching fellows, denoting the increase in teaching-only contracts. This data snapshot demonstrates an overall numerical increase in women academics but with continuing disciplinary differences and a greater likelihood of being in teaching-only roles.

Despite changes over time in women's representation that may suggest progress, it is also critical to delve more deeply into the experiential side of academic work, as done in the two earlier studies. The quotations included in this chapter indicate some similar and some different concerns at two points in time. In the RGAL study, in the late 1990s, women, often with fewer qualifications than required today even for an entry position, worried about how they would transition from a teaching-oriented to a research-oriented profile. As the RAE/REF became more integrated into their work lives, their worries turned to establishing research collaborations, finding mentors, securing grants and publishing, all in sufficient numbers to secure promotions and be entered into the RAE/REF. For Ms Chandler in the RGAL study, not being entered into the RAE simply meant that she needed to improve for the next iteration. But by 2013, when the MCA study was conducted, not being entered into the REF could threaten academic identity and job security, meaning that research had to be prioritised, despite the continuing expectations for teaching and especially the administrative and leadership responsibilities that so often fell to women, even in early career. Extensive strategising was required to secure the 'right' grants, find the best collaborators, build up to larger research designs and work with the growing support infrastructure in the university. This kind of workplace learning is not explicitly conveyed, and some individuals are more successful than others in deducing it.

Moreover, the RAE/REF requirements were altered in each iteration, adding a general sense of anxiety. By 2014, demonstrating 'impact' was added to the list of requirements (on a group basis but with more prestige for impact 'leaders'); by 2021, being submitted per se was less of an upfront concern as all research-involved individuals were to be submitted, along with a formula that might allow some to produce less than others, but accompanied by a greater threat or belief that less productive individuals might be forced into less prestigious teaching-only contracts. We lack up-to-date research on the REF-related concerns of contemporary UK (women) academics in an EDI context. How might the pandemic, often regarded as differentially affecting women's research time (Carruthers Thomas, this volume; Pereira, 2021), influence their abilities (and desires) to maintain their research profiles?

Warnings have been published of a 'radical shakeup' in the next REF (Else, 2022), now planned for 2029, carrying the potential to unsettle academics once again. It is anticipated that the submission rules will change and that the weighting of 'outputs' will be reduced and 'environment' (research culture) increased (Grove, 2023). The relative marginality of EDI concerns needs to be addressed not only through Athena Swan, the Race Equality Charter and other initiatives but also within the structures and cultures of institutions and across academic research communities. UKRI's (2023a) focus on 'building the evidence base' for EDI is an important response in this regard that has the potential to shape a more equitable future.

Notes

1 UKRI is a public body that also includes seven disciplinary research councils that offer additional research funding on a competitive basis plus Innovate UK, which funds businesses involved in innovation. Research England manages the REF on behalf of funding bodies for Scotland, Wales and Northern Ireland as well as England. See UKRI (2023b) for more details about UK research funding.
2 All names of institutions and individuals in these studies are pseudonyms. Naming conventions differed between the two studies. All participants in the MCA study held doctorates, although this is not evident from the first-name pseudonyms used.

Acknowledgements

I would like to acknowledge the work of my colleagues Professor Angela Brew, Professor David Boud and Dr Karin Crawford on our joint study of academics in Australia and the UK, from which some quotations have been used in this chapter.

References

Advance HE. (2021, June 30). *A step-change for gender equality – the transformed UK Athena Swan Charter is launched today.* https://www.advance-he.ac.uk/news-and-views/step-change-gender-equality-transformed-uk-athena-swan-charter-launched-today

Bhopal, K., & Henderson, H. (2021). Competing inequalities: gender versus race in higher education institutions in the UK. *Educational Review, 73*(2), 153–169. https://doi.org/10.1080/00131911.2019.1642305

Brew, A., Boud, D., Lucas, L., & Crawford, K. (2018). Academic artisans in the research university. *Higher Education, 76*(1), 115–127. https://doi.org/10.1007/s10734-017-0200-7

Brew, A., Boud, D., Namgung, S. U., Lucas, L., & Crawford, K. (2016). Research productivity and academics' conceptions of research. *Higher Education, 71*(5), 681–697. https://doi.org/10.1007/s10734-015-9930-6

Chubb, J., & Derrick, G. E. (2020). The impact a-gender: gendered orientations towards research impact and its evaluation. *Palgrave Communications, 6*(1), Article 72. https://doi.org/10.1057/s41599-020-0438-z

Else, H. (2022). Mammoth UK research assessment concludes as leaders eye radical shakeup. *Nature*, *605*(7911), 603. https://doi.org/10.1038/d41586-022-01310-0

Fagan, C., & Teasdale, N. (2021). Women professors across STEMM and non-STEMM disciplines: navigating gendered spaces and playing the academic game. *Work, Employment and Society*, *35*(4), 774–792. https://doi.org/10.1177/0950017020916182

Grove, J. (2023, June 15). REF 2028 reforms set to end requirement to submit all researchers. *Times Higher Education*. https://www.timeshighereducation.com/news/ref-2028-reforms-set-end-requirement-submit-all-researchers

Heijstra, T. M., Steinthorsdóttir, F. S., & Einarsdóttir, T. (2017). Academic career making and the double-edged role of academic housework. *Gender and Education*, *29*(6), 764–780. https://doi.org/10.1080/09540253.2016.1171825

Higher Education Statistics Agency. (2023, January 17). *Higher education staff statistics: UK, 2021/22*. https://www.hesa.ac.uk/news/01-02-2022/sb261-higher-education-staff-statistics

Hicks, D. (2009). Evolving regimes of multi-university research evaluation. *Higher Education*, *57*(4), 393–404. https://doi.org/10.1007/s10734-008-9154-0

Kandiko Howson, C. B., Coate, K., & de St Croix, T. (2018). Mid-career academic women and the prestige economy. *Higher Education Research & Development*, *37*(3), 533–548. https://doi.org/10.1080/07294360.2017.1411337

Khan, R., Ross, F., & Parkes, T. (2022, July 8). All voices matter – what REF 2021 can tell us about the involvement of people from Black, Asian and Minority Ethnic communities in research assessment. *REF Blogs*. https://archive.ref.ac.uk/about-the-ref/blogs/all-voices-matter-what-ref-2021-can-tell-us-about-the-involvement-of-people-from-black-asian-and-minority-ethnic-communities-in-research-assessment/

Leathwood, C., & Read, B. (2009). *Gender and the changing face of higher education: a feminized future?* Society for Research into Higher Education/Open University Press.

Leathwood, C., & Read, B. (2013). Research policy and academic performativity: compliance, contestation and complicity. *Studies in Higher Education*, *38*(8), 1162–1174. https://doi.org/10.1080/03075079.2013.833025

Loftus, A. (2006). RAE-ification and the consciousness of the academic. *Area*, *38*(1), 110–112. https://doi.org/10.1111/j.1475-4762.2006.00664.x

Lucas, L. (2006). *The research game in academic life*. McGraw-Hill/Open University Press.

Macfarlane, B., & Burg, D. (2019). Women professors and the academic housework trap. *Journal of Higher Education Policy and Management*, *41*(3), 262–274. https://doi.org/10.1080/1360080X.2019.1589682

Morley, L. (2016). Troubling intra-actions: gender, neo-liberalism and research in the global academy. *Journal of Education Policy*, *31*(1), 28–45. https://doi.org/10.1080/02680939.2015.1062919

Müller, J., & Tzanakou, C. (2022, March 15). As gender equality becomes a priority for EU research funding, does Europe need Athena SWAN? *LSE Blog*. https://blogs.lse.ac.uk/impactofsocialsciences/2022/03/15/as-gender-equality-becomes-a-priority-for-eu-research-funding-does-europe-need-athena-swan/

Naidoo, R. (2018). The competition fetish in higher education: shamans, mind snares and consequences. *European Educational Research Journal*, *17*(5), 605–620. https://doi.org/10.1177/1474904118784839

National Institute for Health and Care Research. (2020, September 10). *NIHR responds to the Government's call for further reduction in bureaucracy with new measures*. https://

www.nihr.ac.uk/news/nihr-responds-to-the-governments-call-for-further-reduction-in-bureaucracy-with-new-measures/25633

Pereira, M. do M. (2021). Researching gender inequalities in academic labour during the COVID-19 pandemic: avoiding common problems and asking different questions. *Gender, Work & Organization*, *28*(S2), 498–509. https://doi.org/10.1111/gwao.12618

Research Excellence Framework. (2019). *Guidance on criteria and submissions.* https://archive.ref.ac.uk/guidance-and-criteria-on-submissions/

Research Excellence Framework. (2022). *Equality and Diversity Advisory Panel final report.* https://archive.ref.ac.uk/media/1863/ref-edap-final-report-2022-final11.pdf

Research Excellence Framework. (ca. 2022). *Key facts.* Retrieved on 12 January 2024 from https://archive.ref.ac.uk/media/1848/ref2021_key_facts.pdf

Research Excellence Framework. (2023, July 13). *Analysis of inclusion for submission, representation in outputs attribution and scoring.* https://archive.ref.ac.uk/media/1919/ref-2021-analysis-of-inclusion-for-submission-representation-in-outputs-attribution-and-scoring.pdf

Rollock, N. (2021). "I would have become wallpaper had racism had its way": Black female professors, racial battle fatigue, and strategies for surviving higher education. *Peabody Journal of Education*, *96*(2), 206–217. https://doi.org/10.1080/0161956X.2021.1905361

Sikes, P. (2006). Working in a 'new' university in the shadow of the Research Assessment Exercise? *Studies in Higher Education*, *31*(5), 555–568. https://doi.org/10.1080/03075070600922758

UK Research and Innovation. (2023a, January 30). *Building the evidence base.* https://www.ukri.org/what-we-offer/supporting-healthy-research-and-innovation-culture/equality-diversity-and-inclusion/evidence-base/

UK Research and Innovation. (2023b, May 16). *Research England: how we fund higher education providers.* https://www.ukri.org/publications/research-england-how-we-fund-higher-education-providers/

Wolf, A., & Jenkins, A. (2021). *Managers and academics in a centralising sector: the new staffing patterns of UK higher education.* https://www.kcl.ac.uk/policy-institute/assets/managers-and-academics-in-a-centralising-sector.pdf

Yarrow, E. (2018). Gender and the Research Excellence Framework. In J. Robertson, A. Williams, D. Jones, L. Isbel, & D. Loads (Eds.), *EqualBITE: gender equality in higher education* (pp. 63–68). Brill. https://doi.org/10.1163/9789463511438_012

14

RESEARCH FUNDING ORGANISATIONS AS CHANGE AGENTS FOR GENDER EQUALITY

Policies, practices and paradoxes in Sweden

Liisa Husu and Helen Peterson

Access to competitive extramural research funding is one of the main elements in developing research careers. In analysing the research funding and gender nexus, research funding organisations (RFOs) are key actors of interest. Leading research funding organisations in Europe and beyond, as well as the European Research Area (ERA), are increasingly engaged with gender equality and diversity, and the Nordic countries, specifically Norway and Sweden, have been pioneers in this respect since the 1980s (Directorate-General for Research and Innovation, 2009; Global Research Council, 2022; Hermansson et al., 2021; Husu, 2019a; Husu & de Cheveigné, 2010).

In this chapter, we draw on our recent empirical research on the Swedish Research Council (SRC), a Nordic RFO characterised in 2009 as a 'global gender equality leader' (Directorate-General for Research and Innovation, 2009, p. 5). What progress, if any, and in which areas, has this leading RFO made since then in its engagement? Which challenges and dilemmas remain? (For a Canadian comparison, see Tamtik and Sutherland in this volume.)

The Swedish context provides an interesting setting for the study, being characterised by what has sometimes been referred to as the Nordic paradox (cf. Husu, 2019b), with very high research intensity, high overall societal gender equality and long-term political will to promote gender equality, contrasting with persistent gender inequalities in academe and elsewhere.

The Swedish policy setting

Sweden ranks high in international indicators of overall societal gender equality. According to the Global Gender Gap Index of the World Economic Forum, Sweden has the fifth smallest societal gender gap, and has ranked highest in Europe in societal gender equality in the European Institute for

DOI: 10.4324/9781003330431-18

Gender Equality (n.d.) Gender Equality Index since 2010. Gender equality is prominent in the policy agenda, with the Swedish government from 2014 up to the elections in September 2022 declaring itself to be a 'feminist government' (Socialdepartementet, 2016). The principle of gender mainstreaming has been applied since 1994 and means that gender equality work needs to be integrated into all policies and actions rather than run on a parallel track (Swedish Gender Equality Agency, 2022).

Equality between women and men is addressed by both general laws and regulations and by specific laws and regulations for the higher education and research sector. Gender equality is also specifically mentioned in the government ordinance of the four public national RFOs, among them the SRC. The production of gender statistics is also a legal demand: for over two decades, public authorities, including RFOs, have been legally obliged to present person-based data by gender.

Foregrounding of gender equality in research and development is evidenced in the Swedish Research and Innovation Bill for 2021–2024, which lists four main measures to meet the key challenges for research and innovation (Utbildningsdepartementet, 2020): open science, non-material resources, gender equality, and positive and attractive conditions for research careers in higher education. The bill mentions gender equality in research and innovation in several contexts, including the need to continue to work towards the government's goal of gender parity at the professorial rank by 2030. In Sweden, professor is the highest academic position, corresponding to full professor in international contexts, and applies to 16% of all academic staff in 2020. Sweden has seen a slow but steady increase in the proportion of women among professors in recent years, from 17% in 2006 to 31% in 2020 (Bengtsson et al., 2022; Stening, 2020).

We consider the Swedish policy setting and legislative framework as highly beneficial and supportive for RFOs to become engaged as organisational change agents for gender equality.

Organisational change agents for gender equality

In this chapter, we explore the conceptual model of organisations as change agents by analysing the measures, activities and policies of the SRC. The concept of change agent (for gender equality) is typically used to refer to individual organisational members who play an important role in promoting gender equality and achieving sustainable, structural change within their own organisations (Dahmen-Adkins & Peterson, 2021; Peterson, 2014). An organisational change agent for gender equality is an organisation that has taken on the role of change agent for gender equality with significant influence on other organisations, on the whole sector and on society. These organisations constantly develop and implement innovative measures, activities and policies, and are driving change towards gender equality within the realm of their own organisations and beyond. In this chapter, we investigate the extent to which the SRC could be defined as an organisational change agent for gender equality.

Method, material and analysis

Data for our research are the SRC's policy documents, research funding call texts, statements and approaches, guidelines for applicants and reviewers, and news and newsletters, all publicly available on the SRC website (https://www.vr.se). These materials were explored with qualitative content analysis involving coding relevant texts to provide a systematic overview of the content of the documents. The analysis was guided by a sociological frame analytical approach, which involves a focus on how gender equality, as a multi-dimensional social phenomenon, is interpreted, defined and translated into measures, activities and policies in these organisations (Goffman, 1974). Studying policy frames involves, for example, investigating the rationale, scope, content and targets of policies.

In addition, we draw on six semi-structured interviews. Three of these interviews were conducted with SRC staff members, including one senior research officer and two senior advisors. The aim of these staff interviews was to gain a comprehensive understanding of the current approach to gender equality within the SRC, the ways this approach had developed and the challenges that remain. We also interviewed one member from each of the three SRC scientific councils: the Scientific Council for Humanities and Social Sciences, the Scientific Council for Medicine and Health, and the Scientific Council for Natural and Engineering Sciences. These councils meet six times a year to decide which research funding calls are to be made and to select and appoint the members of the review panels that examine and prioritise the applications. The councils consist of between nine and eleven active researchers with a high level of scientific expertise within their field and are elected by researchers at Swedish higher education institutions. These members hold their positions for three years but can be re-elected for three more years (SRC, 2022). The councils also follow up, evaluate and develop strategies for research in their areas. The scientific councils make the final decision regarding which applications will be awarded grants, but they rarely oppose the suggestions from the review panels. The panels are composed of Swedish and international researchers established within their scientific field (full professors or associate professors) with previous experience in assessing and evaluating science.

The data were collected in fall 2020 and spring 2021 within the framework of the European research project Grant Allocation Disparities from a Gender Perspective (GRANteD). The interviews were performed in English by the two chapter authors using videoconferencing software.

Background, history and governance of the Swedish Research Council

The Swedish Research Council is the largest of several major Swedish research funding agencies and in 2022 awarded total grants of 8.1 billion SEK (about £584 million; SRC, 2023).[1] Its grant portfolio includes project funding, career and mobility grants, and infrastructure support for research of the highest quality in all fields. Established in 2001 as a state authority, the SRC merged several previous national disciplinary research councils. One of these preceding national research councils, the Medical Research Council (MRC), was heavily criticised in the mid-1990s after it was challenged by researchers due to a lack of transparency in peer review and bias against female applicants, a case drawing international attention (Abbott, 1997; Wennerås & Wold, 1997). This case led to the dissolution of the MRC; it was described by one of our informants as 'a huge scandal'.

When the SRC was established, gender equality was already on the agenda. Gender research was, for example, explicitly mentioned in the funding framework of the SRC with a specific funding programme for gender research, as well as a Gender Research Committee. In the first year, 2001, a total of 9.6 million SEK (about £693,000) was awarded to gender research projects (SRC, 2002), gender research became a specific funding category in the SRC budget (which lasted until 2012) and funding (a total of 81 million SEK during a five-year period; about £5.8 million) was allocated starting in 2007 for three Centres of Excellence in Gender Studies (SRC, 2011).

Nonetheless, it took a few years before broader and more comprehensive activities and goals related to gender equality were initiated, most clearly in 2006. Drivers came from both governmental directives and individual SRC staff members and leaders. The interviews confirmed continuous strong support and interest in gender equality from the top of the organisation and from members of the scientific councils as one interview participant noted: 'There's a big interest in these questions from everyone.'

According to government ordinance, the SRC must promote equality between women and men within its sphere of activity and, when relevant, promote gender equality in the research the council funds (Utbildningsdepartementet, 2009). Each annual report, all available on the SRC website (in Swedish only), includes a section on gender equality activities as well as gender statistics concerning the different funding instruments and a commentary about these trends (see for example SRC, 2023).

Since 2013, SRC has been included among the 60 public authorities to which the Swedish government has given a gender mainstreaming duty (SRC, 2014). In a national evaluation of the authorities' gender mainstreaming efforts by the Swedish Agency for Public Management, SRC was regarded positively for having implemented new measures and improved working processes (Statskontoret, 2018). The evaluation commended SRC for having revised all strategic and steering documents to ensure that they support the gender equality strategy and having integrated tailor-made gender equality training for all actors involved in all processes concerning research funding.

Policy frames in the Swedish Research Council

SRC has two gender equality plans: one concerns research funding and one for SRC as a governmental agency. We focus here on the former. In the current SRC gender equality strategy, established in 2014, gender equality in research is defined both as a fairness issue and a quality issue (SRC, 2014). The strategy includes a key statement of equal research capacity among women and men and notes that equal participation brings benefits to research itself. Specifically, the SRC is directed to achieve an equal gender distribution in evaluation panels, ensure percentages of applicants reflect the gender balance in a potential applicant pool, confirm that women and men have the same average success rates and grant amounts (taking into account the research type), and integrate a gender equality perspective into analyses and evaluations as well as in the council's external communications (SRC, 2014, p. 1). The SRC strategy also underlines the importance of continuity and vigilance in the promotion of gender equality, expressed as 'a persistent, long-term effort and continuous attention to assure that the ground gained towards equality is not lost' (SRC, 2014, p. 2).

Measures, activities and practices at the Swedish Research Council

Responsibilities and accountabilities

The SRC Board has the responsibility for implementing the strategy. Its objectives require the involvement of the entire agency, including the three scientific councils already mentioned as well as a fourth, the Council for Research Infrastructure. The responsibility is anchored to the highest level in the organisation: unless otherwise specified, the Director General is responsible for advancing the efforts towards achieving gender equality. A cross-cutting coordination group for gender mainstreaming is charged with obtaining an overall perspective on gender equality activities and identifying potential synergies and gaps, as well as suggesting further measures to strengthen the agency's work on gender equality (SRC, 2023). The accountability inside the organisation is outlined in detail in the SRC gender equality policy (SRC, 2014) and the annual reports. These documents describe how the outcomes of the grant decisions are analysed from a gender equality perspective and indicate that the scientific councils are responsible for reporting back to the board regarding approval rates and average grant amounts awarded to women and men. If gender inequality appears in these reports the scientific councils need to comment on and explain such divergences and consider measures for correction.

In practice, however, responsibilities and accountabilities are not always clear. An interviewed staff member emphasised the importance of developing clearer responsibilities:

> I think the strategy hasn't been super clear internally: what are the responsibilities, who was asking what ... who was responsible, who reports to whom, what do we follow-up? It's not extremely clearly written so I think that could be an improvement.

Monitoring and evaluation

Regular monitoring, reviewing and accountability are explicit parts of the SRC gender equality policy. In accordance with the legal demand on Swedish public organisations, the SRC regularly collects and publishes gender statistics on applications and success rates and the amount of funding granted on all funding calls by discipline, as well as time series. The gender statistics of different funding instruments are included in the SRC annual reports.

The gender composition of the applicant pool is constantly monitored against the potential applicant pool. Currently, women and men apply for funding in the proportion they are represented in the potential applicant pool; according to the strategy, measures are to be taken if this changes. However, according to one of the interviewed SRC staff members, altering application patterns was a difficult task for an RFO to take on:

> There are some things we can do to try to get women to apply but a lot of that is beyond our scope of what we can do. But there are signals you can send to the universities. You can work together with the universities so I think it matters, but I can't say how much.

In the Swedish Agency for Public Management's evaluation of the SRC gender mainstreaming efforts, it was noted that the SRC primarily has changed its own internal processes, with only limited effect on society (Statskontoret, 2018, p. 41). Several interviewees touched upon dilemmas regarding both influencing and being influenced by society, or more specifically, the culture and structure in academia. The problem in this context was primarily understood as men predominating in the more senior academic positions.

Gender-equality observation studies and observers

As an innovative measure, between 2008 and 2019 the SRC conducted seven gender-equality observation studies in the panels, using the results to develop and improve the review process (Ahlqvist, Andersson, et al., 2015; Andersson et al., 2012; Söderqvist, Ahlqvist, et al., 2020; Söderqvist, Baard, et al., 2017). These studies, described as 'a breakthrough' by one of the interviewees, go beyond the narrow focus on success rates of women and men and concentrate instead on the dynamics related to bias and fairness in the review process. In addition to these more comprehensive gender observation studies using ethnographic methods for participant observation, one or more members of the scientific councils attend each panel meeting as observers, ensuring that the discussion follows the guidelines and policies of the RFO and answering any practical and formal questions regarding such policies. They do not, however, participate in the assessment or contribute in any other manner to the discussion during the meetings.

An interviewed research council member who also had served as such an observer described the observer's duties as follows:

> To observe and see to the requirement in terms of fairness and the guidelines we give to the reviewers are followed, and that the conflict of interest is respected. ... So that it is fair and respectful discussion ... and that everybody is having a good and fair evaluation.

The observers write reports and submit them to the scientific councils, which use them to develop recommendations to improve the review process.

The observation studies have pointed out gender-based patterns in the panel discussions, for example, how parental leave and dependence/independence of the applicant were discussed significantly more often for female than for male applicants (Andersson et al., 2012). A tendency for men panellists 'to propose women to a lesser extent for the awarding of grants than when women are the proposers [i.e. the lead panellist/reviewer on an application]' was also remarked upon (Andersson et al., 2012, p. 7; see also Roumbanis, this volume). During the 2019 observations, performed in 15 review panels, it was noted that the discussions in the panels were characterised by fairness and engagement (Söderqvist, Ahlqvist, et al., 2020). Despite this, observers also documented how different expressions were used in describing the skills and personal abilities of women and men; men were described as 'excellent' or 'genius', whereas women's abilities were evaluated more critically and with greater hesitation: 'she seems competent', 'is she really...', 'I'm not sure she can do it' (Söderqvist, Ahlqvist, et al., 2020, p. 30). This pattern was particularly conspicuous in the panels for natural sciences and engineering and for medicine and health. However, on a more positive note, the use of informal information and rumours about the applicants, recorded in previous years (Andersson et al., 2012), was always interrupted by the SRC personnel or the panel chair.

According to one of the staff members, when the first of these observation studies was published (Andersson et al., 2012), the reception was 'shock', both in the organisation and in society, because they revealed 'how it might look like in a panel meeting'. Another informant described the first study as 'an eye-opener for many'. The importance of these observation studies was emphasised by the staff: 'The Director General has underlined that these observations have improved our work and our processes.' Another staff member described how the self-image of the SRC was influenced by these studies: 'We are not perfect, but we are trying, like a learning organisation.' A third staff member described that they were 'proud' of the gender-equality observations, as they were making a difference by raising consciousness and awareness 'in the long term'.[2]

The recommendations based on the observation studies included, among other things, developing procedures for the use of predetermined seating arrangements for panels to promote a good discussion climate (Ahlqvist, Andersson, et al., 2015), drawing up explicit guidelines for the structure of evaluation meetings (Ahlqvist, Andersson, et al., 2015) and increasing efforts to encourage more researchers of the under-represented gender to apply (Söderqvist, Baard, et al., 2017). Many of the recommendations were implemented during subsequent years. The interviews with staff members, however, indicate that responsibility to implement the recommendations can be 'a little bit confusing'. Notwithstanding, the efforts made were also emphasised: 'The Department for Research Funding [the SRC department which plans, prepares and coordinates the SRC's calls for grants, and handles the applications that are received] implements to a large extent the recommendations, and this has made a huge impact.'

SRC has conducted several other studies related to gender equality in research, and gender equality issues are regularly addressed in its online magazine *Curie*. In July 2023, the SRC listed 18 gender equality reports on its website available in English and 45 publications in Swedish (with the search word 'jämställdhet', which is Swedish for gender equality) (SRC, n.d.).

Formalisation and professionalisation of the funding process

Clear division of responsibilities and decision-making, detailed handbooks for panels, and monitoring are examples of how the research funding process has been formalised. At the time of the first observation study, training was not provided for the staff attending the panel meetings nor for the panellists. An interviewed SRC staff member reflected on how the formalisation of the research funding process had developed since then:

> [The panel meeting] has to be very carefully designed, and I would say that was not the case [earlier]. It was, if I may exaggerate, that you just let 12 professors into a room and they handle the process. This is not the case today.

Today, SRC's gender equality strategy emphasises that all evaluation criteria should be clear and explicit. The criteria are also published on the SRC website with instructions to reviewers on how to apply them. The guidelines for the assessments of applications also state that career stage instead of biological age is used as an eligibility criterion, and parental leave and other similar leaves are considered when assessing eligibility.

In addition to this change, a scientific council member interviewee explained the importance of regulating and controlling the interaction among the panellists, describing the panel meetings: 'I think they are very structured. We try to create a lot of structure to make sure that everyone gets a chance to speak.' This structuring prevented the problem when some 'people talk and talk and talk and take all the air'. The interaction between the reviewers outside the meeting room was also identified as important to regulate, as described by one of the informants, to prevent the reviewers trying to influence each other: 'Nowadays we of course inform them [reviewers] that "you are not allowed to talk about the applications, not during coffee breaks, not during dinner, not ever".' Generally, the importance of formalisation of the review process, including the panel meetings, was emphasised by the informants: 'I think we do quite a lot of work on that, and I have the sense most of the time that it works well and that it's efficient.'

Gender dimension in research

In 2018, the government ordinance to SRC was changed to include a new paragraph (2 §13) with instructions to consider the gender dimension in research content and to promote a sex and gender perspective in funded research whenever relevant (Utbildningsdepartementet, 2018). Since 2020, most of the funding calls from the SRC require the applicants to clarify if a sex or gender perspective is relevant in their research (SRC, 2023, p. 24). The SRC website gives guidance on this, providing examples of how sex and gender perspectives can be applied in research (Ahlqvist, Birberg, et al., 2020, p. 13). SRC also emphasises that this initiative is part of its work to strengthen the quality and renewal of research (Ahlqvist, Birberg, et al., 2020, p. 5). One informant, however, thought the rules allowed applicants to 'take the easy way out' with the option to declare that a gender perspective might not be relevant, without having to explain why. Some interviewees also touched upon additional challenges with the initiative, as it was considered by some as threatening academic freedom, described as 'the most important' by one of the interviewees. A staff member explained: 'We shouldn't affect the content of the research. We should fund anything that is of high quality.' The informant also suggested that some disciplinary cultures might find it more difficult than others to integrate gender equality initiatives into their research.

A scientific council member described similar dilemmas discussed within the council:

> Science should not be governed by politicians. Science should be free. … We should all be able to apply to SRC for whatever [project we want] and it should be evaluated on its merit as a scientific proposal unbiased. At the

same time, we have society saying we need to focus on gender theory. ... These are two good forces that don't really converge and there is a tension ... that's very hard. ... Maybe it's the thing we think about most at the moment in the council.

Internal and external communications, partnerships and networks

The SRC gender equality strategy emphasises the need for awareness-raising and communication of the policy to members of the scientific councils and members of review panels. Along with external partnerships and networks, these communication efforts exemplify the change agent role of SRC that we argued for early in the chapter.

Members of the review panels are to be instructed about gender equality during the information meetings prior to their evaluation work. The SRC handbooks for reviewers are accessible to reviewers and applicants on the SRC website, and they contain details on review process rules, guidelines, budgets and SRC policies, including the gender equality strategy and conflict of interest regulations (SRC, 2014).

One of the staff members emphasised the role SRC has in promoting gender equality in the scientific community more broadly, by communicating the results from their monitoring efforts and observations: 'In that way we can influence and spread knowledge that there is no neutral ground, and we are all influenced by norms that exist in society in general, for example, norms about women and men.' It was seen as particularly important to influence and communicate with universities, as explained by a scientific council member: 'I think also that we need to encourage the universities to do their share of the work because the research council alone ... cannot solve all the problems.'

Furthermore, the strategy also emphasises that a gender equality perspective should be integrated into all external communication and clearly communicated as a perspective promoted by the SRC and a goal that the SRC works to attain (SRC, 2014). Diversity of role models in SRC communication is also mentioned in the strategy: 'The external image conveyed by the Swedish Research Council should be gender-neutral and not reinforce gender stereotypes of, for example, researchers or subject areas' (SRC, 2014, p. 5).

As an additional example of change agent practice, the SRC's work for gender equality is strengthened by active engagements in collaboration and dialogue with other Swedish funding stakeholders on gender equality. One example of a formalised collaborative initiative is the coordination of a gender equality network for Swedish public funding organisations. These collaborations also extend beyond the national realm, most notably through the SRC's active participation and key role in GENDER-NET Plus (n.d.), an EU network of funders on gender equality and research funding.

Paradoxes and challenges in policy implementation at the Swedish Research Council

Gender made visible and invisible

Several of the interviewees mentioned what could be interpreted as a dilemma or paradox for gender equality work in the RFO: whether to put emphasis on gender or to make sure that gender is *not* emphasised or noticed. To begin with, the reviewers are instructed 'not to talk about gender in the discussion of individual applications', in the words of one of the staff members. The staff member explained, however, how gender was both present and invisible during different phases of the panel meetings:

> We try to keep gender out of the discussion. … We don't show the gender of the applicant in the list of applications, but we keep track of it so when they [the panel] start doing the ranking, that is when the research officer also looks at that [gender distribution].

One of the members of a scientific council explained similarly the process of suppressing the gender of the applicants to have an 'unbiased' evaluation.

Gender was thus made seemingly invisible during large parts of the panel meetings. This approach to gender was also reflected in one observation study (Söderqvist, Ahlqvist, et al., 2020), highlighting that the opportunity of 're-ranking' applications was in practice rarely discussed in the panel meetings. Re-ranking in this context means that applications from the under-represented gender should be prioritised when several applications are assessed as being of equal quality (Söderqvist, Ahlqvist, et al., 2020). Gender equality is thus a 'borderline condition' (SRC, 2020, p. 5), which, according to one of the interviewed staff members, could not be used to 'shift totally a ranking' but to rearrange and lift 'an application from a female applicant with lower scores on merits of the applicant but the same scores on scientific quality, novelty and originality of the application'. The applicant's 'merits' is one of four evaluation criteria (besides scientific quality, novelty and originality, and feasibility of project) and includes assessing the scope of the scientific production while only including the 'active research years' (thus leaving out time for parental and other leave) (cf. SRC, 2020, p. 37).

Given the complexity of assessing merits, especially in the type of comparison required by re-ranking, panellists seemed hesitant to try it. One of the interviewed members of a scientific council, however, suggested that 'they shouldn't really re-rank', emphasising that the scientific quality of the application should always override any other assessments. The panels had to define what they meant by equal quality of applications, which possibly contributed to uncertainties about the re-ranking procedure and its infrequent use. Another explanation for the cautious use of the re-ranking procedure could also be the vagueness regarding the goal. The goal was not to reach an equal success rate for women and men every year and in every call. Instead, relative success rates are monitored over three-year periods during which a trend is evaluated.

Continued improvements or progress come to a halt?

The staff members and scientific council members had ideas about future new initiatives for the SRC, regarding, for example, anonymous application processes, excluding the merits of the applicant from the evaluation, or doing a lottery among the top-ranked applications. One of the scientific council members explained the need to continue to develop the SRC gender equality work and to act as a change agent, driving the work also being done in universities:

> We need to be always aware that where we are now today is [because of] the work of many others before us … and I think we should not just be happy with what we have today. We must seek to improve to make it even better.

Despite the initiatives, the drivers and the commitments, the future of engagement with gender equality within SRC was not unproblematic. An interviewed staff member described signs of an organisation where people had settled and 'had lowered their ambition', based on assumptions that 'there is not much more to work on' (i.e. diminishing returns). This attitude was manifested, among other things, in that the observation studies became performed on a less regular basis: instead of every second or third year, they would be done every fourth or fifth. Another staff member implied that no major revisions were planned to update the 2014 strategy:

> We want to continue the work we have done but also increase it, improve it, and look for new ways. But I don't think it's going to be revolutionary. It [the strategy] is probably going to be quite similar to the one we have. That we continue doing what we do well and develop that.

Discussion

We conclude that the SRC has rightfully been described as an organisational change agent, acting as a driver for change in the research and development sector by developing and implementing innovative and transformative policies for over two decades.

The SRC policy has a very broad scope, clearly operationalised goals and a wide palette of measures to promote gender equality as a comprehensive strategy based on gender mainstreaming. Implementation of the newest element of the current SRC strategy, that is, gender in research content, is clearly more controversial than the more established elements of the strategy and includes several challenges, even though it is in line with current EU research policy.

However, it is noteworthy that some issues at the forefront in international discussions on gender and research funding are not yet addressed by the policy. These areas include an emphasis on gender balance in research teams, intersectional approaches and non-binary understandings of gender. Sweden is part of the European Research Area, where all these questions are increasingly addressed in the policy debate and documents. For example, in the seven-year European research framework, Horizon Europe, that began in 2021, gender balance is strongly encouraged within research teams, including leadership roles, and is considered as a ranking criterion to distinguish proposals with similar evaluation scores (Directorate-General for Research and Innovation, 2021). Horizon Europe also includes inclusive gender equality plans demanded as an eligibility criterion for funding and provides funding for gender and intersectionality research.

The SRC is characterised by strong, long-term societal and governmental support for gender equality as an important value. As a public funding organisation, the SRC is experiencing demand from the Swedish government to gender mainstream all its activities and is accountable for reporting annually on the progress and actions in this respect. These factors thus constitute an incentivising context for an organisation to become a change agent. But the SRC is also going beyond what other Swedish RFOs have been doing and has been a pioneering change agent, both nationally and internationally.

One of the most distinct displays of the SRC taking on the role of a change agent is the implementation of ethnographic observation studies of the review panels. This is a significant best practice that has evoked much interest internationally and could be adopted by more RFOs. Drawing on the experiences of the SRC, however, this initiative should be implemented with awareness of possible resistance not only from panellists but also from within the organisation. The interviewees described the results of the observation studies as an initial 'shock' and an 'eye-opener' for the organisation, which learned that it was 'not perfect'. One of the interviewed SRC staff therefore suggested that if other RFOs implement observation studies of panels, they should be prepared for 'tensions', as the critical lens is also turned to the practices of internal organisational actors (e.g. research officers). A less provocative strategy for other RFOs to adopt (initially) could instead be to use the type of external panel observers that are always included in the SRC panels. These observers do not collect and analyse ethnographic data, but instead ensure that formal rules, including gender equality guidelines, are followed. Instead of publishing public reports on their findings, they produce internal evaluation reports to the scientific councils.

Despite demonstrating high commitment and engagement on a formal level in the SRC, the analysis has also identified paradoxes, challenges and resistance regarding the implementation and the process by which policies become organisational practice. The SRC strategy emphasises the importance of persistence and long-term efforts to ensure that 'the ground gained towards equality is not lost' (SRC, 2014, p. 2). Our analysis suggests that there may be some risk that the organisation might be lowering its ambitions, and instead of continuing to innovate and drive new initiatives, could be scaling back on already established routines. On the other hand, the active participation of the SRC in proactive international networks of research funders around gender equality, such as GENDER-NET Plus, demonstrates continuous ambition, taking organisational change agent efforts beyond the national context.

Notes

1 Additional sources of research funding include other councils, public and private foundations, industry and the European Union. Sweden has a high percentage of researchers in the population and is one of the Organisation for Economic Co-operation and Development countries with the highest expenditure on research and development in relation to GDP (SRC, 2019, pp. 11–12). Yet the system coexists with a high degree of insecurity for researchers (see Griffin, this volume; Sveriges Universitetslärarförbund, 2021).
2 See also Roumbanis, this volume, for a study of interaction patterns among panel members and Peterson and Husu (2023) for a discussion of the impact of holding panel meetings online.

Acknowledgements

The data of this article were collected within the European Horizon 2020 funded research project, GRANteD, grant agreement No. 824574: Grant Allocation Disparities from a Gender Perspective (www.granted-project.eu). We thank Helene Schiffbänker and Angelika Sauer for their collaboration in research design and data collection.

References

Abbott, A. (1997). Equality not taken for granted. *Nature, 390*(6656), 204. https://doi.org/10.1038/36647

Ahlqvist, V., Andersson, J., Söderqvist, L., & Tumpane, J. (2015). *A gender-neutral process? A qualitative study of the evaluation of research grant applications 2014.* Swedish Research Council. https://www.vr.se/english/analysis/reports/our-reports/2015-04-03-a-gender-neutral-process.html

Ahlqvist, V., Birberg, W., Lagerholm, M., Sundin, A., Sundström, C., & Söderqvist, L. (2020). *Uppföljning av Vetenskapsradets implementering av köns- och genusperspektiv i forskningens innehåll* [A follow up of the Swedish Research Council implementation of a sex and gender perspective in research content] (Dnr 3.3-2018-05687). Swedish Research Council. https://www.vr.se/analys/rapporter/vara-rapporter/2020-02-06-uppfoljning-av-vetenskapsradets-implementering-av-kons--och-genusper spektiv-i-forskningens-innehall.html

Andersson, J., Hahn Berg, C., & Kolm, C. (2012). *Jämställdhetsobservationer i fyra beredningsgrupper 2011* [Equality observations in four review groups in 2011]. Swedish Research Council. https://www.vr.se/analys/rapporter/vara-rapporter/2012-04-02-jamstalldhetsobservationer-i-fyra-beredningsgrupper-2011.html

Bengtsson, A., Gribbe, J., & Wintgren, H. (Eds.). (2022). *Universitet och högskolor: årsrapport 2022* [Universities and colleges: annual report 2022]. Universitetskanslersämbetets publikationer. https://doi.org/10.53340/UKAP-5

Dahmen-Adkins, J., & Peterson, H. (2021). Micro change agents for gender equality: transforming European research performing organizations. *Frontiers in Sociology, 6*, Article 741886. https://doi.org/10.3389/fsoc.2021.741886

Directorate-General for Research and Innovation. (2009). *The gender challenge in research funding: assessing the European national scenes* (Report EUR 23721 EN). European Commission. https://doi.org/10.2777/36195

Directorate-General for Research and Innovation. (2021). *Horizon Europe, gender equality: a strengthened commitment in Horizon Europe*. European Commission. https://doi.org/10.2777/97891

European Institute for Gender Equality. (n.d.). *Gender equality index*. Retrieved on 12 January 2024 from https://eige.europa.eu/gender-equality-index/2022/compare-countries/

GENDER-NET Plus. (n.d.). *GENDER-NET Plus: promoting gender equality in H2020 and the ERA*. https://gender-net-plus.eu/what-is-gender-net-plus/

Global Research Council. (2022). *Statement of principles and actions promoting the equality and status of women in research*. https://globalresearchcouncil.org/fileadmin/documents/GRC_Publications/Statement_of_Principles_and_Actions_Promoting_the_Equality_and_Status_of_Women_in_Research.pdf

Goffman, E. (1974). *Frame analysis: an essay on the organization of experience*. Harvard University Press.

Hermansson, K., Jacobsson, C., & Österberg, R. (2021). *Gender equality in research funding: a study of 11 European countries, Israel and Canada* (Deliverable No. 6.3). GENDER-NET Plus. https://gender-net-plus.eu/wp-content/uploads/2021/04/GNP-Deliverable-D6.3-Gender-Equality-in-Research-Funding-plus-Coun try-reports-final.pdf

Husu, L. (2019a). Gender challenges in research funding. *Global Dialogue, 9*(2), 25–26. https://globaldialogue.isa-sociology.org/articles/gender-challenges-in-re search-funding

Husu, L. (2019b). Gender equality in Nordic academia: advances and challenges. In D. Vujadinović & Z. Antonijević (Eds.), *Rodna ravnopravnost u visokom obrazo-vanju: koncepti, prakse i izazovi* (pp. 63–73). Akademska knjiga.

Husu, L., & de Cheveigné, S. (2010). Gender and gatekeeping of excellence in research funding: European perspectives. In B. Riegraf, B. Aulenbacher, E. Kirsch-Auwärter, & U. Müller (Eds.), *Gender change in academia: re-mapping the fields of work, knowledge, and politics from a gender perspective* (pp. 43–59). VS Verlag für Sozialwissenschaften. https://doi.org/10.1007/978-3-531-92501-1_4

Peterson, H. (2014). "Someone needs to be first": women pioneers as change agents in higher education management. In V. Demos, C. W. Berheide, & M. T. Segal (Eds.), *Gender transformation in the academy* (pp. 395–413). Emerald Group.

Peterson, H., & Husu, L. (2023). Online panel work through a gender lens: implications of digital peer review meetings. *Science and Public Policy, 50*(3), 371–381. http s://doi.org/10.1093/scipol/scac075

Socialdepartementet. (2016). *Makt, mål och myndighet: en feministisk politik för en jamställd framtid* [Power, aims and authority: feminist policy for a gender-equal future] (Ministerial letter 2016/17:10). https://www.regeringen.se/rattsliga-dokument/skrivelse/2016/11/skr.-20161710

Söderqvist, L., Ahlqvist, V., Andersson, J., Bergström, M., Johansson, H. S., Svantesson, M., & Österberg, R. (2020). *A gender-equal process: a qualitative investigation of the assessment of research grant applications 2019.* Swedish Research Council. https://www.vr.se/english/analysis/reports/our-reports/2020-05-07-a-gender-equal-process.html

Söderqvist, L., Baard, P., Hellström, A., & Kolm, C. (2017). *A gender-neutral process: gender equality observations in the Swedish Research Council's review panels 2016.* Swedish Research Council. https://www.vr.se/english/analysis/reports/our-reports/2017-05-09-a-gender-neutral-process.html

Statskontoret. (2018). *Utvärdering av regeringens utvecklingsprogram för jämställdhetsintegrering i myndigheter* [Evaluation of the government's development program for gender mainstreaming in agencies] (Report 2017/230–235). https://www.statskontoret.se/siteassets/rapporter-pdf/2018/2018-17.pdf

Stening, E. (2020). *Uppföljning av rekryteringsmål för professorer 2017–2019* [Follow-up of recruitment targets for professors 2017–2019] (Report No. 111-263-20). Universitetskanslersämbetet. https://gamla.uka.se/download/18.224b0bb7171a c322a8ee693/1591250510175/rapport-2020-06-04-Uppf

Sveriges Universitetslärarförbund. (2021, May 27). *I skuggan av osäkerheten: om externfinansiering, osäkra anställningar och arbetsmiljön i akademin* [The shadow of uncertainty: external funding, precarious employment and work environment in higher education]. https://sulf.se/nyhet/rapport-i-skuggan-av-osakerheten/

Swedish Gender Equality Agency. (2022, December 22). *Gender mainstreaming.* https://swedishgenderequalityagency.se/gender-equality-in-sweden/gender-mainstreaming/

Swedish Research Council. (n.d.). *Gender equality: equal opportunities in research.* Retrieved on 12 January 2024 from https://www.vr.se/english/applying-for-funding/how-applications-are-assessed/gender-equality.html

Swedish Research Council. (2011). *Evaluation of "Centres of Gender Excellence".* https://www.vr.se/english/analysis/reports/our-reports/2011-04-11-evaluation-of-centres-of-gender-excellence.html

Swedish Research Council. (2014). *Strategy for gender equality at the Swedish Research Council.* https://www.vr.se/download/18.781fb755163605b8cd29c9ea/152948056 6477/Strategy_Gender_Equality_SRC_2014.pdf

Swedish Research Council. (2019). *Future choices for the Swedish research system: knowledge, quality and integrity.* https://www.vr.se/download/18.12596ec416eba1fc845cc8/1576071269880/Future-choices-for-the-Swedish-research-system-2019.pdf

Swedish Research Council. (2020). *Peer review handbook: International Postdoc 2020, fall.* https://www.vr.se/download/18.1af93abe17437c1d3f4ea4/1600768275348/Peer%20review%20handbook%20IPD%20fall%202020.pdf

Swedish Research Council. (2022). *Årsredovisning 2021* [Annual report 2021]. https://www.vr.se/analys/rapporter/vara-rapporter/2022-02-24-arsredovisning-2021.html

Swedish Research Council. (2023). *Årsredovisning 2022* [Annual report 2022]. https://www.vr.se/analys/rapporter/vara-rapporter/2023-03-01-arsredovisning-2022.html

Utbildningsdepartementet. (2009). *Förordning med instruktion för Vetenskapsrådet* [Governmental instructions for the Swedish Research Council] (Regulation SFS 2009:975). https://www.riksdagen.se/sv/dokument-lagar/dokument/svensk-forfattningssamling/forordning-2009975-med-instruktion-for_sfs-2009-975

Utbildningsdepartementet. (2018). *Förordning om ändring i förordningen (2009:975) med instruktion för Vetenskapsrådet* [Ordinance on amendments to the ordinance (2009:975) with instructions for the Swedish Research Council] (Regulation 2018:1881). https://www.lagboken.se/Lagboken/sfs/sfs/2018/1800-1899/d_3404497-sfs-2018_1881-forordning-om-andring-i-forordningen-2009_975-med-instruktion-for-vetenskapsradet

Utbildningsdepartementet. (2020). *Forskning, frihet, framtid: kunskap och innovation för Sverige* [Research, freedom, future: knowledge and innovation for Sweden] (Proposition 2020/21:60). https://www.regeringen.se/rattsliga-dokument/proposition/2020/12/forskning-frihet-framtid–kunskap-och-innovation-for-sverige/

Wennerås, C., & Wold, A. (1997). Nepotism and sexism in peer-review. *Nature, 387* (6631), 341–343. https://doi.org/10.1038/387341a0

INDEX

academic capitalism: external funding imperative 3, 66, 70, 87, 99, 196–197; global masculinity discourse 6, 135–136; ideal academic subject 68, 114, 120, 122, 131–132, 134, 138–139; job security/precarity 8–9, 12, 38, 117–118; managerial practices 7–8, 66–67, 128, 192; resistance 39–40, 92, 122–123, 139; valuation of male-dominated fields 25, 99; work intensification 90, 117–118, 120, 123, 192. *See also* audit culture; neoliberalism; precarity

academic excellence discourse 22, 24, 100, 167–168, 214–215. *See also* research excellence

academic façade, strategies 135–136. *See also* affective economy

academic fields: gender segregation 23–24, 25, 38, 75, 99, 100, 134; research funding differences 178. *See also* disciplinary hierarchies; networks/networking

academic freedom 134, 139, 212–213

academic housework 23, 88, 90, 148, 193

Academic Researchers in Challenging Times (project) (Canada) 9–10, 115

Academy of Finland (AF): competitive funding standards 71, 74–75; gender equality plans 68–70, 76; gender parity in success ratios 71; health technology grants 103; parental leave/work flexibility 12, 69, 71–72

accountability: equity, diversity and inclusion action plans, institutional 181–184; higher education funding 143; industry funding 104; university performance reviews 189. *See also* audit culture; research excellence

Acker, Joan 21–22, 39, 40, 47

Acker, Sandra 10, 11–12, 120

Adam, Barbara 52

administrative work: academic housework 23, 88, 90, 148, 193; non-academic/clerical work devaluation 13, 118–119, 122, 124n3; as senior leadership role 116, 124n2

advocacy. *See* equity-seeking groups

affect cafés (focus groups) 13, 128–133, 135–137

affective economy: as analytic framework 127; anxiety creation 14, 133–134, 137, 194–196, 200; care work in research 23, 121–122, 128, 137; ideal academic subject 68, 114, 120, 131–132, 134, 138–139; othering processes 21, 130–131, 135, 137; research strategies 13, 135–137. *See also* gender-based status inequalities

Ahmed, Sara 6, 127, 135, 137, 147

Arendt, Hannah 170

ARIA (Advanced Research and Innovation Agency) (UK) 55

222 Index

Asian-background academics (UK), appointment types 52, 61n2; funding award rates 83, 142; peer-review panel composition 150–151, 162, 191

Athena Swan (Scientific Women's Academic Network) (UK) 6, 25, 145, 154n6, 191, 201

Attaran, Amir, 180–81

audit culture: growth 37–38, 143; performance-based funding 7–8, 59, 82–83, 100, 174, 192. *See also* academic capitalism; peer-review process; research excellence

austerity agendas, gender conservatism 46–47

Australian research 21, 27, 75, 194

Bacchi, Carol 177
Badenoch, Kemi 153
Becher, Tony 110
Behtoui, Alireza 162
Benschop, Yvonne 22
Bhopal, Kalwant 6, 193
bias: control of 24; implicit 160, 170n1; in recruitment and promotion 66, 68; in research funding 24, 26, 71, 100, 175–176, 207; status-related 159–160, 168–169; systemic 178, 179; training for 151, 181; "unbiased" evaluation 214; unconscious 150–151, 154n8, 193. *See also* gender bias

Black academics: peer-review bias 144, 150–152, 193; research funding award rates 83, 142, 144; UK professoriate 142, 154n1

Black women academics: funding inequities 13, 14, 144–146, 149, 153; institutional funnelling 6, 146, 148; mentorship 145–147, 152–153; peer-review biases 150–152; peer-review panel composition 162, 191; precarity and contract status 52, 58; race research discrimination 6, 146–147, 149; reduced workload, inequities 144, 148–149; workloads 23, 148, 153. *See also* misogynoir

Bloch, Charlotte 135
Boncori, Ilari 85
Bosch, Anita 25
bounded change, concept 40
Bourdieu, Pierre 160
Brexit, precarity 12, 53–60
British Academy (research funding) 82, 196

Business Finland 69. *See also* Finnish Funding Agency for Innovation (FAI)

Butler, Judith 52, 57, 60

Calvard, Thomas 56
Campisi, Caitlin 13
Canada, higher education: federal funding overview 6, 8, 174, 185n4; precarious labour growth 9, 124n5; provincial responsibilities 8, 174; research council grant requirements 117, 124n3; research positions defined 11, 13, 113, 116–119, 121–122. *See also* Canada Research Chairs Program (CRCP); Canadian Institutes of Health Research (CIHR); Natural Sciences and Engineering Research Council of Canada (NSERC); Social Sciences and Humanities Research Council of Canada (SSHRC)

Canada Research Chairs Program (CRCP): CRCP College of Reviewers 175, 176; equity, diversity and inclusion policy changes 6, 177–182; equity targets 180–184, 185n4, 185n5; external peer review 175–176, 179; gender balance focus 14, 178–179; human rights settlement 177, 179–180; institutional nominations 175, 179–180, 184–185; male dominance in peer review 176, 178, 184; programme description 173–175, 178–179, 185n2; research excellence metrics 25, 175–176, 178–179, 183–185

Canadian Human Rights Commission, complaint 177, 179–180. *See also* equity-seeking groups

Canadian Institutes of Health Research (CIHR) 174, 178, 181, 185n4

career progression: COVID-19 and research productivity 12–13, 21, 81, 84–86, 89–93; funding framework changes 14; interruptions and support 71–72, 180; parental leave practices 12, 66, 69, 71–77, 191; publication record 82, 85; research group leaders 102–105; research-intensive universities 101, 178

caregiving/childcare 23, 59, 84–85, 89–92, 94, 114, 167. *See also* COVID-19 pandemic; motherhood

care-related work: conflicts 13, 14; 'careless academic' ideal 68, 114, 120, 122; pastoral care/student support

88–90; professional caring work/ project care 121–23; racialised and gendered patterns 23, 114. *See also* mentoring
Carruthers Thomas, Kate 12–13, 21
Ceci, Stephen J. 24
Chan, Hannah 21
charitable organisation funding 82
Chubb, Jennifer 193
Clavero, Sara 21–22
collaboration: health technology 102–103; Horizon Europe eligibility (UK) 54–56, 60; and multidisciplinary imperative 131; research–industry 69, 72–73, 197; women's international 13, 91–92, 108, 213; work overload 42–43, 45
commercialisation 66, 101. *See also* industry funding
Commission on Race and Ethnic Disparities (UK) 153–154
competition/competitive ethos 7–8, 99–100, 127–128, 135–137, 139. *See also* affective economy
contract status, overview 9, 11, 52, 61*n*1, 118
core funding, performance-based 7–8, 82, 83, 100, 174
corporatisation. *See* academic capitalism
Council for Research Infrastructure (Swedish Research Council) 208
COVID-19 pandemic: funding relief bias 56–58; gendered repercussions 58, 81; precarity and 12, 59, 91; related projects and grant holders 83; research funding policy analysis 53; research productivity in 12–13, 21, 81, 84–86, 89–93; women's caregiving responsibilities 58–59, 84–85, 114
crisis temporalities framework 93
critical policy analyses (CPA) 176–77, 184
critical race theory 153–154
Cruz-Castro, Laura 25–26
cultural/identity taxation 23
culture wars 27, 153–154
Curie online magazine (Sweden) 211

Dear Diary project (UK) 82, 85–89, 93
de Beauvoir, Simone 169
decolonisation and anti-racism approaches 150–153, 194
Degn, Lise 101
Derrick, Gemma E. 193
diary study 13, 85–86
digital communication technologies 91–92

digital humanities (DH): bounded change 40; infrastructure requirements 45–46; interdisciplinarity 12, 38–39; personal accounts 42–47; precarity in 12, 37, 38, 39, 40, 47–48
digitalisation, societal 39
Dimensions (Canadian EDI framework) 6
disabilities, persons with 180–182
disciplinary hierarchies: applied vs non-applied rhetoric 57, 138; career status and gender 110; external funding opportunities 23–25, 56–57, 179; research strategies and career opportunities 133–34. *See also* academic fields; male-dominated fields; STEM (science, technology, engineering and mathematics)
discourse analysis 53, 54, 55, 57, 143
distance-taking strategy 139
division of labour, academic: academic housework 23, 88, 90, 148, 193; gendered 22–23, 88–90, 99–100, 114; public–private during COVID-19 pandemic 84–85; thinking vs clerical work 119–120
doctoral students, precarity 9, 41, 116
double standard 169
dramaturgy approach, social 160, 161

early-career researchers, experiences 74–76, 100, 101, 121–122
Economic and Social Research Council (ESRC), funded projects 144, 196, 199
Education Reform Act, 1988 (UK) 189
elitism, academic 110, 147, 151, 185
emotional labour. *See* affective economy
entrepreneurship 101
Equality and Diversity Advisory Panel (EDAP) (UK) 150–151, 191
equity, defined 8, 15*n*1, 181–182
equity, diversity and inclusion (EDI) in research requirements 6, 177–182, 191. *See also* Canada Research Chairs Program (CRCP); Research Excellence Framework (REF)
equity-seeking groups: about 174, 185*n*1; on career interruptions 180; human rights complaints 177, 179–180; institutional targets 180, 181, 182, 183, 185*n*5; on research excellence bias 175–176, 210; role in policy change 177, 182, 184; from targets to consequences 14
Etzkowitz, Henry 39, 46, 47

224 Index

European Commission, funding policies 15n2, 44, 68
European Institute for Gender Equality (EIGE) index 204–205
European Research Area (ERA) 204, 216
European Research Council (ERC) 135
European Science Foundation 40–41
European Union (funding body) 54, 60, 67–69, 103, 144, 217n1. *See also* Brexit; Horizon Europe funding

Fagan, Colette 192–193
fast professors, concept 120
Federation of Finnish Learned Societies 8
fellowship, research 14, 82, 142, 143, 144–145, 147, 151
feminised labour 56–57, 113, 196. *See also* academic housework; care-related work
feminism, intersectional 6–7, 22, 26–27, 51, 216. *See also* gender mainstreaming
Finland, higher education: academic careers and stages 11, 12, 66, 68; gender equality plans (GEPs) 67–69, 76, 110; men's closed networks 46–47; parental leave and childcare 12, 66, 69, 71–72; temporary and fixed-term contracts 9, 100–101, 107; tenure system 8–9. *See also* Academy of Finland (AF); Finnish Funding Agency for Innovation (FAI); Finnish university funding
Finland, Ministry of Education and Culture 69
Finnish Funding Agency for Innovation (FAI) 69–73
Finnish university funding: core and external 5, 8, 68–69, 76, 103; gender equality policies 128–129; research and innovation funding 70, 71, 75; research–industry collaboration 68–69, 72. *See also* Academy of Finland (AF); Finnish Funding Agency for Innovation (FAI)
fixed-term contracts,52, 101, 107
Formas (Swedish research funder) 44
Foucauldian discourse analysis 53
foundation funding, independent 44, 70, 134, 136, 217n1
friendly rivalry, concept 163, 170n5
funding. *See* research funding bodies; research funding ecosystems
Funding Agency for Innovation (Finland) 72
Further and Higher Education Act 1992 (UK) 83

Gabriel, Deborah 145
Galligan, Yvonne 21–22
gender-based status inequalities: about 159–160; age and research profiles 163, 165–166, 169; disrespectful/patronising treatment 164–165, 168
gender bias: disciplinary assimilation imperative 138; genius/superstar ascriptions 169, 210; grant-funding agencies 25–26, 178; peer-review process 104, 144, 147, 159, 193, 210; research work opportunities 113–114; review panels 24, 159–162, 166–168, 170n2, 210–212; unconscious bias training 151, 181. *See also* bias; disciplinary hierarchies; misogynoir; research excellence
gendered labour. *See* caregiving/childcare; care-related work; division of labour
gender equality policies: audits and 191; implementational variation 22; institutional targets 6, 180–183; Nordic paradox and 5, 15; as organisational change agents 205–206, 213
gender-equity seeking groups 183, 185n5
gender mainstreaming: explanation 5, 15n2, 68–69, 205; gender equality plans (GEPs) 25, 68–70, 73, 107, 109–110; government legislation 5, 67, 205; grant evaluation panels/outcomes 208; parental leave and 12, 66, 69, 71–77, 191; resistance 212–213, 215–216
GENDER-NET Plus 213, 217
gender neutrality 25, 135–136, 139, 175–176, 213–214
gender segregation: academic fields 23–24, 38, 75, 99, 100, 134; contract status and professorships 22, 41, 68, 100, 142, 154n1, 205. *See also* care-related work
Gill, Rosalin, 118
girl minimising, funding success 104
Global Britain discourse 54, 55, 61n3
Global Gender Gap Index (World Economic Forum) 204
global masculinity discourse 6, 135–136. *See also* academic capitalism
Global North focus 27, 58
Goffman, Erving 161
government research funding 7–8, 23, 82–83, 100, 174.
Grant Allocation Disparities from a Gender Perspective (GRANteD) project (Europe) 206

grant applications: gender composition of 209; informal and formal supports 109–110; neutrality impact 25, 175–176, 213–214; overhead costs 44–45. *See also* peer-review panels

grant-funding success: autonomy and job security 109–110; formal and informal knowledge 99, 109; individualised failure 20, 21; national comparisons 10. *See also* disciplinary hierarchies; gender bias; gender segregation; networks/networking

Griffin, Gabriele 5, 6, 11, 12, 40–41

Griffin, Kimberly A. 23

Gutiérrez Rodríguez, Encarnación 151

Haake, Ulrika 8

health impacts, career 90, 92, 149

health technology: academic mothers' experiences 67, 70; interdisciplinarity 100; medical faculty conflicts 104, 107; research centre autonomy 13, 101, 103–104; research funding 103; women's external funding opportunities 13, 102–110

Helgesson, Karin Svedberg 9, 22

Henderson, Holly 6, 193

Hey, Valerie 120

Higher Education Funding Council for England (HEFCE) 190

Higher Education Funding Council for Wales 143

higher education institutions (HEIs): funding restructuring 37–38; neoliberalism and 7, 9, 12, 25, 51–52, 100, 138. *See also* academic capitalism

Higher Education Statistics Agency (UK) 151

hiring and promotion: career interruptions 90–91; grant-funding success 99; publication record and 8, 82, 85, 90, 196–198; research profile 195–197; structural inequality 22

Hokka, Johanna 13

home schooling, COVID-19 pandemic 84, 90

Horizon Europe funding (EU) 54, 82, 144, 216. *See also* Brexit

Hübinette, Tobias 6

human rights complaints. *See* Canadian Human Rights Commission

Husu, Liisa 14–15, 24, 217n2

ideal academic subject 68, 114, 120, 131–132, 134, 138–139. *See also* academic façade

Ikonen, Hanna-Mari 12

imperialism 54, 60

implicit bias. *See* bias

imposter syndrome 108, 110–111, 139

independent researcher/lecturer position 41

Indigenous academics 23, 25, 180–182

Indigenous perspectives 25, 184

individualism, competitive 21, 99, 122–123

industry funding, private 38, 69, 72–73, 82, 103–104, 197

inequality regimes 22, 39, 40, 46–47, 145–146

infrastructure funding 45–46, 175

Innovate UK (business funding) 154n4, 201n1

innovation and resistance 39–40

Insight Grants programme. *See* Social Sciences and Humanities Research Council of Canada (SSHRC)

instrumentalism 122–123

interdisciplinarity 12, 38–39, 77, 107, 110, 134

international research funding (EU) 54, 82, 144, 216

intersectional feminism 6–7, 22, 26–27, 51, 216

intersectionality: approaches/perspectives 6–7, 67–68, 83, 129, 135, 137; culture wars 135, 153–154; and imposter syndrome 110–111; inequality regimes 22, 145–146; institutional equity and diversity plans 182–183

Ireland and Brexit 54

Ireland, Department for the Economy (funding body) 143

ivory tower, critique 131, 139

Jenkins, Fiona 22

job security: precarity vs 8–9, 12; research career stages 40–41. *See also* precarious labour; tenure-track systems

Johnson, Boris (government) 153–154

JuFo (publication forum Finland) 8

Kemelgor, Carol 39, 46, 47

Kerridge, Simon 123n1

knowledge production: decolonising/ antiracist approaches 150–153, 184; as core value (eros) 134; Indigenous perspective, 25, 184; masculinised models 55

Kone Foundation (Finland) 136
Korvajärvi, Päivi 12
Kurtti, Elisa 13

laboratory settings 100–101, 103, 107
Larivière, Vincent 24
leadership roles: manager-academics
129–133, 135–137; research centres
39–40, 43–44, 46, 101–104; White
men 13. *See also* research-group
leadership positions
Leathwood, Carole 12, 21, 193
Leivestad, Hege Høyer 162
Leslie, Larry 66
Letherby, Gayle 88–89
Leyser, Dame Ottoline 55
liability of newness 40
Lucas, Lisa 14
Lund, Rebecca 134, 135
Lynch, Kathleen 114, 120, 122

Mackay, Fiona 39–40, 46, 47
Mählck, Paula 6
male-dominated academic units:
motherhood myths/risk 68, 73,
75–77; old boys networks 75; women
in 12, 100, 107
male-dominated fields: COVID-19
funding relief 56–57; grant success
rates 24–25, 51–52. *See also* STEM
(science, technology, engineering and
mathematics)
manager-academics/leaders 129–133,
135–137
Marginson, Simon 58
marketisation, research 37, 46, 66,
135–136. *See also* academic capitalism
Massey, Doreen 52, 53
maternal ideology/maternalism 89, 122
maternity leave provisions 71–75, 90
Matthew effect in science 24, 109
McAlpine, Lynn 109
McGinn, Michelle K. 10, 15n4, 20, 120
media analyses 51, 53–55, 58
Medical Research Council (MRC)
scandal (Sweden) 207
medicine and health, review panels 210
mentoring: dearth of Black women
academics 145, 153; early-career
funding success 109, 153; old boys
network 5, 12, 43, 46–48, 75, 107;
pay inequity 120; White male networks
56; women in life sciences 101–102.
See also networks/networking
merit evaluations 212–215

meritocracy 159–160, 170
methods/methodologies: case study 177;
content analysis 15, 206; critical policy
analysis 173, 176, 177; diary and
interview 13, 85–86; discourse analysis
51, 53, 143; ethnographic observation
14, 161, 209–211, 216; focus group
13, 128–130; interview 12, 13, 14, 15,
42–43, 70, 100–101, 115, 128,
193–194, 206; media analysis 12–13,
51, 53; qualitative vs quantitative
strengths 3–4, 26; questionnaires
84–85, 143; sense-making and
story-telling 100–101
metrics, funding 8, 59, 175–176,
178–179, 183–185
Mid-Career Academics Project (MCA)
194, 196, 197–198, 199, 200
Ministry of Education and Culture
(Finland) 8, 100
minoritised academics, terminology
28n1, 52, 61n2, 154n2, 154n3, 181
misogynoir, institutional 14, 145–151
mobility, researcher 56, 60, 99, 132
motherhood: career progression 66–67;
careless academic as ideal 68, 114,
120, 122; COVID-19 pandemic 21,
23, 59, 84, 89–90, 92; male-
dominated academic units 68, 73,
75–77; parental leave practices 12, 66,
69, 71–77, 90, 191; productivity gaps
in peer review 167, 191, 212; return to
work 12, 70, 73–74. *See also*
caregiving/childcare
multidisciplinarity imperative 131, 134, 139

Naidoo, Rajani 99
National Institute for Health and Care
Research (NIHR) (UK) 83, 191–192
National Sciences and Engineering
Research Council of Canada (NSERC)
174, 178, 181, 185n4
nationalism. *See* Global Britain discourse
neoliberalism 7, 12, 37–38, 51–52. *See
also* academic capitalism
nested newness 39–40, 46
networks/networking: cross-border and
Brexit 53–54; GENDER-NET Plus
213, 217; in health technology
102–103; informal old boys 5, 12, 43,
46–48, 75, 107; international 213;
masculinised discourse 135–136;
White-only 56, 147; women's online
opportunities 91–92. *See also*
collaboration

New Frontiers in Research Fund (NFRF) (Canada) 6
news media on pandemic productivity (UK) 12–13, 21, 56–57, 84–85
Nixon, Rob 93
Nokia, industry funding 38
Nordic countries: gender equality and diversity 128–129, 204; university research funding in 37–38, 40–41; welfare provisions 5, 12, 66, 76; work time parameters 45. *See also* Finland; Sweden
Nordic gender paradox, 5, 15, 204, 213–214
Nordic universities: four-stage research career model 40–41; gender equality plans (GEPs) 25, 68–69
Northern Ireland Protocol (Brexit) 54
Norway researcher positions 11, 14

observation studies 14, 160–161, 209–210, 212, 214–216
Olsson, Pia 13
online course delivery 84, 87–88
organisational practices: change agents framework 205–206, 213; and history framework 39–40; overview 23–26
Organisation for Economic Co-operation and Development (OECD) 39, 217n1

parental leave policies: Finnish legislation 71; gender mainstreaming and 12, 66, 69, 71–77, 191; job/funding precarity 12, 74–76; male-dominated academic units 73, 76–77; peer-review process and 167, 191, 212; return to work differences 12, 70, 73–74
pastoral care/student support 88–89, 90. *See also* care-related work
pay and hiring freezes 59
Pebdani, Roxana N. 85
peer-review process: career interruptions 178–179; decolonisation and antiracism approaches 150–153, 184; gendered patterns 7, 24; institutional, 147; research excellence and systemic bias 166–168, 175–176, 210, 214–215; unconscious gender bias 159–160, 193. *See also* gender-based status inequalities; peer-review panels
peer-review panels: composition 10, 150–151, 162, 170n2, 191; disrespectful treatment within 161, 164–165, 168; double standards 164, 169; formalisation and

professionalisation 211–212; hierarchical status 14, 24; men's friendly rivalry 163; merit negotiations 166–167, 210; observation studies 210–212, 214–216; ranking consensus 162, 214. *See also* Canada Research Chairs Program (CRCP); Research Excellence Framework (REF); Swedish Research Council (SRC)
Pelkonen, Antti 15
performativity, equity policy 6
Pereira, Maria do Mar 114
Peterson, Helen 14–15, 24, 217n2
Picard-Aitken, Michelle 180
Pondayi, Georgina 25
postdoctoral researchers 41, 43, 45, 74–75, 129
power geometries: Brexit consequences 53–54, 57–60; neutrality discourses 25, 135–136, 139, 175–176, 213–214; resource distribution 176–177. *See also* temporal/spatial analysis
precarious labour: contract status 9, 52, 58, 61n1; dependency/reliance on 52; in digital humanities 12, 37–40, 47–48; funding regime changes 9, 12, 38; racialised and gendered patterns 23, 58, 68, 114, 118
precarity: funding, gender and 47–48, 51, 74–76; funding shortfalls and women's 9, 12, 46–47, 107; neoliberalism and 9, 12; parental leave and 74–76, 90; research careers/stages 12, 39–41; social 12, 51–52, 57–58. *See also* academic capitalism
professional staff, 13, 113, 128. *See also* manager-academics/leaders; research administrators
professorship, full: Black women, prevalence 142, 150, 151; as career stage 41, 68, 109–110, 154n1, 174, 205; in international comparison 10–11, 108, 142; status hierarchy 10–11, 104, 105; women, prevalence 22, 100, 205
publication imperative 8, 82, 85, 90, 196–198
Puhakka, Antero 69

race and ethnicity, terminology. *See* minoritised academics, terminology
race and racism: academic work organisation 119–120; culture wars 27, 152–154; ethnicity minority language

147, 154*n*2; human rights settlement 180–181; as research area 6, 146; university diversity plans 193; White faculty regimes 145–146. *See also* misogynoir
Race Equality Charter (UK) 6, 145, 154*n*6, 201
racialised academics: contract teaching burden 114; cultural taxation 23; ethnic minority categorisations (UK), 142, 147, 154*n*1, 154*n*2, 154*n*3; institutional targets 180–182; women's research work 120. *See also* Asian-background academics; Black academics; Indigenous academics
Ramsay, Karen 88–89
Read, Barbara 12, 193
redundancy (job cuts) metrics 59
relational work, research administrators 116
research administrators: gender equity concerns 120; roles/responsibilities 113, 115–116, 123*n*1; self-identities/ identification 116, 119; valuation by academic researchers 116–118, 121–122
Research Assessment Exercise (RAE) 14, 189, 190–191. *See also* Research Excellence Framework (REF)
research centres: autonomy 103–104; provisional funding and job security 39–40, 43–44, 46; women's funding success 101–104
research chair. *See* Canada Research Chairs Program (CRCP)
research council grants: about, 7, 8, 10, 12, 15. *See also* government research funding
Research Council of Finland. *See* Academy of Finland
Research England (audit body) 59, 143, 154*n*4, 201*n*1
research environment criterion 82, 143–144, 190–191
research excellence: decolonisation and antiracist approaches to 150–153, 184; as funding success 99–100; gender/ neutrality discourses 25, 135–136, 139, 175–176, 213–214; Indigenous perspectives 25, 184; metrics and bias 25, 164, 166–168, 170*n*6, 175–176, 178–179, 214–215; national profiling/ profiles 6, 135, 143, 173–176; racialised and gendered inequalities 150–153, 184; resource concentration

8; university profiles 8, 130–131, 174–175, 189–190. *See also* academic excellence discourse; Canada Research Chairs Program (CRCP); Research Excellence Framework (REF); Swedish Research Council (SRC)
Research Excellence Framework (REF) (UK): audit culture 8, 51–52, 59, 82–83; decolonising/antiracist approaches 150–153; description 8, 14, 189, 190–193; Equality and Diversity Advisory Panel (EDAP) 150–151, 191; funding inequities 24, 144, 148, 195; outputs and impact criteria 82, 89–90, 143, 148, 154*n*6, 190–192; peer review and 8, 190, 198; research environment as criterion 143–144, 201; research impact criterion 82, 143, 190, 191, 200; women experiences of 193–195, 200
research foundation funding 44, 70, 134, 136, 217*n*1
research funding bodies: as change agents 76, 204, 213; decolonisation and antiracism 150–153, 184; gender bias 25–27; gender equality outcomes 6, 173, 204–205, 208; Indigenous perspectives 25, 184. *See also* government research funding
research funding ecosystems: applied vs non-applied rhetoric 57; gender equality frameworks 5–7; general information 4–5, 11, 15, 25; short-termism 47; stratification 82–83, 189; women's success rates 11, 24–25. *See also* Canada; Finland; Sweden; United Kingdom
research funding imperative 99, 195–197
The Research Game in Academic Life (Lucas) 189, 192, 193, 194
Research Game in Academic Life project (UK) 192, 193, 194, 195, 197, 198, 199, 200
research-group leadership positions 104–107
research-intensive universities: career progression 101, 175–176, 178; dearth of Black women 148; higher funding rates 83, 143; informal male networks 193–194; institutional support differences 89–90
research outputs criteria 82, 89–90, 190–191
research productivity: caregiving responsibilities and 21, 89–90, 114,

191; COVID-19 pandemic 12–13, 21, 81, 84–86, 89–93; teaching and service work 22–23; teaching-intensive universities 90; work intensification and 120, 123, 192

research profile requirement 22–23, 195–200

research strategies: competitive ethos 131–132; disciplinary hierarchies 138; inclusion and exclusion practices 130–134; legitimation practices 134; manager-academic perspectives 129–133, 135–137; researchers' perspectives 129, 131; university profiling and strategic planning 8, 13, 130–131, 189

research temporalities, gendered 89–91, 92, 93

research work: care work value within 121–123; feminised labour within 113, 115; institutional supports 117–118, 198–199; teaching, caring and service work 22–23; thinking vs administration 118–119, 120, 122

resistance 137, 139, 145

Ridgeway, Cecilia 160

Rollock, Nicola 193

Roumbanis, Lambros 14, 24, 217n2

Russell Group universities (UK) 83, 143, 148. *See also* research-intensive universities

Salminen-Karlsson, Minna 11, 21

Sang, Katherine 56

Sanz-Menéndez, Luis 25–26

Sato, Sayaka 26

science and engineering. *See* STEM (science, technology, engineering and mathematics)

Scientific Council for Humanities and Social Sciences (Sweden) 206

Scientific Council for Medicine and Health (Sweden) 206

Scientific Council for Natural and Engineering Sciences (Sweden) 206

Scientists for EU, pandemic 58

Scottish Funding Council 143

Scott, Stephanie F. 123n1

The Second Sex (de Beauvoir) 169

service (administration) work. *See* academic housework

sexual orientation and gender identity 6, 52, 135, 145,150, 179, 181–182, 183, 185n5

Silander, Charlotte 5, 8

Sjögren, Ebba 9, 22

Slaughter, Sheila 66

Smith, Cameron 116

social justice researchers 115, 120, 122–123, 147

social media, façade 136

social precarity 52, 57, 60. *See also* precarity

social production of research 10–11, 15

social sciences and humanities (SSH): applied-research imperative 128, 134, 138; core value of 133–34; external funding inequalities 23–25, 56–57, 179; masculinised academic ideal 131–132, 134

Social Sciences and Humanities Research Council of Canada (SSHRC) 10, 118–119, 124n4, 174, 178, 181, 185n4

sociological approaches 160–161, 206

Søndergaard, Dorte Marie 165

Stadmark, Johanna 25

Standing, Guy 39

Starr, Karen 75

status hierarchies: academic vs non-academic research work 122–123; as analytic framework 160–163, 168–169; decision-making authority 138, 165–166; full professorship 10–11, 41, 68, 104, 105, 109–110, 154n1, 174, 205; gender-based 159–160, 163–169; review-panel interactions 163–165; work intensification and 120, 123, 192

Steinþórsdóttir, Finnborg S. 25

STEM (science, technology, engineering and mathematics): European career model 40–41; funding review panels 14, 210; gender equality training 213; informal knowledge networks 21; laboratory settings 100–101, 103, 107; male dominance/masculinisation of 55–57; Matthew effect, funding 24, 109; pandemic funding relief 56–57; techno-science policy context 128; women's early career choices 101–102, 105–106. *See also* health technology; social sciences and humanities

stereotypes, gender: genius 169, 210; ideal academic subject 68, 114, 120, 131–132, 134, 138–139

strategic planning, university 8, 13, 130–131, 189

student experience discourse 87

Sugimoto, Cassidy R. 24

Suopajärvi, Tiina 13
Sutherland, Dawn 14, 24
Sweden, higher education: career/tenure system 8–9, 11; gender equality policies 159, 204–205; humanities and social sciences funding 44; precarity 12, 47–48. *See also* Formas; Nordic countries; Swedish Research Council (SRC)
Swedish Agency for Public Management 207–208, 209
Swedish Research and Innovation Bill (2021–2024) and gender equality 205
Swedish Research Council (SRC): as change agent 15, 170, 204, 213, 215–216; composition and responsibilities 206–209; funding allocations/parameters 41–42, 44–45; gender equality goal 5, 162, 170n3, 207–208, 213, 217; gender mainstreaming duty 5, 15, 67–68, 72, 76, 205, 207–209, 215; on gender research content 212–213, 215–216; gender-equality observation studies 14, 160–161, 209–212, 214–216; merit/excellence criteria 164, 166, 170n6; review panels and bias 24, 159–162, 170n2, 211–212

Tamtik, Merli 14, 24, 184
Tate, Shirley Anne 11, 14, 23
teaching loads 22–23, 87–88, 90, 200. *See also* workload conflicts
teaching-only contracts: as demotion 192, 195, 200; held by women 52, 83, 148; zero-hours contracts 52, 58, 61n1
Teasdale, Nina 192–193
technicians/technical labour 45–46
technologisation 38, 39, 47. *See also* digital humanities (DH)
temporal/spatial analysis 20, 21, 51, 52, 57, 60, 93
tenure-track systems 8–9, 11, 22, 69, 115, 124n5, 189. *See also* precarious labour
Thatcher, Margaret (government) 189
Tienari, Janne 134
Times Higher Education (THE) 51, 53–54, 55, 58. *See also* Brexit
time/temporal concerns: gendered 89–93; grant-writing 20, 148–149; industry-funding timetables 73; peer-review panel 168; research-time allocations 21, 44–45, 88–89; work

intensification 90, 117–118, 120, 123. *See also* workload allocation model (WAM); work overload
Toffoletti, Kim 75
Tri-agency Institutional Programs Secretariat (TIPS), Canada: administration, external peer review 175–179; EDI action plan 180–184. *See also* Canada Research Chairs Program

unconscious bias. *See* bias
United Kingdom Arts and Humanities Research Council (AHRC) 144
United Kingdom Equality Challenge Unit (2005) 154n6
United Kingdom, higher education: equality legislation and 150–51; gender equality policies 6; government funding 142, 143–144; national ranking 189; neoliberalism 51–52; racialised academic representation 142, 154n1, 154n2; research-intensive universities 83; senior lecturers, PhD requirement 194–195; staffing trends 83, 199–200; stratification 82–83, 90–91; tenure-track elimination 8–9, 189, 192. *See also* Athena Swan; United Kingdom research funding
United Kingdom Higher Education Statistical Agency 52
United Kingdom Research and Development Roadmap 54, 60
United Kingdom Research and Innovation (UKRI): award rates and inequalities 51–52, 55, 82–83, 142–143; equality, diversity and inclusion (EDI) plans 144, 201; fellowships and racial discrimination 144–145, 151
United Kingdom research funding: Brexit and 51, 53–56; COVID-19 pandemic effects 12–13, 51, 56–57, 81, 84–86, 89–93; overview 51, 82, 143–144. *See also* Economic and Social Research Council (ESRC); Horizon Europe funding (EU); Innovate UK; National Institute for Health and Care Research (NIHR); Research Excellence Framework (REF); United Kingdom Research and Innovation (UKRI); Wellcome Trust
United States, funding equity 24, 27, 58
University Alliance (UK) 57
University and College Union (UCU) data 52

University of Liverpool, job cuts 59
University of Ottawa, human rights case 180–181
University of Oxford, precarious labour 58
University of Roehampton, job cuts 59
University of Toronto, tenure-stream 124n5
university profiling strategies 8, 13, 130–131, 189

van den Brink, Marieke 22
Vander Kloet, Marie A. 13
Vehviläinen, Marja 5, 6, 12, 40–41, 46–47

Weber, Max 160
welfare states 4–5, 66, 76
Wellcome Trust 82
Whiteness/White faculty regimes 55–56, 99, 137, 142, 145–146, 151, 154n6
work–life balance: within academia 20, 117–118, 120, 123, 149, 195; private–industry 74–75

workload allocation model (WAM) 88–89
workload conflicts: childcare and care-related academic work 59, 88–92; teaching and administrative load 22–23, 148, 193, 195–197; teaching vs research excellence 87–89, 196–197, 200. *See also* COVID-19 pandemic
work overload: academic researchers 117–118; precarity and 12, 42, 45, 59, 118; research/profile creation 20, 44–45, 196–197, 200; teaching division of labour 22–23; work intensification 90, 117–118, 120, 123; worker welfare policies 45. *See also* precarious labour; research productivity

Yarrow, Emily 190, 193
Ylijoki, Oili-Helena 10, 13, 21, 66, 119

zero-hours contracts 52, 58, 61n1

Printed in the United States
by Baker & Taylor Publisher Services